76

D1481850

TEMPLES OF THESPIS

*Some Private Theatres and Theatricals in
England and Wales, 1700-1820*

by

SYBIL ROSENFELD

The Society for Theatre Research
1978

A

© The Society for Theatre Research 1978
Published by The Society for Theatre Research
14 Woronzow Road, London, N.W.8
ISBN 0 85430 026 0

Foreword

The subject of amateur theatre is one that has been almost entirely ignored by theatre historians, reflecting perhaps the somewhat disparaging attitude sometimes displayed towards it by the theatrical profession. But quite apart from its strictly theatrical importance, it is a subject of the greatest social interest, reflecting as it does the enthusiasm for the theatre that has gripped all sections of English society. In particular, during the period covered by this volume, the popularity of private theatricals reflects the life lived in the great country and town houses of England and Wales during their years of glory, when batallions of servants enabled their inhabitants to pursue lives of healthy activity in the field, in the library, and on the stages of their own theatres.

Theatre scholarship is already deeply indebted to Sybil Rosenfeld for her many contributions to it, and The Society for Theatre Research is doubly indebted for the long services she has rendered it. It is, therefore, with more than usual pleasure that I am privileged to introduce this work.

GEORGE SPEAIGHT
General Editor of Publications
The Society for Theatre Research

Contents

ILLUSTRATIONS

Acknowledgments

In order to discover what relics remained of the past glories of these private theatres, I have worried many of the descendants of those who held theatricals or played in them. They have all been most kind in answering my enquiries and supplying what information they had, though in most instances oblivion has fallen on the theatrical amusements of their forebears. Where so many have given assistance it is impossible to mention names, but I am none the less grateful for all the help and interest that have been accorded me. I have also to acknowledge the assistance given by many public libraries and, of course, by the ever courteous staffs of the British Museum and British Theatre Museum.

Sybil Rosenfeld

Chapter I

Introduction

"There is no subject that we would sooner recommend to any male or female author, in distress for a topic, than a History of the Private Theatres of Europe". So said Tom Moore in his "Essay on Private Theatricals"[1] in 1827, little realising perhaps that his topic would verge on the work of a lifetime and run into several volumes. This book is a small contribution towards Moore's fascinating theme. In place it is confined to England and Wales; in time to the 18th century and Regency periods. And even within these limits, the exigencies of space dictate an arbitrary selection of a few of the most important and splendid private theatres of the time, or of those about which some particularly interesting information, such as eye-witness descriptions or records of payments to builders, decorators, scene painters and costumiers has come down to us. Another volume would be needed to cover all the private theatres and amateur endeavours, within these same geographical and period boundaries, of which we have some knowledge. Their ubiquity was astonishing, and I have records of 120 places in which private theatricals were held. Many more must have gone their obscure way to total oblivion.

It is necessarily the theatricals of the great or famous which have, for the most part, come down to us. They made fashionable news and found their way into the newspapers and periodical columns. For them, printed playbills were issued, a number of which are preserved in Charles Burney's collection;[2] and entrance tickets engraved, some of which found their way into the Banks collection.[3] They were often the talk of the town, and scraps of gossip about them were eagerly passed on, so that many valuable descriptions appear in contemporary letters and memoirs.

Though most of the theatres described in this book are those of the aristocracy or landed gentry, we have to remember that amateur acting was by no means confined to the *haut ton* but was popular in other strata of society. We think of Fanny Burney's[4] amusing relation of her experiences as an amateur actress at her uncle's house, Barborne Lodge, near Worcester. We recall that at Steventon Rectory Jane Austen's family indulged in the pastime of amateur acting in a barn or dining-room when Jane was still a child.[5] In John Rolls's Palladian villa at Camberwell in 1809-11, Charles Mathews played the fool in Shakespearean and other burlesques, written for the occasion by Theodore Hook.[6]

During the Napoleonic invasion scare at the beginning of the 19th century, the officers in the waiting armies organised theatricals in camps and barracks in order to relieve the tedium of winter evenings. At Coxheath they built their own theatre;[7] In Ipswich, Colchester, Deal and Faversham they used the local theatres, and in Canterbury, the Guildhall Tavern since the use of the theatre was refused them. Amateurs, too, in many provincial towns gave performances for charity or their own amusement at the local playhouse. In London and in one or two other big cities speculators ran small private theatres where the stage-struck of all types paid for their rôles in order to satisfy their histrionic cravings. The two best known were in Berwick Street and Catherine Street. These haunts, as described by Dickens in *Sketches by Boz*[8] form a sordid picture of low life; yet Edmund Kean acted in one such; John Pritt Harley, William Oxberry and J. R. Planché tried out at Berwick Street, and Junius Brutus Booth at St. Pancras Street, off Tottenham Court Road. There were also prentices' theatricals which were duly attacked by several correspondents to the newspapers[9] and there were theatricals of country boys for one of which John Cunningham wrote a prologue.[10] School plays are a subject in themselves. Yet, though amateur acting was by no means the prerogative of the wealthy and leisured, it was their theatricals that were the fine flowering of amateur endeavour in this country. It was they who built theatres, such as the Earl of Barrymore's (Chapter I) and the Margravine of Anspach's (Chapter IV), which could vie in splendour with the private theatres of European courts and princes. And they were built with the riches and resources, not of principalities and dukedoms, but of private individuals.

If ever the history of the amateur dramatic movement is written, the contribution of the 18th century and Regency *dilettanti*, as they were called, will form its second volume. Let us briefly survey what would constitute its first, and so put these theatricals in their place in the long story.

In the early development of the drama in England, the amateur played an even more important part than the professional. For were not the priests who mimed the story of the Marys at the Tomb, and the guild members who acted the miracles and moralities in the streets of the cities

8

amateur actors? Even if we define private theatricals more strictly as performances wholly or mainly by amateurs to selected or invited audiences, as opposed to the general public, we remember that our first tragedy – *Gorboduc* – was performed by gentlemen of the Inner Temple as part of their entertainment to the Queen at Christmas in 1591; that *Ralph Roister Doister*, one of our earliest comedies, was written by a schoolmaster for his boys, and that one of our first full-fledged operas, Purcell's *Dido and Aeneas*, was given its début by the young gentlewomen at Mr. Josiah Priest's boarding school at Chelsea. Noble amateurs during the reigns of Elizabeth, James I and Charles I, when they wished to act, usually chose as a vehicle the masque or pastoral rather than a regular play. It has been suggested that this was not only because they considered that masques were more appropriate to courtly manners, but because they were more skilled in dancing than in speaking.[11] Amateur performances of plays in private houses were infrequent events, since, if a play was required, a professional company was called in. Neither is there any record of a play being acted by amateurs at court or given on royal progress except for Latin plays at the universities, until after the death of Queen Elizabeth. The sumptuous entertainments of these royal progresses were sometimes presented by amateurs, but they could not qualify as plays, being merely a *mélange* of rhetoric, mime and dancing. Masques, too, were often given at great houses in honour of a visitor or on occasions such as weddings. In these amateurs usually mingled, in the guise of anti-masquers, with professionals. The popularity of the masque greatly increased in the Jacobean and Caroline periods and Milton's *Arcades*, for instance, was given at Harefield in honour of the Countess Dowager of Derby by her family. The famous production of *Comus* at Ludlow Castle was also an amateur occasion.

Queen Henrietta Maria had a passion for acting which resulted in the two most famous amateur performances at court, those of Walter Montague's *Shepherd's Paradise* at Somerset House and *Florimène* at Whitehall. Mildmay Fane's *Candy Restored* was acted by his children at his house at Apthorpe with scenery in 1640. During the stern régime of the Commonwealth, the dramatic tradition, driven underground, was preserved and nourished in large part by amateurs. Shirley's *Cupid and Death* was performed on ground belonging to the Military Company in Leicester Square, and his *Honoria and Mammon* was presented by "young gentlemen of quality at a private entertainment of some Persons of Honour".[12] In Davenant's semi-private entertainments at Rutland House, amateurs probably joined with professional singers and musicians.[13] In the country William Blundell wrote a prologue for a play which was performed by his neighbours at Christmas 1647 "According to the custom of the time"[14] and Dorothy Osborne played in Berkeley's *The Lost Lady* at Lady Peyton's in July 1654.[15]

Even during the 17th century, private theatricals were not the special privilege of the aristocracy. Shakespeare has immortalised the "rude mechanicals' " efforts in *A Midsummer Night's Dream*. In Oxford, youths of the parish presented *Narcissus, a Twelfth Night Merriment* at St. John's College in 1602, and apprentices, printers and others gave *Cupid's Whirligig* in 1632. Anthony à Wood saw those prentices' successors in *Volpone* at the Town Hall on Twelfth Night, 1663.

During the second half of the 17th century, after the Restoration, we hear less of private theatricals. It has been pointed out that, though the the tradition that amateur acting was popular at the court of Charles II was strong, there are but few traces of it.[16] Pepys saw the Duke of Monmouth act with some court ladies in *The Indian Emperor* in 1667/8[17] and condemned all the women except the Duchess and Mrs. Cornwallis as "fools and stocks", and the men as little better except for one Captain O'Bryan who, above all, danced incomparably. Evelyn, too,[18] heard the Duke speak the prologue to a performance of Mrs. Philips's *Horace* by people of quality at court the next winter. But the most famous of all amateur performances at court at this time was that of *Calisto* in 1675.[19] The principal parts in this lavish production were taken by the Princesses Mary and Anne and a number of court ladies including the future Duchess of Marlborough. Some years later, in 1681, Princess Anne played Semandra in Lee's *Mithridates* when it was acted by nobility at the Holyrood tennis court in Edinburgh.

Outside the court there were other amateur theatricals. Three poems in Thomas Shipman's *Carolina or Loyal Poems*, (1683) refer to performances at Belvoir. The first, entitled "Olympus", was spoken in 1675 by Mrs. P. L. to Lord and Lady Roos before a play; the second was spoken by Ant. Eyre by way of prologue when he acted Almanzor in Dryden's *Siege of Granada* there in 1677, and the third is upon Mrs. Bridget Noel's performance as Almahide on the same occasion. That her appearance was not altogether acceptable may be inferred from one of the couplets which runs:

> That such a Lady on the Stage was seen
> Less'ning her self to represent a Queen.

Duffett, too, in his *New Poems, Songs*, 1676, has a prologue to a play acted privately and a prologue and epilogue to another. In the first criticism is forestalled:

> If any should condemn our harmless sport
> We will not plead high presidents from Court:

10

But with an equal rashness we'll maintain,
If serious, he's a formal Fop, whose brain
Does envy what it never could attain.

In the second prologue censure is considered inevitable:

Our case is hard, we must be censur'd still,
For Acting first, and then for Acting ill.
We want brave scenes, gay Clothes and Confidence,
More fit for players than their Wit or Sence.

Duffett's apologetic and defensive tone shows that people who indulged in private acting were liable to be severely criticised, despite royal example. In the provinces Puritanism had a much stronger hold than in London and amateurs might have to run the risk of outlawry from local society. Perhaps for this reason it does not seem that private theatricals were widespread. There was, of course, always the family party performance on an intimate scale, often for children, such as that which John Stewkeley gave at his house at Preshaw as an outlet for the high spirits of his young daughters.[20] In the first half of the 18th century, too, private theatricals were rather few and far between. Again children played a large part in some of them. Hogarth's famous painting shows a group of children presenting Dryden's *Indian Emperor* at the house of John Conduitt, the Master of the Mint, in 1731. The picture gives an excellent idea of how a room was fitted out for these performances. We shall find, in the pages that follow, children acting at Blenheim in 1718 and Holland House in 1761. In 1749 and 1750 the royal princes and princesses, children of Frederick Prince of Wales, coached by Quin, acted in *Cato* and *Lady Jane Grey* at Leicester House. The future George III played Portius in the former and spoke a prologue[21] by Mallet, in which the value to a future king of acting a poet's plays is emphasised. Prince George was then only ten and his little sister Princess Elizabeth, who played Lucia, was eight and so ailing that she could not stand but had to lean against the side scene.[22] But it was not until the 1770's that the real rage began, so that in 1776 we read,[23]

Since the theatrical resignation of Roscius [Garrick] the rage for dramatic entertainments in private families has increased astonishingly; scarce a man of rank but either has or pretends to have his petit théâtre, in the decoration of which the utmost taste and expense are lavished.

The craze reached its climax in the 1780's, declined somewhat in the 1790's, increased again slightly in the first decade of the 19th century and, after that, petered out.[24]

So important were *dilettanti* theatricals at the height of their vogue that affairs of state were curtailed in order to permit of the audience being in time.[25] These audiences were usually carefully selected and an invitation was considered an honour and privilege. In the remoter country districts the visitors gladly endured fatigue, cold and discomfort on long and hazardous coach journeys over jolty roads, with the risk of having the coach overturn in the winter's night; for a Christmas house party was a favourite occasion for performances.

The vogue roused much puritanical opposition and a violent controversy broke out in the press. This reached its height of fury when the first amateur dramatic society was founded. This was the famous Pic Nic, of which Colonel Henry Greville was manager, and which gave performances of French and English plays at the Tottenham Street Rooms in 1802 and 1803. The opposition which had been smouldering ever since theatricals became popular burst into a flame of hysteria which scorched the newsprints with vituperative paragraphs and lampoons. The flames were fanned by the public theatres who chose to see in this innocent project a dangerous rival to the patent houses. The promoters of the Pic Nic thus raised one of the greatest storms in a teacup of the time.

The main theme of the attacks against private theatricals was that they led to immorality and debauchery; the innocent were corrupted, the licentious given their opportunity: "the open embraces of the Actor are exchanged without difficulty for the private of the Seducer."[26] Here is an unusually moderate argument:[27]

It is a question of great importance, whether private plays are likely to promote virtue and morality. To say nothing of the dialogue and sentiments of Comedies, when impressed on the memory and heart; the necessary liberties of the stage are unfavourable to delicacy; and the giving and receiving promiscuous embraces, tend principally to the interests of the gentlemen at Doctors-Commons. Parents who regard the future and honour of their children should hesitate at their engagements in private plays.

The Rev. Richard Graves in an essay entitled "Theatrico Mania"[28] after testifying to the widespread popularity of the amusement, complained that the example of the great house spread to the tenants who spouted their heroics in barns; rural retreats took on the semblance of public places, whilst the tiring rooms "have been productive of more than one intrigue, and elopements, and improper marriages to the distress of families, and, often, perhaps, the ruin of the thoughtless parties."

They were in fact the usual arguments that had been flung for centuries against the theatre, and there is no evidence that there was any truth in the charges or cause for the fears expressed. 18th century high society was

12

pretty free living and the pictures of innocence corrupted seem hardly to
fit in with it. There was an occasional incident such as Twisleton's unfortunate elopement with Miss Wattell,[29] but, on the whole, for all this smoke,
there was singularly little fire.

The theatricals were attacked by the moralists and sniped at by the
caricaturists. In an age when caricatures flourished, one of their obvious
butts was fashionable pastimes and frivolities. Three of the illustrations
are representative of the work of such artists (plates 2, 8, 9). It was the
Pic Nic that evoked the great spate of prints satirising the pretentions of
the amateurs and their conflict with the patent theatres. This satirical
criticism is a healthy antidote to the fulsome flattery of some of the newspapers.

Satire was not confined to newspapers, essayists and caricaturists. Two
farces were written about the craze. James Powell's *Private Theatricals*,
which was printed in 1787 but never acted, introduces us to the stage
struck Lady Grubb and a performance of *Romeo and Juliet* in which "there
will be more plot behind the scenes than on the stage." R. B. Peake's
Amateurs and Actors was brought out at the Lyceum in 1818, and shows
how the amateur David Dulcet engages, to superintend the theatricals, a
provincial manager, O. P. Bustle, who has nothing but contempt for his
patrons as "barbarous murderers of the drama". The attacks achieved
nothing. Patronised by royalty, indulged in by the highest society, appeal-
ing to deep instincts for dramatic expression in the individual, private
theatricals raged the length and breadth of the country for 35 years.

They were also not without their defenders, though these were greatly
outnumbered. They pointed out that play-acting was a preferable form of
amusement to gaming and drinking and that if the right plays were selected,
their experience might even be elevating and "private Theatricals become
a National Benefit".[30]

There was, however, little constructive criticism. One of the few people
who had thought at all on the subject was Richard Cumberland who
contributed his "Remarks upon the Present Taste for Acting Private
Plays" to the *European Magazine* of August 1788. After treating the amateur endeavours with mockery and irony, Cumberland goes on to consider
what should be their function. His main point is that they should not
attempt to copy the professional stage but

should be planned upon a model new, original, and peculiar to themselves; so
industriously distinguished from our public play-houses, as they should not
strike the eye, as they do, like a copy in miniature, but as the independent sketch
of a master who disdains to copy.

Plays written for the stage, which necessarily dealt with strong character and striking contrast, were not for them. Their plays must be specially written by people with a knowledge of the *locale* and the performers. The dramatics should be part of a fête in which the performers could be relieved and the spectators given variety by intervals of music, dancing or refreshments.

Cumberland deprecates coaching by professionals:

> I revolt with indignation from the idea of a lady of fashion being tramelled in the trickery of the stage, and taught her airs and graces, till she is made the *facsimile* of a mannerist . . . Let none such be consulted in dressing or drilling an honorary novitiate in the forms and fashions of the public stage . . . the fine lady will be disqualified by copying the actress, and the actress will become ridiculous by apeing the fine lady.

Prologues and epilogues should be discarded as "relics of servility", since the poets would not be suitors and the performers would be benefactors. Nothing, in short, should be admitted which could provoke comparison with the public stage.

Concerning the fitting up of the theatre and stage, Cumberland considered that many halls and apartments

> with proper help would be disposed into new and striking shapes for such a scene of action, as should become the dignity of the performers. Halls and saloons, flanked with interior columns and surrounded by galleries would with the aid of proper draperies or scenery in the inter-columniations take a rich and elegant appearance, and at the same time the music might be so disposed in the gallery, as to produce a most animating effect. A very small elevation of stage should be allowed of, and no contraction by side-scenes, to huddle the speakers together and embarrass their deportment; no shift of scene whatever, and no curtain to draw up and drop, as if puppets were to play behind it: the area, appropriated to the performers, should be so dressed and furnished with all suitable accommodations, as to afford every possible opportunity to the performers of varying their actions and postures, whether of sitting, walking, or standing as their situations in the scene, or their interest in the dialogue may dictate; so as to familiarise and assimilate their whole conduct and conversation through the progress of the drama to the manners and habits of well-bred persons in real life.

There is sense here as well as snobbery. Cumberland saw that the amateurs could not hope to rival the professional players on their own ground and believed that they should provide something different based on such natural amenities and advantages as they possessed. Many critics to-day urge amateurs not to attempt to copy west-end productions. Cumberland concluded that the fashion for acting should be cautiously indulged and narrowly confined to certain ranks, ages and conditions.

This, of course, was not the end of the story, though it was the end of a particular chapter in it, before society was overwhelmed by the upheaval of the industrial revolution. The lull in private theatrical activities in the last years of the Regency but marks the transition to those of the rest of the 19th century. Some theatricals such as those at Woburn Abbey[31] bridged the gap; others, as at Little Dalby Hall,[32] were renewed after an interval of years. New and fine private theatres arose such as that at Chatsworth in 1830 which still stands, or that at Burton Constable[33] in Yorkshire which functioned from 1830 to 1850. In another sphere Dickens took his amateur company on tour, and in the succeeding decades amateur dramatic societies arose all over the country. But the years 1770 to 1810 were the golden age. Never again in an industrial world did private theatres make such a stir nor provoke such controversy.

Chapter II

The Earl of Barrymore's Theatre at Wargrave

The most famous of all the private theatres of the 18th century was that of Richard, Earl of Barrymore at Wargrave. The Earl was one of those eccentric and extravagant characters whose personalities and escapades are the talk of their time and who secure, as a kind of legend, a minor immortality.

Born on 14 August 1769, he succeeded to the title and estates as a child of four and, in his youth, was thoroughly spoilt by his grandmother, the Countess of Harrington, who sent him to Eton with £1,000 in his pocket. No wonder that he early acquired prodigal habits and, on the completion of his education, lived in the most extravagant manner, squandering his fortune on his sporting and artistic whims. He soon became an intimate of that other wild and artistic young man the Prince of Wales, afterwards George IV, so that his enemies saw in him the epitome of the profligate and licentious lives led by the Prince's set.[1] He indulged in all kinds of gambling from boxing matches to horse races, and what he won on the turf he lost at cards. He was the finest gentleman coachman and jockey in the kingdom, and his exploits with a hired mail coach by night were the terror of the countryside. Like most rakes he had an adolescent humour which made him delight in puckish pranks such as changing inn signs; but he also had in him a morbid strain which sent him spending nights in the stews, not so much to partake of their debaucheries as to observe the lowest types of mankind. Withal he possessed a strong artistic streak which found an outlet in his enthusiasm for painting, and his passion for the theatre. His flair for spectacle once led him to array his hunting establishment in imitation of that of Louis XIV at Fontainebleau, with four superbly mounted negroes decked out in scarlet and silver, and a performer on the

16

French horn who played Handel in the woods. Or the scene he would devise would be Watteauesque, an aquatic fête to the islands of the Thames, or a pastoral in the woods, when the company would dress their own food, dig up wine previously carefully buried, and dine in a tent. Barrymore's friends found him gay, generous and good-humoured with an excellent mind and a detestation of hypocrisy; at bottom, for all his wildness, a man of sense and education.[2] The strangely contradictory impression that his uninhibited and restless nature made on his contemporaries is well summed up by one of them:[3]

His Lordship was the eminent compound of contrarieties, the most singular mixture of genius and folly – of personal endowment and moral obliquity, which it has been my lot in life to encounter. Alternating between the gentleman and the blackguard – the refined wit, and the most vulgar bully, he was equally well known in St. Giles's and St. James's, and well merited the appellation he received in noble quarters, of the Modern Duke of Buckingham, who was "everything by turns and nothing long."

To such a man the stage, with its opportunities for display, its dramatic contrasts, its largeness greater than life would have an obvious appeal; and particularly pantomime with its tricks, continual movement and spectacle, and comedy, with its witty and stylised exposure of the follies of mankind.

Barrymore enjoyed the society of actors and found it an extraordinary anomaly that they were not usually admitted to the privileges of gentlemen. He counted the Bannisters, Johnstone, Incledon, Munden and Edwin among his friends, and of Mrs. Abington and Mrs. Jordan he spoke rapturously. Pasquin gives it as his opinion that had he not been born a nobleman, he would have become an excellent actor of clowns and wags; and a contemporary print depicts him as the Maecenas of Scrubs and Scaramouches.

One of his early connections with the theatrical world was as part owner of the Royal Circus in St. George's Fields, which had opened in 1782 in opposition to the famous Astley's. The Circus was a failure and Barrymore soon retired from his interest in it, but Carlo Delpini, who wrote and produced its comic pantomimes, was later to play an important part in the Wargrave theatricals.

These theatricals began humbly in a barn with a performance of Garrick's farce *Miss in her Teens* in which Barrymore himself played Flash and his brothers Henry and Augustus played Puff and Fribble, whilst the more intelligent villagers were entrusted with other rôles. The audience was not the bright world of fashion but local tradesmen and farmers and their families. The oldest in the cast was still under 17 so that the theatricals must have taken place before Barrymore's birthday in August 1786. 18 months later the rich young earl employed Cox, who had been carpenter to Covent Garden, to erect that "noble and matchless structure, the private theatre at Wargrave."[4] An entertaining diarist from nearby Henley, Mrs. Lybbe Powys,[5] records on 31 January 1789 that "Lord Barrymore had the last summer built a very elegant playhouse at Wargrave, and had a Mr. Young from the Opera-House to paint the scenes, which were extremely pretty." Tobias Young was a landscape painter who had gained some local reputation at Southampton, where he lived, and later an exhibitor at the Royal Academy;[6] he was also one of the scene designers at the King's Theatre in the Haymarket. According to Angelo,[7] Barrymore's scene painter was Scot, the son-in-law of John Raffael Smith, but there is no other evidence that he was connected with the Wargrave theatre.

On the building itself no expense was spared. Anthony Pasquin mentions the almost incredible figure of £60,000 as the cost of "the most splendid theatre in the kingdom". A hostile pamphleteer[8] stigmatised it as "the most ridiculous, expensive, profuse and prodigal scheme that ever signalised a predilection for private theatricals" and tells us that

The same magnificence that pervaded the structure was systematically extended to every inferior apartment and the most trivial office of the whole; the GREEN and dressing rooms were adorned with a superflux of ornamental furniture in the highest style of elegance; every portable article upon the premises was of the most expensive kind, and the wardrobe alone exceeded *two thousand pounds* in the purchase.

Meanwhile on 10 September 1788 Lord Barrymore disported himself on the Brighton boards as Bobadil in *Every Man in his Humour* for Mrs. Bannister's benefit. Several days before the event not a ticket was to be obtained, though the pit seats were railed in as extra boxes. The theatre was crammed to overflowing and the Prince of Wales and Duke of Gloucester witnessed their boon companion's performance from a pavilion erected on the stage. A critic wittily remarked that, although Barrymore had failed to fill Bobadil, he had at least filled the house. In truth, like so many amateurs he was in large part inaudible.[9] In spite of an adverse press Barrymore made two further appearances as Hob on other benefit nights, a persistence attributed to his desire for popularity. Munden[10] says he even played Harlequin and jumped through a hoop, though there seems no confirmation in contemporary newspapers of this feat.

Fortified by his experience on the professional stage Barrymore opened his new theatre on 26 January 1789.[11] The rehearsals had been superintended by the young comedian John Bannister. Performances were given three nights that week; Mrs. Lybbe Powys was present on 31 January and found the theatre extremely full of neighbouring families. Cake, negus and wines were served between the acts, and the cake for one night alone was rumoured to have cost £20. The play was Vanburgh's comedy *The Confederacy*, the afterpiece Mrs. Inchbald's new farce *The Midnight Hour*. In the cast professionals mingled with amateurs. The actresses were all from the company of Thornton who owned the Reading Theatre, and Mrs. Thornton herself was one. They were treated with the deference due to society ladies and, though placed at a separate table at supper, they were served with claret and champagne. The two professional actors were Ryder and John Edwin junior who played the two old women, Mrs. Cloggit and Mrs. Amlet, in the comedy and well became their transvestite costumes. Edwin, son of a more famous father, was introduced by Angelo for the part of Mrs. Amlet. He quarrelled with everyone but none the less rose to the position of co-manager with Pasquin of the court of folly. Barrymore was accused of inculcating him with dissolute habits and luxurious tastes, and he became as great a reprobate as the most reckless of the Barry brothers. Henry Angelo, the fencer and an ardent amateur actor, played Dick and was pronounced by one critic the only passable actor in the play, though better suited in the farce. He afterwards received a teasing anonymous letter suggesting that he send puffs to the papers of his own acting at Wargrave, as he had done at Brighton, and make them ring with his praise. As for Barrymore himself he showed real comic ability as Brass, wore suitable and elegant costumes, and was tolerably accurate. This was more than could be said for Crowder and Thompson who hardly knew a line of their parts and could not stop laughing. On the other hand Captain Dive spoke the prologue and played the Marquis with ease.

The Midnight Hour had a scene of a moonlit garden which boasted an entire transparent painting, then much in vogue, as background, and this was considered strikingly beautiful and an improvement on its counterpart at Covent Garden. The Theatre itself had recently been improved by the addition of an elegant box lobby. But the living conditions for actors and visitors were uncomfortable and overcrowded. Angelo[12] has thus described them:

The cottage was small, and the room I lay in was called the Barrack Room, from the number of beds in it, which amounted to eight. These he [Barrymore] reserved for his select friends; he considered me one of them, and what he called a star at his theatre. The other visitors were left to scramble sometimes in the cottage for what they could get. This room, instead of being a dormitory, might better have been compared to one of the hells in St. James's Street, from the gaming, rioting, drinking, and swearing, which filled up the whole night, with few intervals of sleep, and these few only from the effects of wine.

The theatricals were new in August. The indefatigable Mrs. Lybbe

Powys attended on 17 August and pronounced that his Lordship played Scrub in *The Beaux' Stratagem* "amazingly well". It was perhaps his most famous rôle, and he was not only much at ease in it and perfectly unembarrassed, but he showed a quite extensive knowledge of the tricks of acting. He was even compared with Yates and Weston in the scene in which Mrs. Sullen cautions him not to approach his master's temples with a razor. Dive as Archer and Blackstone as Aimwell had the advantages of attractive and elegant appearance and "easy and gentleman-like deportment". Blackstone had, however, met with an accident and made a limping, albeit successful, lover; he also wrote and spoke the epilogue. Angelo, who played Boniface, delivered the prologue, and afterwards acted Mrs. Pentweazle in a scene from Foote's *Taste* in the manner of that mimic, and sang a spicy song to a French air. The afterpiece was Lloyd's farce *The Romp* in which Barrymore sustained Walty Cockney. Actresses from Thornton's company again undertook the feminine roles.[13] On 21 August the performance was honoured by the Prince of Wales. He arrived from Brighton, dined and dressed at Wargrave and was ready for the curtain to ring up at 9 p.m. *The Romp* was omitted because of the unusual lateness of the hour. A special box was prepared for His Royal Highness which he shared with Mrs. Bertie and Mrs. Wilmot, and complimentary lines of greeting were added to O'Bryen's prologue. Mrs. Thornton spoke the epilogue that evening in which the plea was put forward:

> What tho' untaught in the theatric air,
> We want the measur'd step, the practis'd stare,
> Fearful t' offend, solicitous to please,
> We fail t' attain an unembarrassed ease.[14]

After the performance a select company of 150 people withdrew to a collation in the supper room, whilst other parties were accommodated in a lesser room. This in turn was followed by a splendid ball in the new ballroom which was opened by the Prince and Mrs. Bertie at 3 a.m. and went on until 7 a.m. Among the guests was the Rev. Mr. Tickell, Barrymore's tutor, and we may well wonder what this sober man thought of his erstwhile pupil's extravagance.

Barrymore's scene painter, Young, was given a benefit at the Reading Theatre in October. On this occasion "a full set of capital Scenes, Pillars, &c., with very rich Appendage, the whole designed and executed by Mr. Young" was displayful and was said to "produce the most striking and astonishing effect" and betoken "the masterly pencil of that very capital and ingenious artist".[15]

The Christmas holidays were chosen for the next theatricals. Angelo was dispatched to Drury Lane to secure the services of Mrs. Goodall which he succeeded in doing. Barrymore was lavish in his inducements, and is recorded to have sent an amateur, whom he wanted, £30 to enable him to come down to Wargrave in style. Mrs. Goodall herself received a handsome *douceur* to which was added a gift of the rich attire ordered for her in the breeches' rôle of Sir Harry Wildair in *The Constant Couple*.[16] She made a great hit with the country audiences and the *Reading Mercury* eulogised her as possessing a classic grace in her figure united with the comic archness of Mrs. Jordan. She also played a spirited Maria in *The Citizen* and spoke the prologue, written by Blackstone on the spur of the moment as he lay in his bed in the barrack room with a wet napkin round his head to counteract the excesses of the preceding night's orgies. Mrs. Goodall's husband, who had never been on the stage before, appeared at Barrymore's request as Jubilee Dicky and as Dapper in *The Citizen*.

The third offering was Delpini's pantomime *Don Juan* which had first been presented in 1788 at the Royalty Theatre. Delpini was henceforth to play an important part in the Wargrave theatricals as manager of the pantomimes whilst his wife acted as housekeeper to the Earl and subsequently herself took part in some of the performances. Delpini, who was born in Rome, had been engaged by Garrick for the Drury Lane pantomimes and later had created and contrived mechanical effects for others at Covent Garden and the Haymarket. In these pieces he acted the clowns, and has been called the best clown of his day.[17] Volatile and eccentric, he was the very type who would make a strong appeal to the Earl, who took him and his wife under his wing and installed them in a cottage near the theatre.[18] In order to accommodate the pantomime, *Don Juan*, the stage was increased almost 20 ft. in length by adding the back buildings to it

the propriety of which was seen in all back views, which required stage room; but in the hell scene of the infernal regions . . . in particular this attraction produced the most striking effect, by enabling the painter to place his scenery at a proper distance for effect which in the former state of the stage would have been too much contracted.[19]

Young, then under article to Barrymore for a term of years, painted new scenery for all three pieces but "the scene of hell exceeded all description." Under Delpini's expert guidance the pantomime was capitally conducted and minute attention paid to the business. E. C. Everard, who was at that time a member of Thornton's company, tells us that it "surpassed all I could conceive". He remarks too on the liberal entertainments and rewards received by the members of the company.[20]

Barrymore had been coached by Delpini in the part of Scaramouch in which he received the "extreme of praise". His acting had improved and as Young Philpot in *The Citizen* his scenes with Mrs. Goodall met with commendation. Mrs. Lybbe Powys, who attended on the third night, 5 January 1790, reported of the three pieces: "My lord acted in all of them as well as possible". She found the theatre "amazingly crowded", and the guests included the Earl and Countess of Craven, General Conway and the Duchess of Bolton. As for the other performers, Ximenes was nervous and embarrassed but Blackstone was a striking figure and succeeded in attaining an ease rare on the stage, whilst Wade's military air and address was just suited to the part of Col. Standard.

On the last night, 8 January, the Prince of Wales again honoured the theatricals. He had a special box erected for him and six additional loyal lines were added to the prologue. After the performance the pit was covered with a platform and a masked ball took place in the theatre to which all the rank and fashion of the county were invited. A display of fireworks completed the entertainment.[21]

No sooner were the entertainments over than Barrymore set about enlarging, and in part rebuilding, his Theatre. By May it was in ruins[22] and in July Horace Walpole was writing "I did hear a deal about Lord Barrymore and the theatres he is building".[23] The other theatre was in Savile Row. Formerly Squib's Auction Room, it had been occupied by the *fantoccini* since January when it had been converted into a pretty theatre with a pit and two rows of boxes.[24] Barrymore had it adapted for live actors, keeping the auditorium as it was, but putting in a new and enlarged stage and scenery. The result was said to be "in every respect more commodious and better arranged than the theatre of the Duke of Richmond". Walpole was present and wrote to Mary Berry on 23 July[25] that he found "Little Burlington Street blocked up by coaches". The Prince of Wales, Mrs. Fitzherbert and all the fashion which the town at that late season could muster, came. The prologue, which was written and spoken by the poetaster and amateur actor, William Thomas Fitzgerald, alluded to the marionettes which had formerly occupied the stage, and to Barrymore as a "Thespian Quixote". Edwin, Angelo and Barrymore himself retained the parts they had taken at Wargrave. Barrymore, though unable to conquer the defect of a bad voice, was lively and his Scrub had a dry humour; he did not force applause by overdoing gesture and grimace. Wade's fine figure was admirably suited to Aimwell, whom he played gracefully but rather seriously. Wathen was rather too eager and bustling as Archer. He had been introduced to Barrymore by the veteran actor Smith as the best amateur of his day, and his appearance as Archer to Barrymore's Scrub is perpetuated for us by an engraving from an original picture by De Wilde (Plate 1). Of the professionals, Rock had a fine Irish brogue as Foigard, and Mrs. Rivers, Miss Richards and Miss Collins from the Richmond Theatre were all praised; particularly Miss

Richards for her pure articulation and fascinating archness as Cherry, and as a lesser Mrs. Jordan in the farce. Edwin, later to become her husband, showed promise in the old men line, though only 20. Barrymore and Delpini danced a burlesque Pas Russe in which Delpini was dressed as the dancer Madeleine Guimard, who had recently come to London, and Barrymore as a "pantalooned Nivelon". Ice, tea, jellies and lemonade were served in the intervals and the curtain did not descend until 1.30 a.m. after which there was a supper party for the elect.[26]

Barrymore's next stage venture was his appearance at the Richmond Theatre on 11 August, at a benefit for Edwin. Walpole wrote contemptuously to the Earl of Strafford:[27]

Last night the Earl of Barrymore was so humble as to perform a buffoon dance and act Scaramouche in a pantomime at Richmond . . . and I, like an old fool, but calling myself a philosopher that loves to study human nature in all its disguises, went to see the performance.

Indeed the notorious Earl's appearance drew the Prince of Wales and crowds from the neighbourhood including all the families of consequence. Such was the crush and the mismanagement that many were prevented from getting in; others made a false entry without paying, and several took a peep through the doors from the lobby. *The Minor* with Angelo as Mrs. Cole, O'Keeffe's *The Poor Soldier* with Wathen as Darby, and *Don Juan* were presented, and Mrs. Wells gave her famous imitations. The entertainments concluded with a shower of fire "not but the house was perfectly warm without it".[28]

George Selwyn[29] wrote to Lady Carlisle that Lady Caroline Campbell and his adopted daughter Mlle. Fagniani had seen

that étourdi Lord Barrymore play the fool in three or four different characters upon our Richmond Theatre. Well, but what did that signify. Nothing to me; let him expose himself on as many stages as he pleases, and wherever the phaeton can transport him; but he comes here, and assembles as many people ten miles around as he can squeeze into a Booth

so that there was danger from the overwhelming heat and from the paucity of exits. Later he reports on the performance:

Lord Barrymore danced the pas Russe with Delpini, and then performed Scaramouche in the petite pièce. I asked how he danced; Mr. Lewis said very ill. "How did he perform the other part?" "Execrably bad." "Do you think", I said, "that he would have known how to snuff the candles?" "I rather think not," says Mr. Lewis. Mie Mie [Mlle. Fagniani] is more satisfied with his talents; she thought him an excellent Escaramouche; ce seroit quelque chose au moins. But

I am more disposed to think Mr. Lewis is in the right, and I hope, for the young nobleman's own sake, that toutes les fois qu'il s'avise de se donner en spectacle, et faire de pareilles follies, il aura manqué à sa vocation.

The wiseacres might shake their heads but society flocked to the display.

The Earl's coming of age celebrations, which commenced on 21 September and lasted a week, were the occasion for the opening of the enlarged Theatre at Wargrave. We know what this Theatre looked like from an engraving of the interior after a drawing by Gabriel Cox which appeared in the *General Magazine* of March 1792 (Plate 7). The description accompanying it stated that it

presents a faithful representation of the inside of the first private theatre in the world ... The dressing rooms, offices &c., are planned with so much judgment, and with such strict attention to elegance and convenience, that no visitor of taste can behold them without admiration ... It is intended to embellish the green room with portraits executed by de Wilde, of the principal performers who have displayed their powers on the Wargrave stage.[30]

The picture of Wathen and Barrymore as Archer and Scrub was probably one of these portraits. This same article says that the theatre could easily contain 700 spectators, but this is probably incorrect as the seating capacity given in contemporary newspapers[31] and by Mrs. Lybbe Powys is 400. The last named was present at the opening on 21 September and enters in her diary:

Went to Lord Barrymore's theatre. The first time of opening since so enlarged. We had been to see the interior parts of it the week before, and most clever and superbly elegant it was. It now holds 400. The play Figaro [Holcroft's *Follies of a Day; or, The Marriage of Figaro*] and Robinson Crusoe, well performed three nights.

According to the *London Chronicle*[32] the Theatre was an exact model of Vanbrugh's King's Theatre in the Haymarket "and the whole is finished with captivating beauty". Christie's Catalogue[33] of the sale of the material and contents of the Theatre adds further to our knowledge. We learn that the west entrance was the principal one and was approached by a flight of Portland stone steps with an iron railing and six iron lamps. The door had a light over it, there were two windows and the whole was surmounted by a Portland stone coping and pediment. The engraving shows two tiers of boxes with five side boxes on each side on both tiers; in addition there were probably four front boxes since the catalogue lists three pilasters and angle pilasters to the front boxes. The two stage boxes were conveniently placed overhanging the orchestra well instead of being on the stage itself.

This enabled a forecurtain to be drawn, shutting off the whole stage from the auditorium, an unusual arrangement for so early a date, and one which forestalled modern practice. The stage boxes were decorated with ornamental iron work just visible on the engraving. The prince's box was furnished with a drawing room and private staircase. As for the stage itself, the proscenium arch is set far back leaving a large forestage flanked by the usual arrangement of proscenium doors with windows above. Behind the proscenium arch was the second curtain: 28 cut glass chandeliers provided the lighting and no footlights are shown on the stage. Rooms attached to the Theatre included a carpenter's room, provided with a bed, dresser and sink, suggesting that the carpenter lived as well as worked there, nailroom, lumber room, property room, printer's room, scene room, musician's room, dressing room and green room. The wardrobe was extensive and elegant. In a spacious salon adjoining the Theatre the company partook of refreshments between the acts and at the end of the performance. In a recess, over which the family arms were emblazoned, six menservants in scarlet and gold served coffee, tea, sweetmeats, orgeat and lemonade.

Many amusing details about the running of the theatricals have been preserved for us.[34] Rehearsals began at 9 or 10 at night, were interrupted by refreshments in the early hours, and continued until 3 or 4 a.m. More important rehearsals were held on Sunday evenings when actors from London were able to attend. Dress rehearsals were given to "inferior people" such as "servant maids, dairy wenches, shepherds and ploughboys"; then the pit would be filled with smock frocks and red cloaks whilst the *élite* found entertainment in listening to the remarks of the yokels from the vantage point of the side boxes. Barrymore and his friends would at times disguise themselves and follow the country people out of the village in order to overhear their remarks upon the performances; and with the more objectionable of these they would regale the party at supper. On one occasion Barrymore, muffled in a great coat as disguise, even took tickets at the door. In comparison with those of other private theatres, these tickets are surprisingly plain.[35]

As for the personnel: the pamphleteer and theatrical hack JohnWilliams, alias Anthony Pasquin, appears to have shared the management with young Edwin. Pasquin has also been called the Earl's secretary and the poet laureate of Wargrave, who received a greater, albeit less regular, salary than Southey himself. Delpini continued to superintend the pantomimes, and Thomas Carter was employed as musical director. Carter was the composer of songs which had become famous at Vauxhall and had been musical director of the Royalty Theatre, Wellclose Square, for which he had composed several operas. Barrymore also engaged 16 musicians at nearly £100 each. The carpenter was Reuben Cox and he had six assistants; the prompters were Harwood and Le Brun, the latter a man of dry humour who possessed but one shirt and occasionally walked on as a gentleman; the scene painters were Young and Emmanuel; and the printer, Hopwood. This last printed books of the various plays performed with the imprint "Wargrave: printed by W. Hopwood"[36] but no trace of them has come to light.

A curious appendage to the theatricals was a mock court before which offenders were arraigned and tried in the small hours. Punishments were summary, and both ludicrous and distressing; doubtless horseplay took a large part in them. The court consisted of a Lord Chief Justice, Pasquin; Council for the Majesty of Decency, Barrymore; Council for the Prisoner, Capt. Taylor; Mace Bearer, John Edwin; Crier of the Court, Delpini; Ordinary for the Culprit, Rev. Mr. R—; Jurymen, Hon. H. and A. Barry, Blackstone, Capt. Middleton, Stone, Wade, Constable and Richards.

As we have seen, the performances consisted of *Follies of a Day* followed by the pantomime of *Robinson Crusoe* which has been attributed to Sheridan. Blackstone wrote a prologue,[37] which however was not spoken referring to the enlargement of the Theatre:

> Grateful, he [Barrymore] well remembers when, of late,
> Patient, tho' wedg'd in close array, they sate . . .
> For this, our house – has undergone Reform:
> No sham reform, altho', so strange the case is,
> 'Tis brought about – by multiplying places . . .
> Our humble wish one steady aim pursues,
> Its first, its only object – to amuse.

The actresses, including Miss Richards, were from the Richmond Theatre, and Wathen made his first appearance as Figaro and Harlequin Friday on the Wargrave stage. Barrymore acted a drunken gardener in the comedy and Pierrot and Clown in the pantomime. The new overture to *Robinson Crusoe* was by Charles Dibdin and it concluded with a dance of children, dexterously produced from a cask, in the Temple of Hymen in which Barrymore and Delpini repeated the Pas Russe and kept the audience in a roar with their antics. The performers were for once all perfect, and the scenes of the pantomime were beautiful and its complicated machinery well managed.[38] The company was not numerous as, owing to the death of the Duke of Cumberland, many London guests, believing that the performances would be postponed, failed to appear. Barrymore was attacked for opening the Theatre under the circumstances:

The public are to judge how far this conduct is decent or becoming that while the Public Theatres are shut on account of the decease of one of the Royal Family

26

Private Theatricals should take place under the immediate auspices of a Peer of the realm.

Barrymore merely gave it as an excuse "that the Moon favoured him with her light but refused to lend it him at any other time" and repeated the performances on 23 and 25 September, concluding the festivities with a masquerade on the very day of the Duke's funeral, a defiance which was characterised as only the second part of the *Follies of a Day*.[39] Barrymore, indeed, immediately took advantage of the closing of the public theatres to invite Bannister, Johnstone and Duffey down from Covent Garden. His invitation to his friend Bannister ran:[40]

You will make me very happy if you will come down for a day or two this week. . . . You can have no excuse, my boy, so pray let us see you. You shall have the great bed and every other necessary commodity. . . . I assure you our theatre is really elegant. We play Try Again the last night of our performances; you would oblige me exceedingly if you would procure me the dress you wore and also the Walloon uniform which I will take great care of from Colman.

The two act farce *Try Again* was added to the programme on 25 September. In it Bannister had created the rôle of La Fourbe at the Haymarket and Ryder had performed the hero who assumes the character of an Irish officer in the Walloons. Mrs. Abington was among the guests and is said to have advised Barrymore, when he consulted her, to Try Again and get up a favourite old piece in its place. The three actors from Covent Garden also performed a catch or glee.[41] These last two performances were attended by a numerous company from Reading but also by members of high society from town. On the night of the final masquerade not a room in the worst hovel was obtainable and many were obliged to dress in their carriages. On this occasion

The illumination and ornaments of the theatre were brilliant variegated lamps and flowers were festooned with taste round the pillars of the boxes, and the stage was terminated by a transparency, with the words "Vive l'Harmonie", with the Anchor and the Union Flag surmounted by the Prince's Crest.[42]

The floor was marked out with new ornaments in chalk for the dancing and 500 guests partook of the supper. Barrymore entertained the company in several characters, and songs, catches and glees formed part of the entertainment. It was 9 a.m. before the party broke up.

There were no Christmas theatricals but in January 1791 the members of the Wargrave theatrical club gave a supper and ball at the Maidenhead Town Hall. A transparency representing comedy on a pedestal flanked by Harlequin and Pierrot, all life size, adorned the chimney piece, and Barrymore and his brother, Wathen, Edwin, and Delpini regaled the hundred guests with the ever popular catches and glees.

The next performances at Wargrave were held on 13, 17, and 18 April. About three weeks previously Wathen wrote to Tate Wilkinson asking him to release Miss Richards for a fortnight from the York company, to which she had migrated from Richmond. Miss Richards backed the request by a wheedling and flattering letter and Wilkinson inconvenienced himself and let her go. On 5 April Barrymore apologised for keeping her longer and she did not return to York for some time. When she finally did she was coolly received there and left soon afterwards. Wargrave had gone to her head and caused her to put on airs.[43]

The Rivals was the play and in it Barrymore played Acres; Wade, Capt. Absolute; Edwin, so good at old men, Sir Anthony; Blackstone, Faulkland; Wathen, O'Trigger and Miss Richards, Lydia Languish. This was followed by the first act of *Robinson Crusoe* and then by a completely new pantomime *Blue Beard*. In addition there was a divertissement by Barrymore and Delpini as Pluto and Prosperine in the shades below, and the *Pas Russe* was danced, this time by Mons. Vestris and Madame Hilligsberg themselves. Barrymore made a hit as Acres and proved, according to one critic "that a Gentleman can equal our best Comedians", and according to another "his transitions from the boisterous display of his assumed valour, to the discovery of his natural timidity, shewed a boldness of conception and a happiness of expression which we have seldom seen exceeded". Edwin's tones recalled those of that comic genius his father, whilst Angelo's arch simplicity in the small part of David, and Wathen's Sir Lucius also met with commendation.[44]

The pantomime *Blue Beard*, though ascribed to Barrymore himself, was more likely an adaptation by Pasquin from a popular French original; it was under the direction of Delpini and Angelo confirms that the dialogue and songs were by Pasquin; and the music was by Carter.[45] It seems to have been the first appearance of the story on the English stage though many other versions followed, and this or another pantomime of the same name came out at Covent Garden in December 1791. The scene plot is described in the *Reading Mercury*: first a sea shore, then a transparency in which Genius shows Osmyn his mistress and Bluebeard; Bluebeard's palace falls into ruins and is changed into an excellent view of hell in which Bluebeard is tormented by devils who dance round him with burning torches and finally throw him into the flames; lastly was shown "a beautiful illumination, which crowns the loves of Osmyn and Zelucca".[46] The hell scene was probably the same as that to which Don Juan had been consigned. Newspaper comments were rapturous: "one of the most beautiful species of entertainments we remember", "a superb spectacle", "chaste and charming elegance".[47]

The Prince of Wales, though expected, failed to appear on the opening night and the house, though full, was not crowded. The company lingered on until 2.30 and Mrs. Lybbe Powys did not reach home until 4 a.m.

Barrymore bespoke another benefit for his scene painter Young at the Reading Theatre on 14 June when Delpini appeared as Scaramouche in *Don Juan* for that night only. Young, in addition to the admirable scenery he had already painted for this pantomime, prepared a "new and superb set of rich and most elegant Scenes" on which he is said to have lavished all his art.[48]

The Earl's generosity to his protegés won for him the title of "the Thespian Maecenas." His patronage of Edwin and his family and Richards and his "charming little daughter" are particularly mentioned, as is the good treatment he accorded the members of the Reading company who performed at his Theatre to each of whom he made a present of 10 guineas. Wathen, who was known as his low comedian, acquired the lease of the Richmond Theatre at this time and it was expected that the Earl would assist him. Meanwhile the theatricals due at Wargrave in August were postponed and Barrymore lingered at Brighton. It was reported that he would play there for Iliff's benefit and two days after every seat was sold.[49] He does not, however, appear to have acted though he patronised the performers' benefits more than any other gentleman in the town. His actor friends naturally besought him to appear for them since crowded houses were then assured. The young actor John Bannister wrote to Angelo[50] that his father, Charles Bannister, had resigned from Covent Garden and was going to play for a few nights in Brighton in return for a benefit:

where he flatters himself that he shall experience His Lordship's patronage – and in order most essentially to serve him on this occasion, if his Lordship could be prevailed on to perform, you and myself will endeavour to fill up the last of anything most agreeable to His Lordship.

Edwin married Miss Richards in November and went to Ireland. In spite of rumours that theatricals would not take place until Christmas, they opened on 26 November, but only for a small and select party, with revivals of *The Citizen* and *The Romp* in the former of which Wathen succeeded Angelo as Sir Jasper Wilding, whilst in the latter the Edwins appeared as Barnacle and Priscilla Tomboy. On 2 December Garrick's *The Guardian* replaced *The Citizen* with Barrymore as Sir Charles Clackit, whilst on 3 December *The Guardian* was followed by *Hob in the Well* with Barrymore as Hob and Wathen as Old Hob. The performances were no longer on the same lavish scale and they concluded at 9 p.m. The boot was beginning to pinch the spendthrift host and besides there was a scheme to open the Theatre regularly every Tuesday and Saturday for some months for the entertainment of the Oxfordshire gentry.[51] This season opened on Tuesday 6 December with *Every Man in his Humour* in which Barrymore appeared in his old rôle of Bobadil, followed by *Hob,* and on the Saturday by *Robinson Crusoe. The Beaux' Stratagem* was given on Tuesday 13 December with same cast as at Savile Row except that Mrs. Horrebrow played Cherry. She was a sister of the famous singer Mrs. Crouch, and, though she had been acting for some time in Calcutta where she was known as the Jordan of the East, this was her first appearance on a European stage. Her tones somewhat resembled her sister's but in addition, she had a vein of humour, and her lively and pointed rendering of Cherry was applauded by all the fashionables.[52] The rôles of Boniface and Dorinda were read, a proceeding not unusual even on the professional stage of the time.

The Citizen, The Devil to Pay and *Hob* were given on 17 December and on the 21st the Prince of Wales witnessed a performance of *Every Man in his Humour*. He was due again at *The Beaux' Stratagem* on 28 December but, though a superb box was fitted up for him,[53] there is no record of his having actually attended. The plays continued throughout January 1792, Mrs. Cross succeeding Mrs. Horrebrow. A play bill[54] for the *Rivals* and *The Padlock* on 14 January shows Barrymore as the only amateur among professionals. John Moody, renowned for his playing of Irish characters, had taken over O'Trigger, and, in Bickerstaffe's comic opera, M. Williames and Charles Incledon himself sang. This fine tenor was then the star at Covent Garden which was temporarily closed; he too was restless and eccentric in disposition. On 24 January when *The Mayor of Garratt, The Romp* and *Hob in a Well* were given, Lord Barrymore was suffering from a severe cold and Wathen undertook his rôles in the two latter pieces and hoped that the audience would excuse any inaccuracies. *Every Man in his Humour*, due on 28 January, was postponed. On 30 January the company was further reinforced by Joseph Munden who played Sir Anthony Absolute for the first time, and John Johnstone, Munden's successor in Irish characters on the stage, who played Sir Lucius O'Trigger. An apology had to be made for some of the professionals owing to an unexpected performance at Drury Lane and this may have included the actor William Barrymore billed to fill the rôle of Faulkland. In *The Poor Soldier* Incledon sang Dermot "with sweetness and melody not to be equalled" whilst Johnstone appeared as Patrick.[55]

Barrymore had still not paid in full for his sumptuous Theatre and, on 18 February, Cox sued him for the recovery of £449, the balance due on his building bill. Barrymore's guardian had warned Cox not to execute the building and Barrymore pleaded nonage. It was, however, proved that

The Rt. Hon. The Earl of Barrymore & Capt. Wathen
as Scrub & Archer

Engraved by Jones, from the original Picture painted from life by De Wilde, (by permission
from the Comedy of the Beaux Stratagem,
in the celebrated Edition of Bell's British Theatre, which is now publishing Periodically

THE PASSAGE

Arch: But what Ladies are these?

Printed for J. Bell British Library London July 1791.

1. Wargrave Theatre. *The Beaux' Stratagem.*

"__AY, HERE'S THE MASCULINE TO THE FEMININE GENDER__"

Enter COWSLIP, _with a bowl of Cream_. __Vide. Brandenburg Theatrical__

"As a Cedar tall & slender; __ "Is her nom'tive case,
__ Sweet Cowslips Grace " And she's of the feminine gender."

2. Brandenburgh House Theatre. Mrs. Hobart as Cowslip

he had acknowledged and ratified his debt since coming of age and Cox won his case. Lord Kenyon, before whom it was heard on the King's Bench,

lamented that this young nobleman had, in his minority, been surrounded by designing men, who, instead of storing his mind with useful literature, had, he was afraid, depraved his taste and perverted his disposition. With respect to the tendency of private theatrical entertainments, his Lordship doubted extremely whether they ever inculcated one single virtuous sentiment. He had known instances where they had a contrary effect; and they usually vitiated and debauched the morals of both sexes; the performers seldom retired from the entertainment, but every Romeo knew the estimate of his Juliet's virtue.[56]

Debts and the condemnation of the law despite, performances probably continued, though the next one recorded was not until 16 March when George Colman's melodrama *The Battle of Hexham*, with music by Dr. Samuel Arnold, and *Blue Beard* were presented.[57] A few professionals such as Williames and the Edwins again mingled with tried amateurs such as Wade and Wathen and one or two new players. Barrymore took the comic rôle of Gregory Gubbins and supers supplied the villagers, soldiers, guards and chorus. After the play Moses Kean, the crippled mimic who was the uncle of Edmund Kean, gave his entertainment *The Evening Lounge*. In *Blue Beard* a representation of an Indian procession and wedding was introduced. All that has come down to us of the pantomime is a song with words by Pasquin and music by Carter called "When We're Married" which was afterwards sung to different words in Colman's *Surrender of Calais*. The verses sung at Wargrave were[58]

> This key opes the Casket where Emeralds Lye,
> And this where my costly Array meets the eye;
> With silks far more bright than the Tyrian dye,
> And all shall be thine when we're married.
> But I charge you, by all that is sacred and great,
> Not to open the door, and embitter your Fate,
> If you do, you'll be curs'd by the Furies' full hate,
> And you and I never be married.

The doors were opened at 5.15 and the performance began at 6. Tickets for the next night were ready for delivery at Mrs. Delpini's, so that regular performances must have been taking place. Pasquin tells us that *The Apprentice* was given at Wargrave and it may have been done at this time. Mrs. Lybbe Powys[59] saw an unnamed performance on 16 March and *The Merry Wives of Windsor* on 30 March "both amazingly well performed". In a note she adds that the latter "was the last play acted, as the beautiful theatre was soon after taken down".

31

The Earl's extravagances had brought their revenges at last. On 25 June 1792 the *Gazetteer* reported: "The Theatre of the Earl of Barrymore at Wargrave, with all the dresses and decorations and with the ball and greenroom furniture, have been seized by the Sheriff of Berks, and are shortly to be sold". The *Public Advertiser* five days later gave a mock list of properties purporting to have been comically misinterpreted in the Sheriff's book:

> Thunder entered as set of bowls,
> Lightning pounded resin,
> Shower of Hail, a sieve and dried peas,
> A scene of Hell, A damned hot looking picture,
> The Elysian Fields, The Dog and Duck,
> A General's Truncheon, A Rolling Pin,
> A Conjuror's Gown, A Clergyman's Cassock,
> A Highwayman's backscratch, A Crop,
> A Fool's Cap and Bells, Lord B—re night cap

The Sheriff ordered the sale of the theatrical property by auction and one Hawkes advertised the sale in the *Reading Mercury* on 25 June, the items including

> The superb and elegant Dresses, Decorations, Cut Glass Lustres, beautiful Scenery, excellent Dressing Room, Ball and Green Room Furniture, compleat Printing Apparatus and every other internal accommodation of that much ad-mired Theatre ... Tastefully selected at an immense expense, and recently executed in very superior, and masterly stile, by some of the first artists in the kingdom.

The sale was stopped and, on 11 July, a case was brought before the Hon. Barry Perryn and a special jury at the Abingdon Assizes, in which one Piper sued Messrs. Kealy, Butler and Curtis for trespass and forcible entry into the theatre and house of Lord Barrymore against whose effects they had obtained execution. Damages of £909 were awarded the plaintiff, being the amount of goods already sold by auction subject to deduction of the expenses of the sale. The defendants were ordered to withdraw their officers from possession and to restore to Piper all unsold effects.[60]

On 24 September Christie's advertised the sale of the Theatre, its scenery, machinery and materials on the premises, and on 8 October the date was announced as 15 October with viewing for six days previously. Catalogues were obtainable at the inns and of Piper whose address is given as 11 Howland Street, Russell Place. The wardrobe and dresses, twenty-eight cut glass chandeliers and other theatrical articles could be purchased by application to Mr. Christie direct.[61] At the sale on 15 and 16

October Sir Charles Marsh of Reading bought the traps and scenery painted by Young and Emmanuel, and Thornton of the Reading Theatre purchased the sashes, frames, doors, dressings and enrichments on each side of the stage together with the entablature drapery and columns of the proscenium. Other buyers were Ximenes who had been one of the amateur actors and Delpini. Some of the furniture was eventually purchased for the Chestnut Street Theatre, Philadelphia where it arrived in April 1793.[62] The scenery and machinery comprised 273 pieces in 7 lots.[63] Only one lot is specified in the Catalogue and this contained:

A dessert cloth, a saloon cloth, a sheet complete, 22 borders various, 3 old canvas cloths and rollers, one gauzed; Blue Beard's palace cloth, a moonlight transparent ditto, a transparent glory ditto, a moveable horizon cloth, the several barrels, lines and pullies to ditto, 2 pairs of lamp ladders and lamps, 4 pair of wing ladders, a thunder barrel, 22 iron maces, [braces] for scenery, all the loose and fixed grooves, 2 flat frames, a trick door, flat and irons, 5 trap barrels and irons, a table trap complete, a windmill with sails and 8 small canoes, two stuffed camels, a lamp with barrel, lines, and [added in MS] three painted oil cloths 15 x 14 feet and one 15 x 10 feet.

The moonlight transparent backcloth was probably that used for the garden scene in *The Midnight Hour*, the canoes were most likely properties for *Robinson Crusoe*. The trick door and traps were pantomime effects. The grooves were used for holding the wings. It is interesting to find that gauze heightened the effect of a backcloth. Evidently the scenery and machinery were elaborate even in comparison with professional theatres.

The total proceeds of the sale were only £1,127.10.0, a poor result for "the Compleatest Private Theatre in the Kingdom". As for Lord Barrymore we do not hear of his acting again. On 6 March 1793 at the age of 24 his meteoric career was put to an end by the accidental explosion of a gun whilst he was on duty with the militia. On the day he died he was to have stood sponsor for the infant daughter of the comedian Johnstone. Perhaps it was as well that the fatality happened, since he could hardly have lived happily and soberly in poverty, yet his death, like that of Don Juan, seems to leave the world bereft of some great, dynamic vitality. He was buried in the chancel of Wargrave church on 17 March. A stable and a coachhouse later arose on the site of his splendid Theatre; these in turn have disappeared and the ground on which they stood is now part of the kitchen garden of Barrymore House.

Chapter III

The Theatricals at Richmond House

The theatricals at Richmond House, Privy Gardens, Whitehall, given by the Duke of Richmond in the spring months of 1787 to 1788 differed from those at Wargrave in several respects. They were not given in a specially built theatre but in an adapted room, the Duke himself did not act, and they were patronised by the cream of Georgian society including the King and Queen themselves, so that an invitation was a privilege much sought after and prized by the élite. Indeed they were the most fashionable and exclusive of the private theatricals of their time.

Charles Lennox, 3rd Duke of Richmond, grandson of Charles II and Louise de Kerouaille, was far from being an eccentric rake of the type of Lord Barrymore, nor did he share his passion for the stage. But he was interested in the arts, and, in 1758, had opened a gallery in Richmond House of plaster casts from the antique for the use of artists and students. Primarily he was a politician, who started as an ardent advocate of Parliamentary and franchise reform and then suddenly turned coat into a firm supporter of the *status quo* and a courtier. He had also been a soldier, and his interest in military affairs led him to prepare and push his plans for the fortification of Portsmouth and Plymouth. At the time of the theatricals he was a man of 52 and a member of the Pitt ministry. In 1779 he was described as "tall and comely, wears his own hair, but is rather bald, he has a musical voice, an easy and genteel address, but has a warmth in his temper which sometimes exceeds moderation, and injures a delicate constitution",[1] Horace Walpole[2] found in him the contradictions of a man who was both "intrepid and tender, inflexible and humane beyond example". He was an unpopular figure, accused of domestic parsimony and public extravagance.[3] One of the many satirical paragraphs in the press about his meanness, pictures him carping at the expense of materials for his theatricals.[4] The Duke's family connections took a large part in these entertainments. His wife Lady Mary Bruce was the daughter of Charles, Earl of Aylesbury by his third wife Lady Caroline Campbell, and the Campbells and Mrs. Eleanor Bruce were among the performers. The Duchess's stepfather was General Henry Seymour Conway, and her step-sister the Hon. Mrs. Damer both of whom played a prominent role in the theatricals.

The Duke himself had acted at the age of five with his sisters Caroline and Emily at the family mansion at Goodwood, when de Boissy's *Les Dehors Trompeurs, ou l'Homme du Jour* was presented before a small but noble audience on 26 September 1740.[5]

Unlike those at Wargrave, the Richmond House theatricals had no professionals in the cast. They were, however, professionally coached by Elizabeth Farren. The Earl of Derby, who was one of the principal amateurs, was already in love with her, though he had to wait 10 more years until his wife's death set him free to marry her. Owing to this con-nection she was accustomed to move in the circle of the élite and a foreign visitor[6] remarked that she hit off the air of a woman of fashion exactly and would not be out of her sphere in the most brilliant company; he adds "What will make you downright in love with her, is that they tell me she is as declared a democrat as the noble lord her sweetheart". Indeed there is probably little truth in the insinuations printed in a scurrilous pamphlet[7] on the occasion of her marriage, that she used the chances afforded her by her appointment to superintend the stage business at Richmond House, to push her way into society; though it was most likely a fact that "from this period she began to be noticed even caressed by a very long list of Fashionables".

It was common knowledge at the time that she owed her appointment to the Earl of Derby[8] and she was made much of. Her portrait was in-cluded in the set of fashionables painted by Downman for the scenery of the first play *The Way To Keep Him* and General Conway dedicated his *False Appearances* to her with an acknowledgment of "the advice and patronage you favoured it with as a friend on its appearance in its first form at Richmond House". A niche, known as Farren's niche, was specially erected adjoining the stage with a seat from which she could prompt, though she does not seem to have made use of it and George Selwyn occupied it during the first performance.[9] Far from taking advan-tage of her position, when she came before the curtain in the last act at a public rehearsal, she declined a chair that was offered and stood during the remainder of the performance.[10]

A greater actress than Miss Farren also assisted. Mrs. Siddons gave advice to the ladies about their dresses, at any rate in 1788 when her absence delayed the rehearsals at which she was helping.[11] Richard Yates, the veteran actor from Covent Garden, who had retired from the stage in 1782, is also mentioned as having been associated with Miss Farren in superintending the theatricals.[12]

Rehearsals of Murphy's comedy *The Way To Keep Him* started in February 1787 at the houses of Mrs. Damer and General Conway. It was probably the first time that Mrs. Damer acted though she was to become one of the most celebrated amateurs and to have theatricals in her own house at Strawberry Hill. Storer[13], writing to William Eden on 10 April, expresses surprise at her inclusion:

A play is going to be acted at Richmond House, which occupies the public attention, but will not satisfy the town, as there can only be about eighty persons[14] admitted at a time, and there are to be but three representations. Mrs. Bruce, Hobart, and Damer, Lord Derby, Mr. Edgcumbe, and Sir H. Englefield, are the principal performers. How Mrs. Damer got there is a difficult matter to explain: Mr. Walpole says she will act excessively well; I forgot Mr. Arabin, a famous actor, is to be one of the performers.

The Hon. Mrs. Hobart, the Hon. Richard Edgcumbe and Major Will Arabin were among the keenest *dilettanti* actors of the time and their names appear in the casts of many private theatricals. Lord Derby was considered one of the best amateur actors; he had acted at Preston 14 years previously and for the past seven years had "been much in the habits of Theatric business".[15]

The first open rehearsal, to which a company of 60 select friends was invited, took place on 12 April and lasted from 9 to 12 p.m. Though the performance lacked the smoothness and mechanical continuity of plays at the public theatres, some of the acting would have done credit, it was said, to the most experienced actors. Lord Derby was rather disappointing and the excuse was made for him that he could not understand the Lovemore type of selfish, pleasure-loving husband. Mrs. Bruce was outstanding among the ladies and was so convincing as the sensible rattle of a maid that a countess afterwards remarked to her "My dear, if I did not know you to be a gentlewoman, I should swear you were born a chamber-maid".[16] She thus vindicated the ability of the aristocracy to play, not only rôles in which they were themselves, but those to which they were much addicted from lower life. The final rehearsal was on 18 April, the first performance the night following.

Before describing these let us glance at the place in which they were given. Richmond House stood on the site of what is now Richmond Terrace and was then the southern extremity of Privy Gardens.[17] The Duke employed James Wyatt to convert two rooms on the south side of the house into a theatre and salon which he ornamented splendidly. The arrangement was ingenious. Guests were shown first into the salon from which temporary steps led up to large folding doors. When the play was to begin, these doors were thrown open and the guests entered through them to the back of the auditorium. The descending steps on this further side of the door formed the gradation of seats down to the stage. These ranges of built up benches, "admirably contrived for seeing from the top", resembled the sloping pit of the public theatres. A gallery which accommodated 14 people was erected across a bow window on one side, whilst a corresponding recess on the other was made into a box for the royal family. "The front of the Theatre", that is the proscenium, was reported to be "elegant and lively, corresponding with the furniture of the room". The capacity was rather limited and seems to have been between 125 and 150[18] but this suited the Duke since it enabled him to keep the company very select.

This he went to a great deal of trouble to do by devising an elaborate system of invitations to avoid the "intrusion of improper company". In the first place tickets were limited to 20 for the Duke himself, 12 for the Duchess and for each actress, 6 for each actor and for Generals Conway and Burgoyne, who had respectively contributed the prologue and epilogue, 2 for the Earl of Abingdon, who had written a song for the play, and 1 for Miss Farren, making 125 in all. With the tickets was sent a form letter to each distributor which read:[19]

The Duke and Duchess of Richmond present their Compliments to Mr. Goodenough and have the Honour of sending him His Ticket as a Performer and four Tickets at his Disposal for the Play of the Wonder for Thursday the 7th of February, 1788. Mr. Goodenough is requested to insert in his own Hand Writing, on each Ticket the Name of the Persons to be admitted, and to sign and seal it with his Arms. Mr. Goodenough is also requested to send to Richmond House, on the Day before the Performance, a List of the Persons for whom his Tickets are made out, without which they cannot be admitted.

The Duke in this way had a complete list of the guests and could make sure that no tickets were transferred. The tickets[20] themselves announced that the play would begin at 8 p.m. precisely and that no one would be admitted later than 7.30. The ladies were desired not to wear hats, bonnets or feathers for the high headdresses of the day made it impossible for anyone seated behind to see anything. When the King and Queen attended the ladies were "desired to come in Night-gowns, Robes à la Turque or other dresses without Hoops, and not to wear Feathers or High Caps." The front of each ticket bore the signature of the Duke or Duchess and his seal; the back, the name of the guest and the signature and seal of the person inviting. Both tickets and printing varied in colour for the different performances, those for the rehearsal being distinguished by a green seal. For their own guests the Duke and Duchess had a printed form of invitation on which they merely filled in the name, and the Prince of Wales had a ticket to admit himself and friends at all three performances. Invitations were greatly coveted, and many of the nobility were pleased to get even the promise of a reversion.

So important were the theatricals that a motion in the House of Commons which concerned the finances of the country, tabled for 19 April, was actually postponed owing to its being the opening night at Richmond House. About 120 spectators were present at the public rehearsal when the scenery was not finished nor the dresses as fine as on the succeeding night.[21] On the first night itself the Prince of Wales was present and sat between the Duchesses of Richmond and Devonshire. Among the guests were the Duke and Duchess of Cumberland, Mrs. Fitzherbert, the Sheridans and Miss Linley, Mrs. Garrick, and Pitt and Fox who created a stir by entering together. J. P. Kemble, who was present either this or the next night, was rumoured to have been so delighted that he requested permission to transport the show to Drury Lane.

The prologue was written by General Conway and spoken by Mrs. Hobart. It reviews the disadvantages of the Thespian, Greek and modern public stages: As for the first:

> No Rainbow Silks then flaunted in the wind;
> No Gauzes swell'd before; nor Cork behind;
> No Diamonds then with all their sparkling train;
> No Rouge nor Powder e'en a single grain.

On the Greek stage, it avers, masks would have hidden the beautiful countenances of a Siddons or a Farren. Lastly the public theatres where "Mobs shout above, and Critics snarl below" are adversely compared with

> This fair Garden's calm retreat
> At once the Virtues, and the Muses' seat.

The humble band of players scorned the "noisy plaudits of the croud" in favour of the candour of the select "Whose hearts are partial tho' their judgment's true". Additional lines were added on the opening night in compliment to the Prince of Wales. The epilogue was written by General Burgoyne of the Saratoga defeat, brother-in-law of the Earl of Derby, and as well known as a dramatist, with four pieces to his credit at Drury Lane, as he was as a soldier. Mrs. Damer delivered the epilogue which gracefully alluded to her talents as a sculptress:

> Oh, cou'd my humble skill, which often strove
> In mimic Stone to copy forms I love,
> By soft gradation reach a higher art,
> And bring to view a sculpture of the heart! [22]

The performers who were nervous at the rehearsal, got rid of their embarrassment before their friends and equals. It is not possible to judge of the standard of acting since the newspapers mostly disclaim any intention of being critical; as one put it "If a gentleman player fails, it is no more than was to be expected; if he succeeds in any degree his merit will be acknowledged".[23] The *Town and Country Magazine* pleads in extenuation that "To expect excellence from novices in the practice of an art, which requires great study and experience would be unfair and to criticise upon their errors with severity, would be cruel and unjust".[24] Yet in spite of an attempt to concentrate on what could possibly be considered praiseworthy, a few out-spoken comments made their way into the reports. One critic commends the finely toned voice of Lord Derby and the way in which he spoke the tags whilst another finds objection to his voice, face and figure. Arabin as Sir Bashful Constant used his powers of mimicry to make his performance a pastiche of those of others. Corpulent Mrs. Hobart was vivacious as the Widow Belmour and showed comic talent, and she executed Lord Abingdon's additional song with a turn of much beauty, but she was too rapid in her delivery of the prologue and had not learnt the art of pausing for effect. Mrs. Damer was at times inaudible in the epilogue. Miss Campbell's solo on the harp was her most noteworthy contribution as Lady Constant, but Mrs. Bruce's Muslin was everywhere acclaimed.

The dresses must have been exceedingly rich and handsome.[25] Mrs. Damer wore a plain white robe for morning habit but when dressed "an embroidered gauze on a white ground, a diamond necklace of prodigious value, wheatsheaf ornaments of diamonds in her hair, a girdle of diamonds and stars of the same in festoons for the dress", all "in the most shewy stile". Mrs. Hobart's morning dress was of white gauze, and when dressed she donned "a plain white muslin, diamond flowers in festoons, and diamond girdle, necklace and various ornaments in her hair". Miss Campbell wore "an Indian muslin with gold on a red ground". As for the men, Lord Derby had four changes: a chintz night gown, a brown morning frock, as Lord Etheridge a dauphin colour, embroidered with red and silver flowers with a very brilliant star, and lastly, a rich vest with a light brown coat. As Sir Brilliant Fashion Edgcumbe decked himself out in "a

39

rich embroidered crimson velvet, quantities of rings, seals and diamond pins". Arabin as Sir Bashful Constant had in contrast "a mouse coloured spring velvet with silk flowers, very large muff and plaid ribbons to his watches". The band of 16, some of whom were from the Sussex Militia of which the Duke was Colonel, some his private musicians, was clad in scarlet uniforms. The effect of these rich materials, the men's velvets throwing up the white muslin and gauze of the ladies, and of this profusion of jewels sparkling in the candlelight, must have been fine indeed.

Thomas Greenwood, the scene painter of Drury Lane, and John Downman, the fashionable portrait painter, were responsible for the three scenes. The first scene of Mrs. Lovemore's drawing room was the most famous because it contained four pictures by Downman, "conspicuous for their grace", of Mrs. Damer's friends, and, "in conspicuous place, and with apposite peculiarity on account of her late introduction to this select party – the portrait of Miss Farren stands as just brought home from the painter, and not yet placed on the wall".[26] There appear to have been six portraits in all for a set of six engravings after them was published by M. Lawson at 36s. plain and 3 guineas coloured faithfully to the originals. They claimed to be "exact resemblances of the Original Drawings" and consisted of the Duchess of Richmond engraved by Burke, the Duchess of Devonshire and Lady Duncannon engraved by Bartolozzi, Lady Elizabeth Foster engraved by Miss Caroline Watson, Miss Farren engraved by Collyer and Mrs. Siddons engraved by Tompkins.[27] Downman's actual painting of the Duchess of Devonshire used in the theatricals is in the possession of Mr. Croft-Murray and can therefore be compared with the engraving. It is a large wash drawing, delightfully posed and handled but much too refined for the glare of even a candlelit stage. True it is faded and in bad condition but it is conceived as a portrait small in size and merely enlarged to fit its place on the stage. The engraving is more brightly coloured and has added a background. Downman was a strange choice since his delicate art was quite unsuited to the scale and emphasis of scenery, but perhaps the fact that he was a gentleman as well as a fashionable portraitist had something to do with it.

The second scene, of Lady Constant's apartment, was in red, and the last of the Widow Belmour's dressing room, was striped in gold with landscapes by Greenwood. This too was admired:

The dressing room and the painting of the chairs in particular, which go beyond any description we ever witnessed – have to boast Greenwood, the painter of Drury Lane. In both these [scenes] – nothing is too florid, nothing is overcharged – but the whole admirably calculated for the distance. And in this way too – is the judicious keeping-back of the music – faintly heard – like sounds at a distance.[28]

On the occasion of the royal visit on 17 May the scenery was further improved, the portraits being "thrown into perspective, and hung from festoons in Mrs. Lovemore's apartment. And the heads of Lady Aylesbury and Lady Melbourne – from the charming hand of Mrs. Damer – on the side panels, as if standing on pedestals[29]." Dixon is said to have been the painter of a new apartment, a repository of Mrs. Damer's sculptures but this probably means, not that Greenwood's set was discarded, but that Dixon was called in to paint replicas of Mrs. Damer's two busts in perspective on the side wings. Unfortunately John Bell's project of issuing engravings of the five acts with accurate scenery and likenesses of the performers, and a sixth engraving of the King and Queen and their suite in the royal box, to be drawn by Downman, was never carried out. All we have is the satirical print (Plate 8) which shows from left to right the Duke of Richmond and perhaps the Duchess in the stage box, Mrs. Damer, paunchy Lord Derby, obese Mrs. Hobart and Richard Edgcumbe in the last act.[30] Though no attempt is made to reproduce the actual setting or costumes, the print gives some idea of the performers and their fashions. The decoration on the box obviously alludes to the Duke's fortification schemes and the motto is one which appears on a series of theatrical prints of the time.

The Duke merely presided as host and attended to everything and everybody. After the play a select company was entertained to supper and songs, and toasts continued until 4 a.m.

Further performances were given on 20, 30 April, 5, 12 16, 17 May. Another that was to have been given on 4 May was postponed until the next day as the House of Commons was occupied with the Prince of Wales's business. Thus the finances of the country gave way to Richmond House, but even Richmond House had to give way to finances of the Prince. On the last and most festive night of all the King and Queen, accompanied by the Princesses Royal, Elizabeth, Augusta and Mary, attended as well as various foreign ministers. They were conveyed in seven carriages. Grenadiers were stationed at the gates and the royal guests were received at the door by the Duke. He carried the candle to the King and Lord George Lennox to the Queen when ushering them upstairs to the strains of God Save the King played by the Sussex Band. The royal box had been specially constructed with a crimson canopy, supported by cast iron pillars richly gilt and surmounted by a crown; it was painted by Dixon. A box on each side was fitted up for the Princesses in a similar manner. Seats down to the stage which might impede the King's view were left unoccupied and the gallery was set apart for attendants. Names were placed on all the seats and guests and attendants were asked to be in them by 7.30. The Duke stood in attendance and presented ices and other refreshments at suitable intervals. The usual complimentary lines were substituted in the prologue and epilogue, those in the former referring to the unlicensed amateurs:

> If an Unlicens'd tho' not Venal Band,
> Have dared with zealous, yet with trembling hand,
> Ent'ring with pious awe their hallow'd shrine,
> To raise an Altar to the Heav'nly Nine;
> If, strongly ardent in so fair a cause,
> We have transgress'd, while we revere the Laws,
> E'en Caesar's self, their Guardian and their Friend,
> Would thro' our error see its nobler end.[31]

The Earl of Ailesbury noted in his Diary that "Mrs. Hobart was in want of prompter in prologue. Mrs. Damer in epilogue had monotony of voice, and she did not speak the epilogue well; there was little or no applause."[32]

In further compliment Miss Campbell played on the harp God Save Great George the King with variations. The band was increased and placed on the stage and there were new dresses as well as new scenery. Mrs. Damer wore an elegant salmon coloured chemise with a shining belt, and Miss Campbell a light blue striped gauze over a white petticoat looped up with diamonds, and on her head a cap of feathers, gauze and a wreath of green leaves with diamond flowers. The play began at 8 and at its conclusion Their Majesties went into the salon and congratulated the circle of performers. It was crowded and insufferably hot. After midnight the royal party departed, the season was over, and the scenery folded up to be kept for another occasion.

What was the verdict of the town? Horace Walpole[33] wrote to the Countess of Upper Ossory

I am very far from tired, Madam, of encomiums on the performances at Richmond House, but I by no means agree with the criticism on it that you quote, and which, I conclude was written by some player from envy. Who should act genteel comedy perfectly but people of fashion that have sense? Actors and actresses can only guess at the tone of high life, and cannot be inspired by it ... The Richmond Theatre, I imagine, will take root. I supped with the Duke at Mrs. Damer's the night before I left London, and they were talking of improvements on the local as the French would say.

There is of course, no more truth in his argument that the aristocracy must necessarily act parts in high life better than professionals, than there is in the theory that actual scenery is better than painted, for the simple reason that truth to life as it is lived is not the same as truth to the stage

42

where it is imagined. To General Conway Walpole wrote "The Way To Keep Him had the way to get me, and I would crawl to it, because I had an inclination". One writer spoke of the advantages of presenting the play without cuts and with a nicety of elocution unknown to the public stage.[34] But there were also criticisms. The *Town and Country Magazine* inveighed against the harm that private theatricals did by encouraging the lower classes to imitate their example and thus fall into idleness and dissipation, and by creating competition for the professional actors. The first is the usual puritan argument used against all drama, the second was often used against private theatricals and caused trouble later between the theatres and the amateur Pic Nic Society. Actually it sometimes worked the other way. Thus when Miss Farren appeared as the Widow Belmour the Richmond House amateurs went in a party to see her, and when, the following year, she astutely chose for her benefit, *The Jealous Wife*, which had just been given at Richmond House, she again drew their patronage.[35]

The greatest actor of the day, John Philip Kemble defended the amateurs and praised the production:

the dresses worn by Mrs. Damer were refined models of decoration, frequently suggested both by herself and Mrs. Siddons. And may I be permitted to ask what could equal such an amusement in the circles of fashion, limiting its indulgence strictly to their own rank? It required talent, and it displayed it in the eye of majesty itself. By these entertainments an attempt was made to revive the *gothic* triumphs in the courts of James and Charles, and something was enjoyed beyond a concert or a crowd.[36]

Hannah More[37] indeed thought

It would have made some of the old nobility stare, to have seen so many great personages descended from them, degenerated (as their noble pride would have called it) into geniuses, actors, artists, and poets, [but adds sententiously] Real talent, however, never degrades.

The next play chosen was Mrs. Centlivre's comedy *The Wonder* and this time there was an afterpiece – *The Guardian*. The principals met and read the play on 7 December and by the 18th rehearsals were in full swing every night under Miss Farren's supervision[38] Walpole was as usual, agog with the news and wrote to the Countess of Upper Ossory on 16 December:

The new performers are Lord Henry Fitzgerald, who never played in comedy before but is good in tragedy; a Miss Hamilton, niece of Lord Abercorn, and a Captain Merry. Mrs. Hobart does not play in these pieces, but is to choose her own part in the next.

43

Next day he added,

I was at a rehearsal last night and amazed. Lord Henry is a prodigy, a perfection – all passion, nature, and ease; you never saw so genuine a lover. Garrick
was a monkey to him in Don Felix; then he is so much the man of fashion and
is so genteel. In short, when people of quality can act, they must act their own
parts so much better than others can mimic them. Mr. Merry is an excellent
Lissardo too.[39]

Mrs. Hobart was, after all, called in to take the part of Flora in *The
Wonder* from Mrs. Bruce whose uncle had died. There was some difficulty
in procuring a suitable Ines and Walpole wrote to his correspondent
suggesting that,

If the actress who played Kitty so admirably in High Life Below Stairs
[presumably at Ampthill] is not engaged at either of the theatres at Blenheim or
Winstay, I believe she might have a large salary and free benefit at Richmond
House, where they are in sad want of an Ines.[40]

On 29 December a rehearsal took place at Mrs. Damer's before a
select company which included the Duchess of Leinster (sister-in-law of
Henry Fitzgerald), Mrs. Hobart, General Burgoyne and the parents of
Miss Hamilton.[41] The business and words were nearly perfect at the
beginning of January and the newcomers were gaining confidence.
Rehearsals were as strict as in the public theatres and business and
dialogue were repeated again and again.[42] The death of Lord Gerald
Fitzgerald by drowning, though it threw the Richmonds and Leinsters
into mourning, did not suspend the theatricals, and the opening performance took place on 7 February 1788. It was not given in the rooms
which had been used the previous year. The Duke had since bought
an adjoining house on the west side, and on the middle floor Wyatt
designed a new theatre which was painted and decorated by Greenwood.
"The Stage", we are told, "is the floor – and the Orchestra is sunk
into the room below it – and so, in the same manner is the Pit".[43] The
acoustics were good but the stage, which was only about 19 ft. wide
including the wings, was cramped: "Beautiful as the Theatre is, in the
want of Space and Perspective, there are still Evils, which no art can avoid
nor counteract".[44] The seats all had backs, a degree of comfort unknown
in the public theatres, and they were lined in pea green colour. According
to *The Times* there were front and side boxes, a stage box, balcony and
orchestra. The other stage box was a fake, for the *World* reports

the Deception in the Painting of Stage-Box, on the King's side, and opposite to
that in which the Dutchess of Devonshire sat, on Thursday evening, was admirable – the shade of the door, half opened, was the best effect we ever witnessed;
and so was the drawing of the lattice above.[45]

44

The upper part of the theatre was laid into a large box to accommodate those invited by the Duke and Duchess, in the centre of which a canopy was erected for the King. There were two side boxes flanking this central box. When the King and Queen visited the theatre the lords and ladies in waiting occupied the front box whilst the maids of honour were accommodated over the stage box.[46] The capacity was just over 100.[47] Like many theatres of its time it suffered from poor ventilation and was excessively hot in the warmer months.

This year the allotment of tickets was on a different system: Mrs. Damer had 12, the other actresses 6, and the actors only 4 for the nights they played. On the first night the Prince of Wales came together with the Dukes of York, Gloucester and Devonshire and Horace Walpole. The company "in elegant undresses", without feathers or high ornaments, was bedizened with jewels. The performance finished soon after 11.30 and was followed by a select supper party. There was neither prologue nor epilogue since neither the pieces nor principals were new.

Lord Henry Fitzgerald's acting as Don Felix was by all accounts, outstanding. A nephew of the Duke of Richmond, he had already had experience in the Shane's Castle theatricals[48] though not in comedy. One critic wrote that "Tones more true to Nature – feelings more consonant to Passion – or action more immediately impressive, have not, we will venture to say, ever been witnessed in the memory of the Stage"; another said "his figure, voice and manner united in communicating a true representation of a noble-minded, polished gentleman: his agitations were expressed with variety, discriminated with skill, and the passion of jealousy was never more naturally portrayed."[49] His sister Lady Sophia[50] is a prejudiced witness but nevertheless worth quoting:

Very busy all the morning making up things for the play, dined very early, and at Four o'clock, we went to Richmond House Theatre to secure good places. Mother, Ciss and Mimie were in the Dukes Box, Sophia in the Pit in the first row, in order to see Henry well. He really was more delightful and more charming than can be express'd. Everybody that had seen Garrick thought Henry equal to him, some parts beyond him; but Henry looked much more the character of Don Felix, as he had one great advantage over Garrick, that of having a remarkable pretty figure and looking more like a gentleman, which I understand was not the case with Garrick. Mr. Walpole and all the great critics were charm'd with Henry; and as for the ladies they left The Theatre dying of love for him.

At another performance she was piqued at Mrs. Siddons's reactions: "She rather disappointed us in her praises of Henry, as she said much more about Lord Derby, who is certainly not to be named with Henry. At the same time he is a very good actor, but in a different style". One

45

newspaper expressed the wish that comedians equal to both of them might be found in the public theatres, and such odious comparisons must have been very galling to the professionals, and it is not to be wondered at that their *dilettanti* rivals were unpopular at Drury Lane and Covent Garden. Lord Derby was, indeed, a rather rotund lover but he had improved under Miss Farren's tuition and in *The Guardian* he made a hit, so that it was averred that even Garrick, who had but a poor opinion of amateurs, would have rejoiced in his Heartly. Arabin was to have played Lissardo but resigned the part to Robert Merry who acted it so well that Arabin was not missed. He had been offered the rôle of Gibby but considered it beneath his dignity and it was given to Major Good-enough, an old hand who had played at Sir William East's and Mr. Bowles's theatricals,[51] and who managed to cope with the dialect. Once again in considering Edgcumbe's Young Clackit, the easy coxcombry of the gentleman born was compared with the extravagant buffoonery of the public stage. Among the other actors was Lord Henry's brother, the ill-fated Lord Edward Fitzgerald, who played Don Pedro, and William Ogilvie who had been tutor to the young Fitzgeralds and then married their mother, the old Duchess of Leinster.

As for the ladies Mrs. Damer brought fashionable grace and elegance to Violante, and in her contrasting maid's rôle in the farce was lively and familiar without being bold or vulgar. The Earl of Ailsbury, however, pronounced her "very indifferent".[52] Mrs. Hobart's abigail was pert and sprightly though over-dressed. Miss Campbell, rather nervous as Harriet in *The Guardian*, suggested "the tender anxieties of chaste passion"! As against the praise of the *Public Advertiser*[53] who, expecting only that it would be "well enough for Ladies and Gentlemen", was surprised to find a powerful performance, we have to place the patronising con-donation of the *Town and Country Magazine* which spared "the imper-fections of actors, who being all well pleased with themselves should not be put out of humour even though they failed in pleasing others". In contrast to a great deal of adulation we have to remember Lady Eleanor Butler's impression:

Performance at the Theatre, Richmond House execrable except Lord Henry Fitzgerald, his Don Felix equal to Garrick. Ogilvie as if heaven and Earth were coming together. Mrs. Damer detestable. Mrs. Hobart well in some, indif-ferent in others, horrid in many parts.[54]

Lord Henry Fitzgerald had recently returned from a tour in Spain and so arranged the men's dresses for *The Wonder*, set in Portugal, in Spanish style. He himself wore a white satin vest and breeches with crimson slashes decorated with gold lace, and a richly embroidered cloak of crimson velvet;

whilst a blaze of diamonds shone from his hat. Mrs. Damer and Mrs. Hobart chose their own dresses which had dark satin bodices and muslin petticoats. There were three scenes: a Spanish street, a new room and a beautiful representation of the Terriero de Passa from a sketch made by Fitzgerald. The scene shifting was carried out by picked carpenters drafted from the Duke's corps of military "artiseers". The music was again supplied by the Sussex militia band of wind instruments.[55]

The first evening did not pass off without excitement for a mob collected outside and broke some windows. Whether this was due to the Duke's political unpopularity or was a protest against extravagance and suspected dissipation in high life, we do not know, but the intrusion of the rude world without must have been rather alarming to the distinguished company within. The Duke's lead in London theatricals was championed in high tone by the *Public Advertiser* which claimed that they might prove of importance to national morality since they tended to correct rather than encourage dissipation, and were instructive in comparison with other fashionable entertainments which were a compound of vice and folly. All the same one cannot help thinking that no such moral motive was in the Duke's mind.

The performance due on 14 February was postponed until the 18th owing to the illness of Mrs. Damer,[56] and then, in order to prevent a repetition of the disorders of the previous occasion, the Duke had an outhouse erected for constables and servants.

Seven performances were[57] given in all and the King and Queen attended on 1 March. On 6 March Henry Fitzgerald took over the part of Don Pedro owing to his brother's illness and the crowded house included Walpole and Kemble.[58] Meantime rehearsals of Murphy's *Jealous Wife* had been proceeding apace. This comedy was the choice of Mrs. Hobart as *The Wonder* had been that of Mrs. Damer. Other plays had been mooted. *The Rivals* was to have been altered by Sheridan but he was too busy with the trial of Warren Hastings and could not get it finished in time.[59] Some tragic scenes by Lady Wallace were mentioned but nothing came of this, nor of the rumour that *The Upholsterer* or *High Life Below Stairs* was to be the afterpiece.[60]

The *Town and Country Magazine*[61] thought that the performance was better than that of *The Wonder*. Mrs. Hobart's Mrs. Oakley rivalled Mrs. Damer's Violante, but Mrs. Damer herself made the small part of Lady Freelove more important than it usually was and was particularly good in her hysterical scene. Lord Derby as Oakley was the leading man and it was a part well suited to him. He gave an "elegant and accurate exhibition of a man of fashion and feeling" and made every tone and action appear spontaneous. Lord Henry Fitzgerald had the secondary rôle of Lord

Trinket which he doubled with that of Charles owing to his brother's illness. His performance in the former was compared favourably with that of professional actors who made a pert, affected fop of it savouring of the *valet de chambre*, whilst Fitzgerald was the young nobleman, spoiled by travel and the views of the fashionable world, but with the manners of a gentleman. Only he overacted the drunken scene. Arabin doubled O'Cutter and Paris, and managed the brogue though he wanted the manner of the Irishman. A newcomer was an old stager, Major Fury who had previously acted at Lord Villiers's theatre at Bolney Court, Henley, in 1787 and who as Major Oakley was temperate and sensible in contrast to Merry who overdid the comedy of Russet. Miss Hamilton's chief attraction was her singing. As an actress she lacked animation and spoke too fast.[62] No prologue seems to have been delivered though one was written by W. T. Fitzgerald.[63] The topical epilogue by Miles Peter Andrews compared the Theatre to Westminster Hall, where the trial of Warren Hastings was proceeding, as a place of judgment. It was spoken by Mrs. Hobart whose rendering was rather spoilt by the late arrival of Fox, Lord North and General Burgoyne from the House of Commons.[64]

The dresses were, as usual, superb. There was a new drop scene of a room at the Bull and Gate Inn. This was fixed too far forward and contracted the already confined stage still further.[65] At one performance fat Mrs. Hobart got stuck between the wall and one of the side wings from which unhappy position she was finally extricated "by the extraordinary exertions of Major Fury".[66]

Mr. and Mrs. Piozzi attended on 15 March and the King and Queen, together with the posse of princesses, came on 29 March. They arrived, not at the usual door in Privy Gardens, but through the house of Lord G. Lennox which was specially decorated for their reception. On the last of the five nights, 4 April, Kemble was again present.[67]

The company next turned its attention to verse tragedy in order to give Lord Henry Fitzgerald a chance of showing his talents in the heroic field. He had already played Varanes in Lee's *Theodosius* in Ireland in 1786 and this was the tragedy chosen. It had been adapted for use in private theatres by Edward Tighe, whose alterations involved the omission of several minor rôles and the cutting down of the speeches. George Matthew, brother to Lady Galway, and Miss Hamilton introduced pathetic airs in character, two of which were specially set by Thomas Billington whose setting of *Night Thoughts* qualified him as suitable to compose the music for the solemn rites at the altar.[68] Miss Hamilton also sang the last air composed by Sacchini which had never before been heard in public. She had been in a quandary about the words of this song with which she had to amuse an Empress determined to kill herself. As Mrs. Piozzi puts it:

an English ballad she could not disgrace herself by uttering – her fellow Performers said they would suffer no Italian Song to be pronounced. It was out of Character; & Jane Holman was prepared only with an elegant Air composed by Sacchini. Mr. Hamilton was at his Wits end, & came to me on Wednesday not knowing what would be done. Next day I made Piozzi play the Tune over to me, till I learned & then made verses to it – They suited the Queen's Distress and her Delia's Voice, & gain'd me Admission where Thousands were excluded – at the Theatre.[69]

Verses
Vain's the breath of adulation
Vain the tears of tenderest passion
While a strong imagination
Holds the wandering mind away!

Art in vain attempts to borrow
Notes, to soothe a rooted sorrow,
Fix'd to die – and die to-morrow
What can touch her soul to-day[70]

According to Mrs. Piozzi Miss Hamilton was renowned "for brilliant Execution & pathetic Portamento di Voce".[71]

The chorus was recruited from various choirs and the music was conducted by Major Goodenough who was more famous for his musical than his dramatic talents. Billington's additions to Purcell's original music were pronounced pretty and his setting of "The more than Gordian knot is ty'd" was full of the pathos for which his work was noted.

Though rehearsals had been under way since 22 March, the music was first rehearsed on 5 April and the final rehearsal did not take place until 24 April. The opening night was on 26 April. The acting was said far to exceed that in the comedies since it was "much easier to assume the passions than imitate the humours of mankind", a verdict that brings to the ground Walpole's theory that it was high society's forte to enact fashionable life. So moving were Mrs. Damer and Lord Henry Fitzgerald when the latter fell by his own sword, that Miss Harriet Hobart and Lady Ann Wesley were carried out in a faint,[72] but one may suspect that the heat in the theatre was at least a contributory cause. Fitzgerald, who excelled in the pathetic and whose tones were remarkably sweet, was very suited to the role of Varanes. The praise of the newspapers is confirmed by Storer who told William Eden that "Lord Henry Fitzgerald is as great in this play as he was in the Wonder".[73] Matthew, a newcomer, made the high priest Atticus a part of consequence by his figure, and dignified style; Derby showed feeling and judgment as Leontine, but Halliday as Theodosius forgot his words.

Dresses and scenery were magnificent. The splendid costumes of Varanes and Athenais were well contrasted with the simplicity appropriate to those of Leontine and the High Priest. Mrs. Damer's imperial robe in the last act was of purple on a straw coloured bodice with an embroidery of flowers and was decorated with silver and ermine. In another scene her dress is thus described:

The elegance of taste shewn in Mrs. Damer's last new stage dress beggars all description, and can only be excelled by the attractive graces of the beautiful wearer. The petticoat was of celestial blue crape spotted with silver, ornamented with wreaths of primroses, which were looped up with bows of diamonds; a festoon of primroses went round the bottom of the petticoat, finished with a rich silver fringe. The train was a primrose coloured goffree'd crape spotted with blue crape in relief. The belt round the waist was of diamonds, with three diamond breast bows, and sleeve bows. The head-dress consisted only of a wreath of primroses, and a wreath of diamond lilies, surmounted by an immense panache of white, blue and primrose feathers.[74]

Thomas Greenwood painted three new scenes; "a wood, an Altar, with the Bloody Cross, and the Inscription, In hoc Signo Vinces, and a Palace", all of which enhanced his reputation.[75]

New ventilators had been installed and were a welcome improvement. On the opening night the Duchess of Leinster and the young Ogilvies occupied the stage box with the Keppels over them, whilst the Duke of Gloucester and Princess Sophia were in the front box. Four further performances were given on 28 April, 1, 3 and 6 May; the King and Queen attended the last one.

Though there had been some talk of *The Devil to Pay* as an afterpiece with Mrs. Hobart as Nell, nothing came of it. Mrs. Hobart in fact did not take any further part in the theatricals and there seems to have been a keen rivalry between the Damerites and the Hobartites. Lord Carlisle wrote a prologue for Mrs. Hobart and John Milbanke a prologue and epilogue for Mrs. Damer but whether they were ever delivered or merely added fuel to the flames we do not know.[76]

The final play, *False Appearances*, was a new venture, a translation by General Conway of Boissy's *Les Dehors Trompeurs*, in which, as we have seen, the Duke of Richmond had appeared as a child. The original was compressed and pruned, so much so that one critic found it barren of interest and lacking in incident and the vigorous humour of native comedies; though he hastens to add that his strictures were not "from any wanton wish to repress the attempts of those in higher life to try their hand at dramatick productions". Indeed he felt that the production of a new piece in a private theatre was an auspicious event: "The pursuit of such a propensity may lend a grace to the art dramatick; it cannot, while a mixed audience are judges enfeeble it".[77]

Mrs. Lybbe Powys was at the first night on 23 May and records in her diary,[78]

The prologue and epilogue were both very clever; wrote by General Conway, and spoken with great spirit by Lord Derby, and Mrs. Damer. The whole was amazingly well acted. The house filled with all the fine people in town.

Walpole wrote to the Earl of Strafford of the success of the piece, "The language is most genteel, though translated from verse; both prologue and epilogue are charming";[79] and to Hannah More he wrote "I do lament your not going to Mr. Conway's play; both the author and actors deserved such an auditor as you, and you deserved to hear them".[80]

Fitzgerald again played the lover and this time was compared to Barry and even said to excel him in the beauty of his tones. His commanding figure was well set off by his French regimental uniform of white turned up with green. Derby was commended for his by-play and the neatness and point with which he delivered his dialogue. Merry as the honest M. de Forlis had a good conception of his part and when Pitt was seated in the second row, his references to the minister seemed so aimed at him that not only the audience but the actors burst out laughing. Mrs. Damer's volatile, gadabout Countess was a finished and intelligent performance and her dress was beautiful as usual. Mrs. Bruce, who once again took the maid's part, was considered second only to Miss Pope. The whole comedy had ease and spirit and once more was used as a stick with which to beat the professional comedians:

There is an obvious desire to assimilate, and an apparent ardour to assume and to exhibit, the very feelings the characters are actuated by, that we have again and again remonstrated with the public comedians for not sufficiently attending to, which the performers on such a stage as Richmond House, naturally direct their more cultivated minds to the adoption of. The one, when pleased to do so, can assume fictitious feelings with less difficulty to themselves because it is their daily habit and their avowed art; but they cannot do it with half the impression of persons, who are not in the custom of acting out of their character.[81]

It is Walpole's argument in elaborated form. Other performances took place on 31 May, 10, 12, 14 June. The two last were respectively manager's and author's nights, that is to say all admission tickets were issued by them. Additional contrivances for ventilation rendered the room cooler in the height of summer.

There was trouble with the Sussex band and the catch singers. Their original requests having been considered too heavy, they had agreed to leave their reward to the Duke's generosity. This had finally been arranged as a weekly salary and the run of the kitchen and rooms over the stables for sleeping quarters. However, they quarrelled with the cook so that the Duke proposed an alternative of board wages of 5s. 3d. a week each. This proving inadequate, he then arranged for set victuals to be supplied from a cheap cook house in Porridge Island, Strand. On 9 June the musicians presented a petition in which they complained of the unvarying diet and requested a relaxation of the agreement and some liquid refreshment in the music room after "the intense heat of the Theatre during the performance". Their requests were refused by the Duke. [82]

Conway's comedy was subsequently brought out at Drury Lane with the additional character of the Abbé. But at Richmond House there were no further theatricals. The King's mental breakdown in November put a final damper on their already dubious resumption, and by December it was announced that the theatrical "in spite of all that uncommon skill and fashion could do for it, is no more: the theatre is dismantling and turning into a dwelling house for Colonel Lennox and Lady Charlotte". [83] Miss Campbell, one of the players, died shortly after. Rumours of reopening were afloat from time to time during 1790 [84] but on 21 December, 1791 Richmond House was burnt down, never to be rebuilt. The following year the Duke superintended the building of a theatre in Chichester, near his Goodwood estate, and "generously furnished it, when completed, with some beautiful scenery, painted by first rate artists, for his private theatre in Privy Garden." [85]

The Duke had given a great fillip to the fashion. Frederick Reynolds, [86] returning from Switzerland

found the whole town infected with another mania – Private Theatricals. Drury Lane, and Covent Garden, were almost forgotten in the performances at Richmond House; and the Earl of Derby, Lord Henry Fitzgerald, Mrs. Hobart and Mrs. Damer in the Way To Keep Him and False Appearances were considered, by crowded, and fashionable audiences, equal, if not superior, to Kemble, Lewis, Mrs. Siddons, and the present Countess of Derby.

The Duke's position in society and the cachet given the entertainments by the patronage of the King and Queen caused the theatricals to be widely advertised and discussed. Though on no such fabulous scale of extravagance as the Earl of Barrymore's, they probably were more effective in encouraging the craze.

Chapter IV

The Margravine of Anspach's Theatricals

With the Margravine of Anspach we return to one for whom the stage was a passion and who, in the dual capacity of writer and actress, was herself the centre of her theatricals. Unlike the Duke of Richmond's, her entertainments were not principally for her friends but for herself; she would not have been interested in being merely the aloof hostess. Whereas, too, the Duke could command the best Whig society of his time, the Margravine was under a cloud at court and was not visited, therefore, by the more rigid members of society. Those who did come were supplemented by French *emigrés* who had fled from the Revolution and who introduced a cosmopolitan atmosphere, and several French pieces, into the theatricals.

The Margravine was a vain and egotistical creature with a strong streak of exhibitionism in her nature, who yet was capable, where her happiness was involved, of showing determination and strength of character. At the age of 17, as Elizabeth Berkeley, she had married William Craven, (afterwards Earl of Craven) in 1767 but, after scandals on both sides he left her in 1782. She travelled about Europe for some years until she finally settled at the court of the Margrave of Anspach in 1787 as his "adopted sister". In 1791, only a month after she heard of the death of her husband, she married the Margrave in Lisbon, and persuaded him to give up the ruling of his principality and retire with her and his fortune to England. Her precipitancy was considered indecent and, on her return, she found herself cold-shouldered by the court and high society. The Margrave, a stolid German, who seems only to have wished for a peaceful life, purchased Brandenburgh House, a country villa on the bank of the Thames at Hammersmith, and spent the rest of his days there. His wife

53

built a theatre in the grounds where she could entertain him and at the same time indulge in her favourite pastime of taking the centre of the stage.

She has told us that her attachment to the drama dated from the age of 12. As Lady Craven she organised private theatricals at the family seat of Combe Abbey in Warwickshire with the assistance of the Rev. Charles Jenner and Joseph Cradock. We find her accepting the loan of scenes from the latter who had his own theatricals at his house in Gumley:

> We have fixed upon three different pieces to be acted during the Christmas holydays; the Drummer is one; the Citizen the other; and one musical entertainment. I hope you will do me the favour to play a principal part in one of these, if not in both. I wanted much for you to have been here, and have examined if my playing was worthy to accompany yours.
> As to the scenes, I will certainly accept of them, but at the same time beg we may agree about the time of removing them. In all probability you will act something at your own house this summer and I would not send for them till towards the winter.[1]

We find her about the same time taking part in theatricals at Blenheim Palace where she spoke an extempore epilogue, to *High Life Below Stairs*, in a greatcoat and jockey cap with a whip in her hand, and on 7 January 1773 another epilogue as Rag with Harriet Wrottesley as Tag and the Duchess of Marlborough's little boy fiddler as Bobtail.[2]

She appeared as an authoress five years later when she was living at Benham House, Newbury, and gathered together the local gentry to perform her translation of Pont de Vile's comedy *La Sonambule* at the Newbury Town Hall on 11, 12 May 1778. In the cast of *The Sleep Walker* were Le Texier as the Dutch gardener and Sir Charles Buck, who had acted at Mrs. Hobart's at Nocton and was a well-known character in the literary world, as Lord Vandergrass. The blue stocking, Elizabeth Montagu, described the performance to Mrs. Vesey:

> We went to the play on monday night. Lady Craven acted very well and we had a prologue and epilogue of her writing; they were lively and pretty, but the best of our entertainment was an Opera Comique acted and sung by her Ladyship, Mr. le Texier, and a french man he brought for the purpose. Lady Craven sings and acts admirably, and looks so pretty and has so much french vivacity I am sure all Paris wd be mad after her, if instead of an English Peeress she was turned into a french Opera girl. I was so disordered by the heat of the play House on monday night, that I was obliged to stay at home and take saline draughts on tuesday. . . . On Monday night all the Neighbouring Ladies were at the Play, on Tuesday few but the Newbury people.[3]

The prologue and epilogue by Lady Craven were spoken by her and Sir Charles Buck respectively and were printed together on a broadsheet dated 18 May 1778.[4]

The profits from the performances were given to charity. *The Sleep Walker* was later printed in a limited edition at Strawberry Hill and is a poor piece though with touches of originality in the types. Lady Craven followed this up in 1780 with the production of an original three act comedy[5] entitled *The Miniature Picture*. This was also given for the benefit of the poor at the Newbury Town Hall on 6, 8, 10 April.[6] The receipts surpassed expectation at playhouse prices, and sufficed for the relief of the needy of the town.[7] A new prologue by Wilton and an epilogue by Lady Craven were spoken. Another epilogue written by Jekyll was spoken by Mrs. Hobart at a later performance and was that used at the public performance at Drury Lane in May.[8] The afterpiece was *Three Weeks After Marriage* with Mrs. Hobart as Mrs. Racket and Lady Craven as Dimity. According to the *Reading Mercury*:

The comedy was agreeably and beautifully characterized with vivacity, sentiment, incident and language, and these different qualities of the play were admirably supported as humour, elegance, or grace required.

Lady Craven[9] says that the piece was never intended for the public theatres but that Sheridan borrowed it under pretence of writing an epilogue[10] for it and brought it out at Drury Lane in May against her will, in spite of which she was persuaded to attend its last representation. This was not quite true for it ran for four nights and Walpole[11] has described how on the second one she

sat in the middle of the front row of the stage box, much dressed, with a profusion of white bugles and plumes to receive the public homage due to her sex and loveliness. . . . It was amazing to see so young a woman entirely possess herself. . . . Lord Craven, on the contrary, was quite agitated by his fondness for her and with impatience at the bad performance of the actors, which was wretched indeed.

Undeterred, however, Lady Craven brought out her musical farce *The Silver Tankard or, The Point at Portsmouth* at the Haymarket on 18 July 1781. The fine lady's attempt to depict seaport humours was doomed to failure, and the piece was heard only with difficulty on the first night, though the audience restrained itself from more rigorous condemnation out of respect for a lady's work.[12]

After this Lady Craven again turned her attention to the private stage. In collaboration with William Beckford of Fonthill fame, she produced a five act musical piece entitled *The Arcadian Pastoral*, which was performed at Queensberry House on 17 April 1782 by her children and those of Lords Spencer, Paget and Southampton.[13]

Beckford has provided us with amusing descriptions of the getting up of this piece, its trials and troubles as well as its delights.[14] On 5 April he wrote:

At length, after moving Heaven and Earth and, one would almost think the powers beneath it, Lady Craven has succeeded in obtaining the loan of Queensberry House for the performance of her Pastoral – the words a farrago of her Ladyship's – the music a farrago of mine. Our actors and actresses, Singers and Songtresses are all in their teens without any exception. Burton and Bertoni are drilling them apace under a special commission from me. The "Spectacle" in the last scene will be "ravissant" – not less than twenty or thirty blooming girls and boys appearing together at one time on the stage. . . . We are all at work clearing away partitions and causing as thick a dust as ever was raised by coaches and phaetons on the grand day of Epsom and Ascot. . . . Barthélemon[15] leads our band and manages our chorus; and a nice chorus it is, composed of – his wife, his eldest well-taught brat and seven or eight stray choristers from Westminster and the Chapel Royal. Our "noblesses", though they cut a delightful figure on the stage and open their coral lips very plausibly, are not in reality required to sing – no-no –, the sufficient chorus is behind the scenes, enveloped in mystery. Henry Fitzroy is our principal singer – by far the handsomest of King Charles's breed I am acquainted with . . . he sings from the heart in a delightful contralto and, thanks to our beloved Bertoni,[16] has caught already some of those bewitching appoggiaturas which were probably in high vogue at the opera of Sybaris.

Our Prima Donna, Miss Fawkener (the daughter of a once most fashionable Miss Ashe), has real talent, which is more than I can say of several others, who shall, and deserve to be nameless, and who are – O ye Gods! – how right entirely humdrum. One of these Dowdies [Maria Gavin] begins the opera with a song about twirling a wheel – of my composition alas! but of which I am ashamed most heartily.

Beckford goes on to say that Lady Craven's exertions were made in the hope that society's desire to attend the performances "would dispel a certain film of shiness which was beginning to creep over fashionable faces at her approach" owing to stories that were circulating about her. She succeeded so well that she was besieged with requests to obtain admittance to rehearsals: "The starchest of the starch are fast relaxing into complacency, and the wisest of the wise are foolish enough to stoop down to all sorts of petty manoeuvres to worry an invitation."

First-class talent was called in to coach in various branches: to Garrick's successor John Henderson was entrusted "the task of dis-awkwardising our raw actors"; Pacchierotti joined Bertoni and Barthéle-mon in giving lessons to Fitzroy and Miss Faulkner, but the ballet proved more difficult because Giovanni Gallini, ballet master of the Haymarket, refused to assist. The help of Richard Cosway, the miniaturist, was then enlisted and he "went straight to Drury Lane, and there, from the goodly company of Sylphs and Fairies, selected a bouquet that I think you would style divine." Unfortunately the "fairest rose of all" was forbidden by her mother to appear owing to the bad reputation of Queensberry House and of Lady Craven.

A general rehearsal, to which invitations were issued, took place on 16 April and was "lighted up in style". The company ranged from the Duke of Cumberland, the Archbishop of York and Lord Chancellor Thurlow to Dr. Burney, Sir Joshua Reynolds and Cosway, whilst nearer the stage sat a "formidable array of starch old maids, pattern wives, exemplary matrons and gambling dowagers" and next to the orchestra "three or four baboonical elders". Such an attendance filled "her frolic Ladyship" with "triumphant spirits". The finale, says Beckford maliciously, was sung by the chorus in such perfect tune and feeling manner "that she even forgave the liberty I had taken in writing not only the music but the words to this part of the pastoral." He wishes he had written the whole since it was ten times more insipid even than *The Silver Tankard* so "you will not be surprised at my fits of impatience whist adapting music to such lackadaisycal trumpery." He was even dissatisfied with the music he had composed for it. "Not a single air do I think worth sending you."

The following night Beckford took up his pen to describe the performance on which so much care, talent and expense had been lavished:

As I foretold, the heat was intolerable and the congregation which had received an immense addition of simpering fools, false connoisseurs, and consequential blockheads, – still more so. The "Spectacle" in itself turned out even more charming than I expected. The children were enchantingly well dressed – in the best and that is to say the simplest taste. Among the Figurantes were some of the most nymph-like etherial Creatures you ever beheld – pale and interesting; for I entered a strong protest against rouge, and, as I happen to act a very essential part in the drama, namely that of paymaster general – my remonstrances were attended to. ... The effect of this tender colouring – these evanescent tints – was enchanting. How you would have understood and admired it! How you would have enjoyed the perspective of the stage at that moment when it presented a living parterre – in which the rose and the smooth glossy lily were blended. Bertoni, who presided at the harpsichord, often stole a moment to gaze and Pacchierotti, who has the quickest perception in the world of the beautiful, was so enraptured that he could not resist going behind the scenes and throwing in a few chords as a second to Madame Barthélemon in the finale.

Horace Walpole's[17] praise was milder; he wrote to Mason on 14 April:

Last night before I came out of town, I was at a kind of pastoral opera written by Lady Craven, and acted prettily by her own and other children: you will scold me again for not telling you the title, but in truth I forgot to ask it. There was imagination in it, but not enough to carry off five acts.

The Reading Mercury[18] praised "the elegant simplicity of the language, equally removed from the extremes of unnatural refinement and vulgarity." This paper printed the epilogue, which was spoken by Miss Faulkner as a fairy and concluded:

> Good Heav'ns, I'd nigh forgot – But I was sent
> To ask if with our play you're all content;
> My little trembling friends impatient wait,
> To hear from me your judgment, and their fate.
> *One* too there is, to whom your kind applause,
> As doubly flatt'ring, double joy will cause:
> And *she* to merit most concern appears,
> Who to an *Author's* joins a mother's fears.

One of the Della Cruscan poets, "Arley" (M. P. Andrews), also wrote some stanzas to Lady Craven's children on the occasion.[19]

Her children were acting again in July of this year 1782 in her tamed version of Molière's *Don Juan* which she entitled *The Statue Feast*. The *Reading Mercury*[20] has a full report:

We have had in this part of the world a play; acted by Lord Craven's young family; the sight was altogether the newest and most interesting that imagination can form. The Theatre was made in the wood behind Benham house; the trees formed a canopy, and the darkness and stillness of the night was favourable to the lights and dresses, which were Spanish, and very magnificent. The play was Molière's Statue Feast, but much altered and cut into two acts by Lady Craven, who has, with taste, lessened Don Juan's villany into wildness, and instead of permitting the horrible catastrophe at the end of the 5th act, has caused the Statue to be found the brother of Elvira, who assisted her in her plot of terrifying her inconstant husband from his pursuits. I must observe, however, that Lady Craven's new Statue owes little to translation, the language being her own entirely, and some of the speeches made by Pedro, the servant, contain much humour, which Lady Craven's second daughter did strict justice to.

The interest was heightened

by the Statue presenting a little child to Don Juan (Don Juan's son) which he knew not he was possessed of; the infant was Lady Craven's beautiful youngest son, only three years old, who embraced his theatrical Parents with much grace.

A touching scene, but rather far from Molière. The prologue, said to be written by the hostess, is in romantic vein:

> To this deep shade, this sacred wood belong
> The pow'rs of wit, the harmony of song;

No longer, as in days of yore, the owl
With midnight shrieks affright[s] the calmest soul;
No more the hoarse and death foreboding raven
With croaks disturb the peaceful House of Craven;
A muse, with all a mortal's careless grace,
First decks with artful hand this lovely place. . . .
Tonight Molière appears, à l'Anglaise dress'd,
And if by your applause he is confess'd
A welcome foreigner; perchance your smile
May be an omen to this war-worn isle,
That France and England may once more agree;
Let France give wit, we'll grant it liberty.

The epilogue was an old one to which Lady Craven had added some lines "of delicate satire on the times".

Soon after this Lady Craven, deserted by her husband, went abroad. At the court of the Margrave of Anspach she was once again able to indulge in her taste for theatricals. She had an old riding school converted into a theatre in which the young nobility acted, danced and sang with the help of the court orchestra and "the best machinest in Europe". Lady Craven wrote two petites pièces, *La Folie du Jour* and *Abdoul et Nourjad*, and translated Cibber's *She Wou'd and She Wou'd Not* into French for this Court theatre, herself playing Hypolita. A court lady said that "Sa passion dominante est la comédie, qu'elle joue admirablement; elle a fini par communiquer cette passion au margrave".[21]

On 30 October 1791 Lady Craven married the Margrave and soon after returned to England and settled, as we have seen, at Brandenburgh House. This house had been the scene of private theatricals when, as La Trappe, it was owned by Bubb Dodington. Bentley's comedy *The Wishes* had been acted in the garden prior to its performance at Drury Lane on 27 July 1761.

At Brandenburgh House the Margravine, rejected by the court and ignored by the best society, started to entertain on a lavish scale. In May, 1792 M. le Texier, who had acted with her at Newbury, read a comedy and so delighted the Margrave that he obtained the post of Gentleman in Ordinary to the household at a handsome salary. Le Texier, famous for his French and English readings, then became for two years virtual manager of the Brandenburgh House theatricals.[22] His first effort was a fête in honour of the Duke of Clarence on 17 July when after dinner, whilst the guests strolled in the grounds, the dining room was transformed into a "splendid theatre". A comedy, burlesque, tragedy and burletta all written by Le Texier were performed and in them the Margravine displayed "astonishing and diversified accomplishments", singing in French, Italian and English and playing on various instruments. Her son Keppel took part both in male and female attire, and with Madame

Delavalle and her daughter sang terzettas from Gluck and Grétry's operas. Catches and petites chansons were sung by a French family, Madame Delavalle played on the harp, and fireworks in the garden and a cold supper concluded the entertainment.[23]

On the anniversary of her marriage the Margravine gave another fête at which the house painter Wigstead, later to help with the scenery and decorations of the theatre, sang a song with words by Peter Pindar and music by Shield.[24]

Meanwhile a theatre on the bank of the Thames was arising under the direction of the Margravine's domestic chaplain, the Rev. Mr. Ferryman.[25] On 7 November *The Times* commented:

> The Theatre building by the Margravine of Anspach at Brandenburgh House, will be very pretty when finished. It is already in great forwardness. The outward appearance of it, however, has nothing to recommend it, for one should rather suppose it to be a Bastille, than a temple dedicated to the Muses.

This last remark was evoked by the fact that it was built in the castellated style of the Gothic revival initiated by Walpole at Strawberry Hill. The view of the exterior in a pen and ink drawing by an unknown artist (Plate 10a) gives a good idea of its appearance and of how it was connected with the house by a colonnade.[26] Angelo tells us that it was commodious and beautifully decorated.[27] A water colour of the interior (Plate 10b) shows an unusual and interesting arrangement. In the centre is a large box for the Margrave but at the side there are only four upper boxes each containing five people. Instead of a pit excavated to allow of a low tier of boxes on a level with the stage, a parterre is raised on a shallow platform which accommodated at least three rows of backed benches. The proscenium arch is set right forward in continental fashion without forestage or proscenium doors. Comparison with the engraving of the Wargrave interior (Plate 7), which was only six years its senior, shows its great difference in style from the customary tradition. The Theatre was lit by a chandelier with two circles of candles. The ceiling was said to be too low.

The Theatre was not ready for its intended opening on 17 December, and the project of acting French, Italian and English plays there during the winter had to be abandoned. By January, 1793 Gaetano Marinari was employed on the scenery and Thomas Malton, master of Turner and Girtin, who had painted successful scenery for Covent Garden, was engaged to furnish an architectural scene. His forte was skill in perspective and accuracy in reproducing architectural details, which made his views of London streets and buildings famous. His palace scene proved both in design and execution "his acknowledged superiority in the architectural line" and presented an admirable perspective with the sides so well arranged that every person appeared to enter the stage through an arch. The Rev. Ferryman's mechanical improvements were also commended.[28]

Rehearsals of French petites pièces started to take place in February with the Margravine, Mrs. Hobart and Le Texier in the principal rôles. The Margravine's son Keppel Craven, though only 13, had a leading part but developed measles, so that production was again postponed. Private rehearsals took place on 12 March and 20 April and the Theatre was publicly opened on 25 April with a *Prelude*, and *Fanfan and Colas* and *Le Poulet*, two *petites pièces*. The *Prelude*,[29] written by the Margravine, dealt with the French Revolution and worked up to a compliment to the Margrave, who had retired from the pomp and fatigue of courts to repose on the verdant banks of the Thames. Its scene was a wood with a view of the Thames in the background. After a pastoral opening with Queen Mab, a trophy of arms arose, and furies trampled on the banner of France. They were thus addressed by Queen Mab:

> Desist, ye Ministers of Hell! rebellious fiends
> That tempt the wrath of Heaven. Your sacrilegious hands
> From Royalty would tear the just insignia –
> But here, here your efforts all are vain,
> And, like your Chief, in adamantine chains,
> You're doomed to sink below the light of day . . .
> Rouse not the British Lion's dread revenge,
> Nor tempt the Northern Eagle's waken'd fury.
> United here, they keep inviolate
> The wealth and freedom of this sea-girt Isle.
> From Cassups and the hardy Vandals sprung,
> A warrior fixes here his lov'd abode,
> And Berkeley's daughter hails him all her own.
> While England smiles to see her native child
> Return, with more than birthright dignities,
> She grateful weaves the fragrant myrtle wreath,
> That shall unfading, blow for him alone; –
> To Heav'n-born Poetry she consecrates this place;
> To Harmony, and all its soothing train.
> Here shall her Hero rest, retir'd from pomp,
> And all the pageant falsehood of the Court;
> Here magic scenes shall speak of nought but love –
> Of nought but honour, decency and truth.

The river god then arose from the Thames, the Genius of the Isle descended in a cloud, and the three graces entered preceded by Thalia.

No wonder that the more irreverent paragraphists said that it was "all praise of Spousy and her dear sweet self". It must, however, have appealed to the Margravine's émigré friends. In *Fanfan and Colas*[30] the Margravine

61

in the part of a rustic boy carefully imitated French patois; other rôles were taken by M. le Texier and his wife, Count D'Alet and Keppel Craven. *Le Poulet* was a dialogue between a French valet, played by le Texier, and an English maidservant, played by Mrs. Hobart, in which the latter introduced the sad story of her public fête at Ham the previous summer when drenching rain had turned all her fine creams into milk and water. The proceedings were conducted with great magnificence, a new gold service was prominently displayed, an elaborate supper provided and a surprise masquerade given for which the Margravine had supplied all the dresses. Even the Prince of Wales, who was used to splendid entertainments, said he had never seen one more handsomely conducted. About 120 guests were present, for the Theatre was not adapted for more than a select party of friends. Though the Margravine had succeeded in luring the Prince of Wales to Brandenburgh House, her lavish ostentation did not procure her the patronage of the highest society. The performance was repeated on 2 May when the Margrave occupied the state box round which the company flocked during the intervals.

The Statue Feast, with the Margravine as Don Juan, was revived on 17 December at a grand entertainment followed by a supper and concert, which was attended by the Prince of Wales, Duke of Clarence, Duchess of Cumberland and Duke of Queensberry among others.[31]

When the theatre was reopened on 19 March 1794, the occasion was marked by an elaborate Prologue.[32] The curtain rose and discovered a temple dedicated to the God of Taste, full of priests and votaries with an altar in the centre of the stage. To soft and solemn music, the great priestess entered, attended by four maidens, and invoked the god. But, accompanied by thunder and lighting, Jealousy attended by the Furies arose from the infernal regions and put to flight the priestess and destroyed the altar. The second scene opened in a gloomy wood; the priestess entered dishevelled and in despair fainted in the arms of her attendants. The oracle is consulted and the god is said to have flown to the banks of the Thames. The scene changed to the Thames and the god duly descended in a cloud. This spectacular compliment was suceeded by Jerningham's "historical interlude" *Margaret of Anjou*. Originally written for Mrs. Pope, it is mainly a monologue interspersed with music. The Margravine took the part of Queen Margaret who, fleeing with her son Edward (Miss le Texier) after the defeat and death of Henry VI, encounters a Robber (Keppel Craven) in the forest by whom she is assisted to escape. Jerningham[33] says the rôle "received from the theatrical abilities of her Serene Highness the Margravine the richest colouring and most impressive truth of expression". She eschewed bombast and declamation and drew tears from the assembly. A French comedy followed in which the Countess de

3. Delaval Theatre. Lady Stanhope as Calista.

4. Blenheim Palace Theatre. *False Delicacy*.

Linières distinguished herself in a soubrette part and in which her husband, Count D'Alet and the Le Texiers also found favour. Keppel Craven and the two Miss Berkeleys were other performers.

The final offering was an *Italian Pastorale* by Count Benincasa which was acted by the author, the Margravine, Sapio,[34] the Baron de Parsay, and the Chevalier de la Cainea, the music being under the direction of Haydn's friend, Johann Salomon. The Margravine's inordinate vanity was catered for by an elaborate compliment in which Keppel as the God of Taste re-descended and awarded her a double crown of laurel. A supper and ball followed. The colonnade, which connected the Theatre with the house, had been replaced by a conservatory and the Theatre too had been improved and enlarged. *The Times*[35] described it as

the most elegant thing to be seen; the company was conducted to it through a suit of apartments, and a winter garden of 100 feet in length, filled with magnificent orange trees covered with fruits, and all sorts of exotic plants in full bloom. The tout ensemble of it unites elegance with magnificence, and we cannot be surprised, for when the invention of the Margravine, and the execution of Mr. le Texier are joined the effect must be delightful.

The next opportunity for a grand scale celebration was the election of the Margrave as hon. freeman of the Fishmonger's Company, on which occasion the Margravine entertained the company in her usual sumptuous style on 17 July. The theatricals opened with a prologue by Peter Pindar spoken by Arabin. It was probably then that the person selected to speak the address was too nervous, because of being imperfect, and Arabin delivered it without ever having seen a line of it, prompted by Keppel.[36] *The Yorkshire Ghost*, a five act comedy by the Margravine, was the main piece. The situations, it was said, exhibited the comic powers of Arabin and Le Texier whilst the Margravine supported her rôle "with a spirit never equalled in a private, and rarely excelled in a public theatre". Count D'Alet, Keppel Craven, Morris, Madame le Texier and Miss Berkeley also took part. The epilogue, written and spoken by the Margravine, defends the heroine for trying to capture her lover despite carping opposition, a situation which reflected on the Margravine's second marriage. In honour of the Fishmonger's Company a French piece, *Les Poissardes Anglois*, already used by le Texier for his readings, was given as afterpiece. It was based on an actual incident that happened when some French *émigrés* went to Billingsgate to buy fish cheaply, and the fishwomen not only loaded them with their wares for nothing but raised a subscription for their relief.[37] As the fishwoman Poll, the Margravine sung a song of her own composition of which this is a specimen verse:

I'm a Billingsgate girl – 'tis an odd sort of name,

And my eyes are as black as a coal;
My frankness of heart gives me looks that are game –
But you'll find I'm a good little soul.
Who'll buy, who'll buy?
Who'll buy of this good little soul?

Refreshments between the acts were followed by an elegant supper and then the Great Gallery was thrown open for country dancing and the guests remained "until long after Aurora had shed her beams on Saturday morning".

In 1795 *The Tamer Tam'd*, altered from Beaumont and Fletcher, and *The Sleep Walker* were chosen for the opening night on 9 June. In the former the Margravine played Maria supported by Keppel Craven, Arabin and Madame le Texier. She herself wrote the prologue and M. P. Andrews the epilogue. Two days later O'Keeffe's *Agreeable Surprise* was given, followed by *Les Poissardes Anglois*. In the former Lady Buckinghamshire (formerly Mrs. Hobart) played Cowslip. Poor Lady Bucks., who was very fat, was quite unsuited to play the young girl and became a natural butt for the satirists in consequence. Gillray made a caricature of her in the role (Plate 2) and a lampoonist wrote on "the late chilling Theatricals of Brandenburgh House":

> The House was thin, and much too cool
> Dramatic flow'rs to raise;
> For plants so sensitive as these,
> Requir'd the warmest praise!
>
> The Dame of Bucks in Cowslip vest,
> Expanded to our view!
> The Margravine a Violet sprung
> That look'd a little blue.

Unkindest cut of all the Margravine, jealous perhaps of her rival's acting abilities, composed these verses:[38]

> Tho' her Ladyship's figure,
> Was some little bigger,
> Than Cowslip's; yet all must allow
> That her fat Ladyship,
> Might have cut off the slip
> And famously acted the cow.

It is not surprising that Lady Bucks. never again performed at Brandenburgh House. The Margravine looked beautiful and sang sweetly as Laura and Arabin's whimsical playing of Lingo was laughable. Arabin's son rescued the part of Sir Felix Friendly "from the trammels of buffoonery usually attached to him in the regular Theatre", but whoever played Mrs. Cheshire was insufficiently "giggish" and needed a whip instead of a fan. The dress too was altogether too feminine. The band was conducted by Salomon. A topical laugh was raised by the introduction of Richard Brothers, the prophet who had recently been condemned for treasonable practices, in a procession along with Moses, Wat Tyler and other heroes.

Another piece got le Texier into trouble. An indignant letter appeared in *The Times*[39] complaining that

last week some foreigners, disguised under the assumed character of French Emigrants, were suffered to represent at the Theatre at Brandenburgh House a pitiful dramatic rhapsody, tending to ridicule, and even grossly abuse, the venerable Bishop of St. Paul de Leon, and to calumniate the French Clergy in the most gross manner. To render this strange exhibition still more astonishing, the part of the virtuous Prelate was acted by a sycophant who calls himself a Count.

Le Texier replied[40] that he had written the comedy in order to be of service to the emigrant clergy, that the Bishop was performed by a gentleman of quality, and that he intended to publish the play for the general public to judge. Keppel Craven was praised for his acting as the Abbé Joujou especially in the last act with Count D'Alet and Le Texier.

The Tamer Tam'd was played with *The Agreeable Surprise* on 18 June. *Twelfth Night* was mooted for the next piece but was abandoned in favour of the Margravine's own comedy *The Smyrna Twins* in January, 1796. About this time Le Texier was succeeded as manager by Count D'Alet, an elderly man who was usually cast as the heavy father. The Margravine thought him the best actor she had ever seen and he reminded Angelo of the celebrated French comedian Belville.[41] The performance of *The Smyrna Twins* celebrated the Margrave's birthday on 25 February. The Margravine and her son played the twins. The Turkish scenes and distant view of the sea were executed by Henry Wigstead from a sketch by the Margravine. Wigstead was painter to the Prince of Wales and had been appointed house painter to the Margravine, in which capacity he had helped with the decorations of the Theatre in 1792.[42] The magnificence of the dresses "was particularly seen, from the lights being arranged so as to produce an effect never yet seen on an English stage". Joseph Mazzinghi, musical director of the King's Theatre, Haymarket, and composer of operas, ballets and songs, was in charge of the music and composed three or four arias for the Margravine. He played the harpsichord and conducted a band of well known musicians in which Dragonetti played the double bass, Harrington the oboe, Pieltain the horn and

Holmes the bassoon. The prologue, written by the Margravine, was delivered by Plaistow.[43]

The programme also included Marivaux's *Le Jeu de l'Amour et du Hazard* which was acted by the Counts de la Roche Courbon, D'Alet and Benincasa, M. du Chasset and the Countess de Linières. These French plays were something that the public theatres did not, and could not, provide, but which were made possible by a number of French *émigrés* in London, many of whom had taken part in them in France. The Margravine was complimented on her lead in presenting them and it was even suggested that a subscription theatre should be formed for the purpose.[44] In addition the services of Harry Angelo were enlisted for the first time and he sang a song and personated a Jew with much humour.[45]

Some novelties were added on 21 March when *The Smyrna Twins* and *Le Jeu de L'Amour* were repeated: the Margravine sang an additional patriotic verse to a Turkish melody; the comedian Joseph Munden, in his original role of Peregrine Forester, rendered the Traveller's Song from Pearce's operatic farce *Hartford Bridge*, and a burlesque was put on of the new opera, Cimarosa's *I Traci Amanti* in which a dance by Craven and others caused much laughter.

The newspapers were indulging in sarcastic comments on the Margravine's attempt to win back her position in society by attracting the *bon ton* to her sumptuous entertainments. When *Chrononhotonthologos* was given on 7 April 1797 it was pronounced not creditable to her taste:

There was an attempt at a whimsical procession, but it was tedious in the extreme. The Audience was by no means of the higher order, and performances which lasted from ten o'clock till near three, were, upon the whole "stale, flat, and unprofitable".[46]

The Margravine was accused of trying to console the public for the loss of Miss Farren who had just married the Earl of Derby. Another paragraph ironically lauds the Margravine's taste which, superior to the works of Shakespeare, Congreve, Vanbrugh and writers of the day, "presented her Noble and Literary Friends ... with the exquisite repast of Chrononhotonthologos". A less hostile critic says that the farce succeeded and that Angelo's Aldiberontiphoscophornio, Wathen's Rigdum-Funnidos, Craven's Bombardinian, Wynn's King and the triumphal entry of the conqueror caused much amusement. Simons wrote, for his rôle of the Queen, a mock mad scene in which he burlesqued Mrs. Siddons so that Wathen, who was lying on the stage, could barely suppress his laughter. The Margravine had had a handsome suit made for Simons and herself shone in her own jewels.[47] She spoke and wrote the prologue in which, robed in deep black, she pronounced:

Too long the Comic Muse, in numbers gay,
Has here obtain'd uninterrupted sway.

Some time during this season[48] an alteration of Kenrick's sequel to *Henry IV*, *Falstaff's Wedding*, was brought out with the Margravine as Ursula, Madocks as Falstaff and Angelo as Shallow. Joseph Madocks was a Welsh amateur of wide experience who had acted at Wynnstay and elsewhere. Wathen, whom we have met at Lord Barrymore's Theatre, had now become a professional. The next season Wade, who had also played with Lord Barrymore, appeared at Brandenburgh House. Thus, in place of the émigrés, the Margravine had gathered together some of the best *dilettante* talent of the time. The new piece, put on on 28 February 1798, was an opera, *The Princess of Georgia*, of which the fairytale libretto and part of the music was written by the Margravine. Others who had a hand in the music were Sapio, who was the leader of the orchestra and played the harpsichord in it, Sarti, Guglielmi and Paesiello. The Margravine's fancy once again turned to the gorgeous east, her knowledge of which helped her in the designing of the dresses and decorations. She played the good fairy in which she sang her songs with great taste. Simons, as the black chief of the harem, got into trouble because he refused to encore a song "not remarkably decent". When he reminded the Margravine that he had her command never to repeat a song in the Theatre, she characteristically replied "Ay, but this is my own piece!"[49] With the opera was given a one act piece by Molière with Craven, D'Alet and the Margravine, to the fun of which "the whimsicality of the French dresses of the last centry" contributed. Angelo[50] describing the theatricals, says

The Margravine on all occasions was the prima donna, and mostly performed the juvenile characters; but whatever she represented the heroine or the soubrette, her person and talents captivated every heart. ... The excellent acting of the Hon. Keppel Craven, aided by his youth and elegant appearance, made both the French and English pieces go off with éclat. ... The Count [D'Alet] generally played the father; the Margravine the daughter or pert chambermaid; Keppel Craven, the lover or the intriguing lackey.

On this occasion, at any rate, the Margravine had the satisfaction of seeing her Theatre crowded at an early hour, whilst leaders of society unable to gain admission, were compelled to perambulate the avenues of the garden during most of the performance. A repeat was given on 8 March.

The Margravine, who had so far stood out against tragedy, then gave way to the constant solicitations of her son, and allowed him to arrange and direct a performance of Schiller's *The Robbers* which she had translated and adapted.[51] Though she carefully purged the drama of any possible Jacobinical sentiments she was attacked by the press who hinted

67

that the original tendentious speeches had not been cut. She therefore had her version published so that the public could judge of "the ungenerous and false aspersions" that had been cast on it. She also wrote the prologue and epilogue which were spoken respectively by Wade and herself. As Emilia she gave a performance full of feeling and pathos in which "she displayed all her powers of sensibility and both in her scenes of tenderness and passion shewed very fine acting". Keppel admirably portrayed the contending passions of Charles Demoor, and, during his scene with Old Demoor, a lady in the upper boxes fainted "overcome by the illusion of the Stage". Two new scenes, one of sunset on the banks of the Danube, the other of moonlight in the forests of Bohemia, were painted by Pugh who was scene painter at Drury Lane, and admired for their masterly execution.[52] The afterpiece was Oulton's farce *All in Good Humour* with Miss Berkeley as the Young Lady and the Margravine as a Country Girl. The first performance was on 29 May, the second on 6 June. The weather was sultry and the audience so uncomfortable that it was announced that, after one further performance, the Theatre would undergo improvement and enlargement.

The next year, 1799, having given Keppel his fling, the Margravine reverted to comedy with a three act version of *The Provok'd Wife* on 29 May. Mrs. Abington herself was invited to play Lady Fanciful. So keen, nevertheless, was the Margravine on remaining the centre of attraction that she cut out the conclusion of the second act in order to make her rôle of Lady Brute the principal one; whereupon the outraged Mrs. Abington ordered one of the attendants to carry a table on the stage and went through the excised scene with applause, much to the Margravine's annoyance.[53] Mrs. Abington gave a finished performance and spoke the epilogue; she was "elegantly dressed in white and silver". The Margravine spoke her own prologue and "varied her dresses several times in the course of the evening's entertainment, on which she displayed a profusion of jewellery". Angelo[54] found Sir Walter James capital as Sir John Brute; he himself was only allotted a trifling part and so was allowed afterwards to sing a song alluding to his character of a tailor with a prelude especially written by Jack Bannister.

The afterpiece was a pantomime, *Puss in Boots*, devised by Keppel Craven,[55] the scene of which was laid, once again, in Turkey and Moldavia. One flattering critic went so far as to say that "perhaps finer acting and attitudes were never witnessed". Craven danced some merry dances in style but called down the reprobation of the *True Briton*[56] which characterised one dance as odious and disgusting and expressed the hope that in future it would be danced, not by two men, but a man and a woman. Major, who was in charge of the music, chose and arranged the performers and himself played the harpsichord with exquisite tones.[57] Both pieces were repeated on 12 June and *Puss in Boots* was performed a third time with a French *petite pièce* which resembled Dunlop's *Tell the Truth and Shame the Devil*.[58]

Between these performances and those of June 1800 the Theatre underwent improvement under the direction of Wigstead. It was afterwards reported to be

> simply elegant. One row of boxes encircles the House; the Margravine's is in front. The curtain is of pink silk; in the centre, the Spread Eagle, emblematic of the family arms, appears encircled by a sprig of laurel and oak; the effect was much admired.

From the hall of the house, where a medallion of Comus in a niche bore an inscription by its former owner Lord Melcombe, the guests entered the greenhouse filled with plants and flowers in ornamental stands, and thence progressed through three apartments, in two of which refreshments of tea, lemonade and negus were served.[59]

Performances took place on 25 June and 2 July at which a revival of *The Sleep Walker* was followed by *Imagination*, a one act entertainment by the Margravine. The rôle of the Dutch gardener in the former, originally played by Le Texier, was undertaken by a newcomer, John Nixon, who sustained it with much humour. He was a dabbler in many arts, a painter who designed the entrance ticket for *The Sleep Walker*, a man of taste and talent, and an excellent amateur performer.[60] The Margravine "in the dress of an ancient Dowager" well expressed the haughty arrogance and ridiculed the affectation of greatness in an unusual type of rôle for her. At the end she came forward "dressed in a simple robe of white muslin, with gold chain trimmings, head-dress plain (Grecian) with a diamond star in front and a plain one at her breast", and spoke the epilogue with animation. The epilogue, though its opening resembled the original, had been practically rewritten.[61] *Imagination* included a masquerade interspersed with singing and dancing in which Sir Walter James and the Margravine performed a minuet, Craven danced, Angelo sang his Cranbourn-alley Duet, Wathen supplied a song about a country club, Walsh Porter sang a specially composed Venetian air to a guitar and the whole ended with a chorus from the *Princess of Georgia*. As 300 people were present the Theatre's capacity must have been doubled.

No theatricals were held in 1801 owing to Craven's illness and to the Margravine's subsequent absence abroad.[62] They were resumed in 1802 when *The Statue Feast*, *The Two Officers* and *Imagination* were presented on 11 June. The only new venture, *The Two Officers*, was a *petite pièce* taken from the French by the Margravine; in her epilogue she acknowledged her debt to her French originals. The masquerade this time included a burlesque sung in the Italian style by Maynard of Doctor's Commons, a song by Angelo entitled "Lord Mayor's Day" in which he made game of the new amateur society the Pic Nic, a *pas seul* by Craven and a display of grace and agility by Miss Darville. The band was led by Spagnioletti. A supper followed the plays, at which one servant "splendidly attired" in royal livery was apportioned to each pair of guests. About 250 people came including many foreigners, and the festivities did not terminate until 2 a.m.

The Margrave's birthday on 24 February 1803 was the occasion of the next play. However it was not given in the Theatre but in the great gallery adjoining the dining-room fitted up under the Margravine's direction. At the upper end of this room a temporary and confined stage was set up which measured only 22×20 ft. and was raised 3 ft. 6 in. from the floor, with a small orchestra in front.[63] According to the *Morning Herald*[64] the Margrave did not welcome the idea but was cajoled "into a kind of silent consent". A grand rehearsal was given to local fashionables three days before and the performance itself was followed by a supper and ball. Each actor was allowed six tickets for the play and Angelo[65] relates how he enjoyed being able to take his friends to see the supper preparations between it and the afterpiece.

On these occasions [he adds] the dramatis personae, who came down from London to render their gratuitous services, were invited to dine with the margrave and margravine, when the dinners were elegant, and their attention to their guests most engaging. One of these parties, I particularly remember, was very gay, being assembled on the birthday of the margrave; all the amateurs who performed on her ladyship's splendid little stage were invited to celebrate that anniversary. The festivities over the dessert were not a little enlivened by the wit and humour of John Nixon.

The play was a three act comedy called *Nourjad* taken by the Margravine from Frances Sheridan's The History of *Nourjahad*. It was printed for E. Roberts at Hammersmith in 1803 but is a rare volume.[66] Sometime before the overture is finished the curtain slowly rises on Nourjad's room whilst the theatre is gradually darkened. The play opens with a song by the Genie. The young Nourjad, played by Angelo, has been brought up by the Sultan and is his bosom friend. The Sultan is angered because, when he asked Nourjad what best could make men happy, the latter chose material and sensual pleasures. The Genie, taken by the Margravine, appears to Nourjad and offers him inexhaustible riches and immortality on condition that he must sleep for periods of 40 years. He accepts but the treasure he obtains causes him to fall out of love with his wife Fatima (again the Margravine) and purchase two beautiful, singing slaves (the Mlles. Mortellari). He is just commencing to regret his conduct when he falls asleep, and awakens to find his slaves old hags, his wife, son, servant Ali and the Sultan dead. The scene changes and discovers the Sultan (Col. Berkeley) on his throne surrounded by nobles. Nourjad is summoned, tells of his grief and repentance, and of his conviction that pleasure is not happiness. He asks the Genie, who reappears, to take back her gifts and let him see his wife, whereupon she unveils and reveals herself as Fatima. It was all a hoax engineered by the Sultan to make Nourjad realise his folly. The play ends with Nourjad's presenting his service of gold plate to his friend, a device for displaying the Margravine's own service. The part of the hero was so long that for some time no-one could be persuaded to undertake it. Angelo at last agreed to do so but unfortunately had to rise from a sick bed to play this fatiguing and unsuitable rôle. Apologies had to be made for him. He describes how in the last scene

while I was seated in all my grandeur surrounded with my courtiers, a numerous procession followed in the Turkish costume, and as they appeared, making their salam, they place at my feet the plate, which a few hours before decorated the table I had left.[67]

The Margravine was encored for the opening song "Laurel immortal, Apollo be thine" with music by Mlle. D'Alpy. Little Chatterley, as the black slave, was admired for his *pas seul;* he later went on the stage.

The scenery consisted of a change of curtains "the first representing the entrance of a hall, with fireboard, flowerpots, a clock &c. Second the interior of a palace forming a dome, with shaded pillars and columns". Green baize served for the side scenes.[68] The temporary Theatre, fitted up under the Margravine's direction,

was decorated with flowers, and near to the Orchestra some elegant sofas were placed in the Turkish style, and a table, covered with a superb desert, and all sorts of wines, was provided for the refreshment of the company during the performance.[69]

The Turkish dresses were splendid as usual. The music, partly composed by Corri, partly by the Margravine, was under the direction of G. Ashley. Signor Michele Mortellari was at the piano and Ashley jun. played the violincello. The audience is variously reported to have numbered 97 and 200.[70] They entered the Theatre at 9 and did not leave it until 1 a.m.

Two new pieces were given on 17, 20 June; a farce in two acts entitled *Poor Noddle* translated from the French by the Margravine, and a pantomime *The Release of Eblis* by Craven derived from the Arabian Nights. In the former, Craven impersonated a clownish footman, the Margravine was the heroine and a newcomer, Robert Kerr Porter the traveller, made his first appearance here. *Poor Noddle*, "received with rapturous applause" at Brandenburgh House, met only with "disgust and contempt" when transferred to the Haymarket under the title of *Nicodemus in Despair*.[71] The three act pantomime was printed by E. Roberts "Bookseller, Stationer, and Paper Hanger" to the Anspachs.[72] It is an involved Persian story with "Gouls, Wicked Spirits Haunting Cemetries and feeding on Corpses" and with music selected from Haydn, Kozeluch, Edelman, Nicolai and Devienne. Craven, as the Spirit of Evil, danced with his usual excellence and ease, and the Margravine sang several airs. Between the acts Angelo diverted the company with a ludicrous "Duet of Street Ballad Singers". On 17 June the theatricals were followed by fireworks on the lawn, at which 400 were present, and a supper; on 20 June, 150 guests were conducted through the suite of apartments elegantly lit with lamps and through the orangery to the Great Gallery where supper was served on gilt and silver plate. Scenes of fabulous magnificence were realised in these entertainments.[73]

The Margravine had persuaded her husband to purchase Benham House, to which she was much attached, from the Craven family, and on 27 November 1803 she wrote from there:

The Theatre I alluded to here is within a circular manège I made for the Margrave – & it is very pretty . . . 'tis not the Theatre in Newbury, 'tis in my garden behind this house.

Four years later she told Elliston that the Theatre in her wood was "of a construction . . . peculiarly pretty".[74] No trace of it is left, nor is it known what performances took place there, but the references to it afford further evidence of the Margravine's indefatigable ardour for the stage.

Poor Noddle and *The Release of Eblis* were repeated for the first performance of 1804 on 24 May. Miss Shuttleworth replaced Mrs. Burke as Sophia in the former, otherwise the casts were the same. The pantomime was a brilliant spectacle in which the Margravine was attired in a vest of "white and gold, with shoulder straps of diamonds, and her headdress a magnificent tiara of brilliants". Chatterley was complimented on the comic naivety of his Noddy in the farce and his dumb but graceful acting in the pantomime.

This was followed on 15 June by two new pieces: *'Tis Well They Are Married*, a one act play from the French whose action takes place at an inn just after the battle of Rosbach, and *The Gaunlet*, a three act drama

72

said to be from the Spanish.[75] An address to the latter by the Margravine speaks of "a modest youthful" author: "By my example, in our native land, He join'd *Melpomine's* respected band".[76] Scenery, decorations and dresses were reported to be first class and Nixon in the comic part of an old woodman was particularly effective.

The two pieces were revived in 1805,[77] Angelo as a captain of banditti had to be killed in a duel by Craven, a prince disguised as a woodcutter. He considered himself entitled to a dying speech but did not dare to say anything to the Margravine at rehearsal. Madocks advised him to make one of his own and suggested some appropriate sentences which Angelo spoke at the performance; but he fled when he heard that the Margravine was in a passion about it. He was duly informed, to his surprise, of the next performance, but when he arrived for the customary dinner was reprimanded by the Margravine and had to promise not to utter a word more than was in the text. He took his revenge by imitating instead the groans of a bear and giving a few queer kicks which raised the laughter of the house. He escaped disgrace but this was his last appearance in the theatricals.

On 5 July 1805 a full programme of comedy, farce and ballet was presented in all of which the Margravine played the heroine.[78] The comedy was called *Love in a Convent* and was taken from the French by the Margravine. It convulsed the house with laughter. The Margravine and Craven had never acted better, Joseph Madocks was excellent as Juanillo, so were Simons and Morris in a drunken scene, whilst Hamilton played a porteress. The pantomime ballet, *The Princess and the Slave*, proved a great attraction with delightful music, and Miss Shuttleworth was an excellent mime. The composition by Craven afforded proof of his knowledge of dramatic effect and the dresses and decorations of this "impressive spectacle" reflected credit on the Margravine's taste. The performance was repeated on 15 July when the Duke of Sussex occupied the Margravine's box.

This was the end. The Margrave died on 5 January 1806. The Margravine's chief audience was gone and she had no heart to continue. Besides the expenses were enormous. The Margravine had delighted in her husband's enjoyment though she speaks too of her own satisfaction: "My taste for music and poetry, and my style of imagination in writing chastened by experience, were great sources of delight to me".[79]

The Theatre did indeed open its doors once more on 16 May 1810 to introduce Miss Jane Cramer who gave a recital of acting and singing assisted by the Duke of Kent's band. The *Morning Post*[80] pronounced her

one of the brightest stars that ever yet appeared in the theatrical hemisphere;

her talent in singing is equally great; she sung the Soldier Tir'd in a style that would have reflected credit on the first singer in Europe; also a most difficult Italian song in an equally refined style.

The Margravine herself seems never to have acted again. She ceased to reside at Brandenburgh House in 1819 and died at Naples on 13 January 1838. On 15 May 1822, after the death of the unfortunate Queen Caroline, last tenant of the house, materials of the building and theatre were sold by auction[81] and both were soon afterwards demolished. A copy of the sale catalogue is in the Wallace Collection Library[81] where I have been kindly allowed to examine it. Unlike the Wargrave sale the theatrical properties are not itemised. "The Scenes, Curtains, Side Slips, Rollers, Lines, Pullies and certain Machinery belonging to the Stage" were sold as one lot to Howe for £77 (lot 77). Other items of interest in the building are: "A twenty-four pannel framed shutter, boxes and pullies to the large Gothic window" (369); "The frame work that carries the rollers of the scenes under the roof" (374); "A boarded partition, and 2 steps at the back of the orchestra and a plaster and wood floor" (379); "The front and winged frame of the Stage, 2 orchestra boxes and fittings and flight of steps" (380); "The linings round the side box, a piece of wainscoting in front, and the battening" (382); "Fronts and fittings of 2 boxes adjoining the principal box" (383); "Principal Box 1¼ deal floor & joints, circular front and quartered partitions". The service of chased silver gilt dinner and dessert plate designed and executed by Green & Ward which the Margravine delighted to display on the stage was sold on 27 July 1818. On 8 May 1823, the theatrical dresses, properties and scenery of the Theatre were sold by Robins of the Piazza, Covent Garden. The sale was advertised as

Dresses and Properties, embracing a well-selected assortment of Character those for the first Tragic Business got up regardless of expence, the property of an amateur deceased, the whole adapted to the entire arrangement of numerous Stock Pieces, suited to the views of a respectable Amateur Company. Also, the entire Capital Scenery from Brandenburgh House painted expressly by the celebrated De Loutherbourg, with wings, sky and room borders, lamps, float forms, rollers, and an infinity of well-adapted Machinery, Material, and Properties, on a scale suited to a Country Theatre, not too small.[82]

This is the only evidence we have that De Loutherbourg, who lived in Hammersmith, may have been engaged on the scenery for Brandenburgh House. He is generally supposed not to have painted scenery for the theatre after 1785. If indeed he did it is strange that it was never advertised. There is the possibility that he did not wish it to be known but, even so, one would have expected some reference to it in the journals of the time, since members of the audience would have recognised his style. Whether or not he did provide some of the scenery it is evident that it was on a fair-sized scale since it was suitable for a medium-sized country theatre.

Chapter V

The Wynnstay Theatricals

The theatricals at Wynnstay in Denbighshire were different from any of those we have so far considered in that they were the entertainments of a country squire far removed from the metropolis. Neither actors nor audience were confined to high society and the atmosphere was that of country house festivities in the Christmas holidays in which not only the guests but the servants joined. They were also the most long lived of all theatricals of the time, the first period falling in the lifetime of the 4th baronet Sir Watkin Williams Wynn, from 1770 to 1787, the second in that of the 5th baronet from 1803 to 1810.[1]

The fourth baronet, who had succeeded to the estates and title when he was only five months old in 1749, was a man of taste and culture. A keen musician, he was one of the promoters of the Concerts of Ancient Music; a patron of the arts, he was a friend of Sir Joshua Reynolds, who painted him several times, and a member of the Dilettanti Society. Neither a courtier nor a statesman he was an amiable man of retiring disposition, much beloved.[2]

The celebrations at his coming-of-age on 21 April 1770 were carried out on a vast scale. 15,000 people were given dinner in the park at which a whole ox was roasted, and the entertainments included a poetical contest of Welsh bards, music and, in the way of properties, a triumphal car and Bacchanalian altar crowned with a cask.[3] A special kitchen was erected in the grounds and it was this building which became the first theatre.

After the inauguration of a new organ at Ruabon Church in September 1770 the company were invited to Wynnstay to dinner. Among them, R. Kenyon,[4] who wrote afterwards:

About nine o'clock, we all went to the puppet show, where a handsome

76

theatre and good music were exhibited; but as to Punch, I have seen him much more entertaining for a penny, and never crucified four hours more stupidly in my life. It would have done you good to see how many grave senators were entertaining themselves with the old history of Babes in the Wood ... The whole must have cost Sir Watkin a couple of thousand at least, and was meant to please every body, but whether calculated rightly for that purpose, or to answer any good end, I much doubt.

These puppets were sent to Wynnstay by Roger Johnstone of Drury Lane who was also employed, from August to December, in fitting up a playhouse and painting scenery. The following entries occur in the account book of the butler Samuel Sidebotham for 1771-2.[5]

1771. Feb. 14   pd Mr. Roger Johnston for 18 weeks painting the Scenes & fitting up the Playhouse at Wynnstay from Augst 8th to Decr 12 1771 [sic][6]   £61. 0. 0.

Mar. 15   pd Mr. Johnston's Bill for Sundry Scenes, Puppets &c. sent to Wynnstay last Augst his time 4 weeks fixing them up & for what he did in London in full & all Demands   £300. 0. 0.

The plaster work was by Joseph Bromfield and "Rolling Scenes" were painted by Paul Sandby[7].

The first company of players was a professional one. On 6 January 1771 Sidebotham records:

pd Mr. Randle Jones the Wrexham Players Expences & 5 Guineas given them, playing at Wynnstay   £8.9.0

This throws an interesting light on the kind of sum paid by a gentleman for a private performance at his house. Further entries about the Theatre occur in the autumn and winter of 1772:[8]

Sept. 16   pd Carriage of a large Sash Line for the use of the Playhouse from Ches[r]   £0. 0. 4.

Sept. 29   pd Mr. Richards for 2 scenes he brought to Wynnstay   £50. 0. 0.

Dec. 31   pd Mrs. Hughes, what she Paid in Monmouth Street for 2 Silk Sacks [women's dresses] for the Playhouse Wardrobe at Wynnstay   £6. 6. 0.

pd Mr. Johnston for 5 Noble Venecien Dresses 3 caskits &c. for the Playhouse   £18. 3. 3.

The dresses may have been hired for they were considerably cheaper than those used at Little Dalby Hall which cost £10 to £18 apiece.[8] Evidently *The Merchant of Venice* was performed that winter. Richards was in all probability John Inigo Richards who was to succeed Dall as chief scene painter at Covent Garden in 1777 and who was one of the original members of the Royal Academy.[9] He stayed in Wynnstay to paint more scenes but was not paid until 26 November 1772 under which date there is an entry:

> Pd Mr. Richards for 24 Days Scene painting at Wynnstay Sep[r] 1771 at 2 Guineas p[r] Day & expenses there & Back   £62.5.0.

James Gandon was also employed and, on 2 January 1772, was paid for work which included a design of the Theatre for Wynnstay. Gandon was later architect of many of the important buildings of 18th century Dublin. His mother was a Welshwoman named Wynne, and when at school he often painted scenery and stage decorations for performances by his schoolfellows, but we know of no other connections with the theatre.[10] On 16 June Mrs. Coade was paid 16 guineas for two vases of artificial stone for the niches which are visible in the picture of the play-house.[11]

To the early days of the Theatre must belong a small undated playbill[12] printed in red which announces that

> By Particular Desire by the Cavalieri Gugliemis Company of Comedians At the Theatre at Wynnstay will be perform'd The Minor, written by Samuel Foote, Esq. to which will be added By Mynheer Hogan Voghan's Company of Comedians, The Chaplet. With Entertainments. N.B. No Person to be admitted without a Ticket for the Day.

The curious names represent Williams and Vaughan who were both amateurs in the Wynnstay theatricals. The first dated playbill[13] is a fragment for 24 November 1773 when *The Merry Wives* was given with Puleston as Falstaff and Sir Watkin as Pistol, followed by Murphy's farce *The Upholsterer*. In the National Library of Wales there is an entrance ticket dated in a contemporary hand "Nov: y[e] 22[d] 1773". As this was a Monday it is probable that the theatricals opened on this date. The entrance ticket, which shows a group of characters dancing round a bust of Shakespeare, was reprinted in the *European Magazine*, along with two others, and is there ascribed to Bunbury (Pl. 12b). Bunbury did not act with the company until 1778, though this does not preclude his having designed tickets for the earlier performances. The figures seem to fit *The Merry Wives* better than any other play with Falstaff, three women (the merry wives and Ann Page), a man with a leek (Evans), and a man with a false nose (Pistol). The only inexplicable figure is the soldier with the large hat, queue and military boots. Could Page have been so dressed?

78

It is interesting to note that one of the women wears a ruff, a slight attempt to be Elizabethan in costume.

The Merry Wives and *The Upholsterer* were repeated on 26 November. The following night *Much Ado About Nothing* with Aldersey as Benedick, Sir Watkin as Dogberry and Miss J. Williams as Beatrice, was presented with *Chrononhotonthologos*.[14] The tickets were to be had of S. Sidebotham at Wynnstay and no person was admitted without them. Sidebotham, the butler, was also an actor. Bob Aldersley, who took leads every year but one, was a barrister, who, Colman[15] says, "was punchy, like Garrick in his latter days – but in other respects – alas! alas!" Griffith of Rhual, Flintshire, who played Claudio and the title rôle in *Chrononhotonthologos*, and Apperley, who was Shallow, were local gentlemen. Carter, who had some minor parts, was the cook and Meredith, who sustained the singing rôle of Balthazar, was a cooper with a bass voice which Sir Watkin had had trained. The domestics and retainers were distinguished in the play bills by the omission of Mr. before their names. The Misses Williams were the leading ladies.

As for the Theatre it has been described for us by Colman[16] as he saw it in 1779:

This building although intended to be temporary, was I know not how many years old when I saw it, and it still I believe exists. – It afforded no capabilities except space, for altering it from a kitchen into a Theatre; the alteration, however, was made with good taste; it represented a plain simple interior, with no work in it . . . and, as it could not boast altitude proportioned with its breadth, and horizontal length, the Audience part had neither Boxes nor Galleries, but consisted, merely, of a commodious pit. This construction had one advantage, which cannot, I presume, be obtained in any of our large publick playhouses, – namely – there was no row of flaring lamps, technically call'd the *float*, immediately before the Performers' feet, in front of the proscenium; but this same float was affix'd to a large beam, form'd into an arch, over their heads; – on that side of the arch nearest to the Stage; – so that the Audience did not see the lamps which cast a strong vertical light upon the Actors.

This light came from a more natural direction and did not throw the shadows the wrong way like footlights, but it could not be adopted where there were upper boxes and galleries because it would prevent the occupants from seeing the stage. The Theatre at Blenheim Palace, as we shall see, solved this problem of "the tormenting line of lamps at the front of the stage which wrongs everything it illuminates" by the use of reverberators at the extremity of the boxes.[17]

There do not appear to have been any theatricals in 1774[18] but six successive performances were given from 9 to 14 January 1775. They were preceded by two dress rehearsals to which the local farmers and trades-

men were invited, a cheering though uncritical audience. Two pro-
grammes alternated, *The Beaux' Stratagem* and *High Life Below Stairs*
on 9, 11, 13 January, *Othello* and *The Upholsterer*, on 10, 12, 14 January.
The leading man, T. Grenville, who played Othello, was most likely
Thomas Grenville, the uncle of Lady Williams Wynn. It is said that
Sheridan studied the part with a view to acting it at Wynnstay.[19] Of the
other newcomers Crewe may have been John Crewe of Crewe Hall who
later had theatricals of his own, and Miss Ravenscroft was a local lady.
The scenes were by Sandby, Richards and Wilkinson. The last named was
a stroller who came annually to Wynnstay as actor and scene painter.
The orchestra was said to be "very complete" and characters performed
with "spirit and justness".[20] The house was filled nightly with over 200
guests from the neighbourhood of Chester, Wrexham and Oswestry of
which last Sir Watkin was Mayor. Robert Vaughan took his leave this
season in an epilogue:[21]

> Gallants, behold a Veteran appear
> To beg dismission from the kind & fair,
> His understanding weak his silver Hairs
> Shew he's no Company for strolling Players
> Let younger heads the pleasing task engage
> And spare the Labour of declining Age,
> Granville and Aldersey have powers to please
> They act with Spirit, Energy and Ease,
> Sweet Desdemona! how her Accents flow
> Soft as the fleeces of descending Snow
> But still true woman her Othello dead
> Relumin'd straight she flies to Cassio's Bed.
> [Mr. and Mrs. Griffith played Cassio and Desdemona]
> Cherry's a sprightly Lass & taught by Nature
> She spoke Love's Catechism in every Feature.
> For Honest Feeble I've a great Regard,
> But Termagant his Merit shall reward.
> Sir Gibbet crown his favoured Bard with Bays
> Who wrote for Fame alone and gained – a Chase
> Shou'd Gibbet rob again, his Bard I hope
> Will in return reward him with a Rope.
> Poor Boniface! he must not be here forgot
> Forc'd to quit Litchfield he has ta'en the Yatch
> May this kind Audience his house support,
> His Anno Domini is good old Port.
> Joy to this Stage – No more I'll act a Part
> My words shall be the language of my Heart.

Feeble and Termagant are characters in *The Upholsterer;* Cherry,
Gibbet (played by Sir Watkin) and Boniface in *The Stratagem.* Boniface,
the landlord of the inn, was taken by the cook, Tom Carter, for whom Sir

Watkin had in fact bought the Yacht Inn in Chester; he spoke an epilogue to *The Beaux' Stratagem* in which he advertised his inn and expressed his gratitude to the Wynn family.[22] He continued to act with the company.

The plays for 1776 were *The Provok'd Wife* and *The Citizen* given on 2, 4, 6 January and on the last night, and *The Busy Body* and Garrick's *Neck or Nothing* given on 3, 5, 8 January.[23]

In September of this year Sir Watkin consulted his friend Garrick[24] about plays for the Theatre:

> I am ashamed not to have thanked you before this time for your very obliging letter with the names of several plays fit for our performance, but I deferred answering it till after the opening of Drury-lane Theatre, when you might be better able to know your own engagements, and whether we might flatter ourselves with the pleasure of seeing you, Mrs. Garrick, and your nephew, at Wynnstay this year.

Garrick finally came in the autumn of 1777 but he refused an invitation to perform. Sir Watkin wrote on 8 July that year:

> I was very much disappointed by a message you sent me by Sidebotham: I wish that you could be prevailed on to change your resolution, as nothing would flatter me so much as your honouring my theatre with your own performance.[25]

Robert Jephson[26] wrote to Walpole in October that Garrick, after attending his nephew's wedding in Staffordshire, was going to Wynnstay to superintend the play. But he did nothing of the kind and was merely a guest. A great resort of ladies and gentlemen gathered at Wynnstay and Garrick was in fine spirits and "the Life of the Company". On 2 October *Chrononhotonthologos* and *The Upholsterer* were presented before him, but "The Theatre, and Design of the Performance was kept an entire Secret from Mr. Garrick till the Moment of the Company's being conducted there." It was a great occasion for the amateurs:

> the House was most elegantly illuminated and fill'd with a very brilliant Audience. The Instant Mr. Garrick entered the Theatre, he was received with Peals of Applause! A Medley Overture struck up; at the End of which, Mr. Griffith of Rhual, came forward, and spoke a most elegant and masterly Prologue, written by himself, complimenting Mr. Garrick on his great Attention to Shakespear's Plays in particular, and echoing the Regret of the whole World for the great Loss they have sustained in his retiring from the Stage.

The mock procession in the burlesque is said to have kept the great actor and the company laughing the whole time.[27] The performance, which was followed by a supper, was evidently one of a series since it was on the last night that Garrick was present.[28] The following week Sir

Watkin took the Garricks to see *The Busy Body* which he had bespoken at the Chester Theatre.

Not long after Garrick had left, Sir Watkin was busily arranging the January season. That the task had its worrying moments is evident from a letter that he wrote to his agent Francis Chambre on 26 November:[29]

There never was anybody so unlucky as I have been in every Application ab^ت my plays this Christmas. We Yesterday wrote to Miss Grenvilles to desire one of them to wait on Mrs. Cotes to invite her to act with us. She will be set out for Woodcote before my Letter arrives. As I must apply again I should be very much obliged to you, if you would inform me whether you or y^r Nephew intend going there either this Week or the Beginning of the next I w^d rather that my Message sh^d be delivered by one of you. I wish y^r Nephew to do Salanio[30] in the Merchant of Venice the other Play cannot be determined till I know whether we can have Mrs. Cotes but will be either The Wonder or Every Man in His Humour if it is the latter, I sh^d be very happy if Mr. Wm Cotes would perform either the Part of Welbred, or Young Knowel which ever he likes best they are both disengaged. If he can speake like a Scotch Man the Part of Gibby in the Wonder is not disposed of.

Sir Watkin begs his correspondent to ride over to Woodcote at the end of the week for a reply: "it would be a very *Charitable Act* to me & my Company & as a Reward you shall be *free* of the House & have as *Many Tickets* to dispose of as you please." He adds a pressing postscript: "If Mrs. C. comes the Plays are to be the Merchant of Venice & the Wonder do send me word if you can go which I hope you *can* & *directly* as time is very *precious*". On 2 December he wrote again[31] urging upon Chambre the necessity of his nephew's going to Woodcote as soon as possible: "I hope he will use *all* his Interest & tell her that the Parts I wish her to do are Violante in the Wonder (which she has performed before) & Portia in the Merchant of Venice". Rehearsals were to begin on 26 December, "tho' some of us shall just run over the Plays the first Days of that Week". It is relief to know that the nephew succeeded in his mission so that Sir Watkin wrote on 5 December: "his success has made me very happy; I have sent him his Books & I hope he will like his Parts".

Mrs. Cotes, the daughter of Viscount Courtenay, had married John Cotes M.P. in October. Her husband was averse to her acting but he wrote to Chambre that, as Sir Watkin had been so pressing, he could not think of opposing her appearance on his stage. Though he assented with good grace it was particularly inconvenient

& indeed at no time the wish of Mrs. Cotes or myself that she should act, and I assure you that the request could have come from no other Corner than Sir Watkin to have prevailed upon her.

82

In spite of the objections, however, she became the leading lady at Wynnstay at every subsequent festival but two.

During this season too the caricaturist Henry Bunbury first acted with the company as Shylock and other characters. He was then a young man of 27, a friend of Garrick and Reynolds. Not only did he act leads at Wynnstay every succeeding season but he designed a series of elaborate entrance tickets, two of which are here reproduced (Plate 12 a-b).

The plays were given for six successive nights: *The Wonder* and *The Author* on 12, 14, 16 January 1778 alternated with *The Merchant of Venice* and *The Mayor of Garratt* on 13, 15, 17 January.[32] Wilkinson painted a new scene for *The Author*.

The following year Sir Watkin induced George Colman and his young son, then a lad of 16, to take part in the theatricals. According to the son, his father did not think much of the amateurs' efforts:[33]

The Company here, when off the stage, was superior to any regulars on it; – but I much doubt whether my father, or any London Manager would have offer'd the best actor among them a good salary.

Colman senior commented on

the awkwardness of the amateurs, and their ignorance in the commonest arrangements of the stage; – they either cross'd behind each others' backs, or ran against one another, in the attempt to change sides.

The under-butler, called in to take a minor rôle, was so clumsy in the business of delivering a sword that Colman, in exasperation, jumped on the stage and showed him how to do it. Thereafter he was engaged to coach the company, being, according to his son, vastly superior to the whole corps.

The amateurs stayed at Wynnstay about three weeks in all. They mustered eight to ten days prior to the performances, acted for a week, and separated a few days afterwards. The house party numbered from 25 to 30, some of whom were actors and some guests. Families flocked from as far as 30 miles away and one night carriages were in such demand that even two mourning coaches were requisitioned, each to transport a merry party of six. One of Colman's own comedies was selected – *The Jealous Wife* – and this was followed by Foote's *The Cozeners*, a programme that alternated with Norris's *The Royal Merchant or The Beggar's Bush* and *Catharine and Petruchio*.[34] Colman senior played Russet and Aircastle incomparably and his son as Paris, Ginks and Biondello gave signs of "a good understanding and ripening judgment".[35]

Another newcomer, Salisbury, had also once been an actor but was then Sir Watkin's house steward. The baronet himself did not act this year. Both *The Jealous Wife* and *The Royal Merchant* had new scenes and decorations. The Colmans continued to take a prominent part in the theatricals for the next two seasons. *The Constant Couple* and *The Devil on Two Sticks* were given on 17, 19 and 21 January 1780, alternating with *Cymbeline* and *The Spanish Barber* on 18, 20 January and finally on 22 January *Cymbeline* and *The Author*. Sir Watkin acted again this year as Tom Errand in *The Constant Couple* and is commended by Colman for much drollery. Indeed, he thought him, after his father, the best actor. Among the newcomers was Robert Nares, tutor to Sir Watkin's sons from 1779-1783. He wrote prologues and epilogues for the plays and an elegy on the death of Garrick, which he spoke this season.[36]

Miss Anne Jones, who played second to Mrs. Cotes, was known as The Sparkler from the brilliancy of her eyes and conversation. She was a protegée, and possibly a ward, of Sir Watkin's, and her early youth was spent at Wynnstay; she later became "a notable lady flitting about the fashionable world of Chester and Wrexham" and married Joseph Greaves. One who remembered her said that "she excelled any of the professional ladies he had seen on the stage".[37] In Thomas Carter's account book in the National Library of Wales[38] there are several items of expenditure in connection with the theatre. Meredith was paid ten guineas for his performance and Stokes, a musician five guineas. Wilkinson's bill, probably for scene painting, was for £22. 15. 0. Shoes cost £1. 17. 6 and swords £5. 14. 9. Dorian was paid £6. 8. 0 for copying the music of *The Spanish Barber*. In 1781 Meredith and Stokes re-appear for payment and one Holliday was paid £9. 18. 6 for hair dressing. In addition to Wilkinson, whose bill was for £20. 15. 2, Richards was once again employed as scene painter, and paid £100. The musicians from Carleton's company of players were borrowed for the occasion and their leader Williams was given 8s. for their lodging at Ruabon. Oil was a big item amounting to £25. 4. 0. The local gentry evidently helped with supplying costumes for Lord Lewisham's servant, who brought a present of clothes, was rewarded with a guinea. Among other expenses were 10s. 6d. to a mantua maker, £3. 13. 0 to Banet for jewels, £2. 3. 8 for Bell's play books, and £3. 10. 3½ to a carpenter.

The year 1781 saw the most ambitious programme to date when three full length plays were undertaken. *Rule a Wife and Have a Wife* with *Bon Ton* as afterpiece was presented on 15, 17, 19 January; *Richard III* and *The Lyar* on 16, 18, 20 January and *The Merchant of Venice* and *Bon Ton* on 22 January. Sir Watkin's eldest son made his first appearance at the age of nine as the Duke of York in *Richard III*. At the dress rehearsal of this tragedy the farmers and tradesmen had a hearty laugh at the King's dying speech though the part was taken by Colman.

In 1782 the programme was further enlarged to three plays and three afterpieces. *Every Man in His Humour* was followed by *Tom Thumb* on 7, 9, 11 January; *Henry IV Part I* by *The Apprentice* on 8, 10, 12 January and on the last night, 14 January, *Venice Preserv'd* was given with *Taste*. This was a pretty arduous undertaking since all were new. Altogether 15 actors and 4 actresses took part. It was announced in *Adams's Weekly Courant* that Thomas Sidebotham of the Eagles, Wrexham intended to set up

Lamps of Offa's Dyke during the Play Week at Wynnstay for the convenience and safety of the town and neighbourhood of Wrexham and others who mean to attend the Theatre and to do it effectively solicits their subscription.[39]

Sometime during 1782 the Theatre was either reconstructed or rebuilt by John Evans. The *European Magazine*[40] states:

The Theatre was erected, as it now appears, in 1782, by John Evans, Esq. It is a small but convenient building and has been employed often for the purpose for which it was appropriated. The time will come when the performances exhibited there will be the objects of enquiry, and it is the duty of a literary journal to supply information for futurity, as well as the present day.

The entertainments, continues the writer,

serve to revive the almost lost ideas of English hospitality; they furnish an elegant spectacle, agreeable both to youth and age; from the time of their exhibition they soften the gloom and horrors of winter, and diffuse innocent amusement at a festival season peculiarly set apart for relaxation.

Evans drew a view of the exterior of the Theatre[41] for one of the admission tickets (Plate 12a). The house is shown in the background. Another ticket in the National Library of Wales, dated in a contemporary hand "January 1776" shows the theatre in the background exactly as in Evans's view. If the date is correct it would prove that no alterations had been made to the exterior.

Three plays and two afterpieces were got up in 1783, On the opening night, 13 January, *The Clandestine Marriage* was played with *The Son-in-Law*.[42] The series of Shakespeare histories was continued with *Henry IV Part II* followed by *Barnaby Brittle* on 14 January and on the last night, 20 January, *Henry IV, Part I* was revived with *Barnaby Brittle*. For the first time Aldersey was not among the actors. Colman senior returned after a year's absence to play Lord Ogleby, and Mum and Vinegar, but his son did not this time accompany him. Sir Watkin's second son Charles made his début at the age of eight as a page in *Henry IV, Part II*, and Sir Watkin himself, as usual, played rather small but telling rôles as Serjeant Flower and Davy. Mrs. Cotes did not act this year and we find The Sparkler curiously cast, probably owing to lack of men, as Silence. A magazine entitled *The Breakfast Courant or Bread and Butter Chronicle*[43] was issued in manuscript during this season. It gives no real information but contains many joking allusions to the theatricals of which this is a specimen:

the Actors are desired not to be too free with the vis comica on the Stage, as the House is expected to be very full and the Audience will not have room to burst their sides.

The following December found Sir Watkin in search of a new actor. The serviceable Chambre was once again employed in the business, and the baronet wrote to him on 4 December:

Can you give me any Information ab^t Mr. Kynersley, whether he w^d chuse to act this Season & thro' what means I am to apply to him perhaps you could see him at Shrewsbury & ask Him the Question. – You may give my Compliments & say that I sh^d be much flattered if he w^d join us.

Two days later Chambre reported the result of his interview:

I yesterday saw Mr. Kynnersley & deliver'd to him your Message about joining the Strollers at Wynnstay. He answer'd immediately he wou'd hold himself in readiness and wait your commands to attend at whatever time and place you shou'd please to appoint; but he seem'd rather anxious to have as early intelligence as possible, what parts he was to perform, that he may be perusing & giving some attention to 'em previous to his coming to learn under the direction of whoever you shou'd please to appoint for that purpose, adding at the same time that he thought himself better calculated for some droll comic Character than anything tragical & indeed when you become acquainted with him you will I believe be of the same opinion that his Countenance was never design'd *to shake his goary locks* in a manner that wou'd not rather create a smile in the beholders, than have a different effect, tho' I rather incline to think he will be no bad acquisition to your Dramatis Personae if you can hit upon the proper character wherein to place him.

The part of Malvolio was considered suitable and Sir Watkin wrote to Chambre on 14 December:

I have sent with this a Letter & the Part of Malvolio for the Bearer to carry to Mr. Kynersley. I wish you could give him an hint if you think *he w^d like to make them up* of the Uniforms the Particulars of which his Taylor may know at

86

Mr. Morris. This must come from you "that the Company have a Uniform". I cannot mention it to him as I do not know him but you might do it when you see him or by sending another Letter by the Boy – is he to come here before the Rehearsals?[44]

This correspondence indicates the seriousness with which Sir Watkin took the theatricals. He cast his net as far as Shrewsbury for Anthony Kinnersley, and did not confine himself to people he knew. He had planned an ambitious season of two of Shakespeare's plays *Twelfth Night* and *Macbeth*. Three water colours by Bunbury (Plates 11 a-c) give a good idea of the production and costuming of *Twelfth Night*. Two of the identical costumes for Viola and Sebastian are dated 1785, a year later than the performance. The Hungarian military busbies were sometimes used in the theatre of the time for romantic characters as may be seen in Hoppner's portrait at Kenwood, said to represent Mrs. Jordan as Viola. The short, cutaway military jackets, and Turkish trousers and curved sword together with a jabot are a curious melange but create an air of fantasy well suited to Shakespeare's Illyria. The third water colour of the duelling scene depicts very mixed costumes. Whilst Blech, Antonio and Fabian are in Vandyke dress (Antonio's dress is described as Turkish in the wardrobe book perhaps for another scene) in an attempt to be Elizabethan, Bunbury as Aguecheek is for some curious reason in contemporary habit and the officers entering at the back have ruffs but Turkish trousers. The scene is played in a chamber instead of a garden setting. The comedy, which was given on 7 January, had as afterpiece *Cross Purposes*, the tragedy, put on the following night, had *All the World's a Stage*.[45] Mrs. Cotes played Lady Macbeth to the Macbeth of Bunbury, and also Olivia. Sir Watkin himself did not perform.

A prompt book of *Macbeth* was discovered in the Folger Library by Professor Charles Shattuck who has kindly sent me a list of the scenes. It opened with lightning, a barren heath in the 2nd wing and a cascade. The witches were discovered in the centre of the stage and descended through a great trap. After a saloon flat in the 3rd wing the witches reappear on the heath by three different traps. There follow Wilkinson's palace, an Etruscan chamber and a castle gate. Later scenes include Sandby's wood, Richards's palace, a cascade, a cave and rocks with a cauldron rising from the great trap, a best chamber, a close wood and Richards's drop. The theatre was able to accommodate 23 changes of scene and 4 traps showing its considerable resources and flexibility.

The Hon. John Byng visited Wynnstay in July this year but was disappointed with the playhouse:

Sr W. does not understand comforts ... The playhouse on whose boards I strutted, which was sheds [sic] us by a very pompous scene shifter, is but a poor one and the scenes are shabby; in the property room is a profusion of wigs, and truncheons.

Professor Cecil Price, to whom I owe the reference, has suggested that Byng's opinion may merely have been the usual disillusionment of someone who sees behind the scenes without the glamour of a performance.[46]

Three plays and two afterpieces made up the programme for 1785. They were chosen, as Bunbury wrote to Dalton. "after twenty changes and disappointments". *As You Like It* and *The Agreeable Surprise* were given on 19, 21, 26 January,[47] *The Confederacy* and *Harlequin's Invasion* on 20 January, and *Venice Preserv'd* and the pantomime on 25 January. The music for O'Keeffe's "little opera" *The Agreeable Surprise* was composed by Dr. Samuel Arnold. Sir Watkin wrote informing Arnold that the piece was to be given at Wynnstay at Christmas, and asking him to approach O'Keeffe for "the words of an air for Compton to sing in the last scene", which he did. O'Keeffe[48] relates an incident that he says, occurred at the performance:

Mr. Colman told me he acted Lingo in The Agreeable Surprise; and one night, just ready to step on the stage in high humour, Sir W. W. Wynne, the master and manager, in frolic, snatched off Lingo's highly powdered wig, which, as Mr. Colman said, put him into a lofty passion. Sir Watkin ran away; and Lingo ran after, to demolish him.

But Colman did not act this season and Lingo was played by Joseph Madocks, so that the incident probably relates to Colman's appearance as Mum and Vinegar in O'Keeffe's *Son-in-Law* in 1783.

Joseph Madocks, whom we have already met at the Margravine's theatricals, was a considerable asset as an amateur of experience; his Pierre is particularly praised and his Lingo displayed much humour.[49] Kinnersley proved an excellent comedian, especially good in the songs. Aldersey had returned and he and Bunbury were spoken of as the most talented actors of the troupe. Miss Williams as Araminta in *The Confederacy* showed elegance and ease. Capt. Greville spoke a prologue to *As You Like It* and, on the last night, Kinnersley admirably delivered another, written by Bunbury with pointed wit. Bunbury again designed an admission ticket which was engraved by Bartolozzi. It shows a windmill on the sails of which are the words "tragedy", "comedy", "pantomime" and "farce"; Harlequin peeps from behind a tree with "Invasion" [*Harlequin's Invasion*] engraved on his hat, and other figures bear the legends of the other pieces, except for *Venice Preserv'd* which is presumably represented by an unlabelled woman with a handkerchief; the border consists of a laurel wreath with masks and daggers.[50] Contrary to Byng's impression of the Theatre, the *Morning Post* reporter found it

finished in a most elegant style, and . . . as complete for its size as any of the Royal Houses. It contains about 300 persons. Nothing could have a more genteel appearance than the audience both nights, every one having gone dressed. The scenes are all fine pictures, and the dresses new and elegant.

The amateurs, far from being rivals of professionals, patronised their performances. John Boles Watson's Cheltenham company visited Wrexham about this time and was constantly visited by the Wynnstay party; and so delighted was Bunbury, "the Wynnstay Roscius", by their playing that Watson obtained sanction to perform in Wrexham and the neighbouring towns every three years.[51]

The next festival was held in December, 1785 when *The Inconstant* and *The Devil to Pay* were given on 20, 22, 26 December, *The Winter's Tale* and *Who's the Dupe?* on 21, 23, 27 December and *As you Like It* and *Who's the Dupe?* on the 28th. Bridgeman, who played Florizel and Jaques, was a newcomer, and was probably the eldest son of Sir Henry Bridgeman who had had acting experience at his father's theatricals at Weston Hall, Staffordshire, 1775-7. Kenyon wrote to his brother on 3 January:[52]

The Wynnstay plays were not so well attended as formerly though crowded on some of the nights. The performers behaved as well as usual, and Mr. Bridgeman is particularly clever. The elegant ticket of the last year admitted on the present occasion.

On the playbills the ladies were requested to come without hats.

Sir Watkin tried to enlist Sheridan to help him with his theatricals in 1787. Whether he actually did so is uncertain. The *Morning Post* reported that visitors were crowding in to see the performances which Sheridan was getting up, and that *The Rivals* was to be given after *The Tempest*, whilst Drury Lane Theatre was furnishing properties that were not procurable at Wynnstay.

On 3 December 1786 Sir Watkin wrote to Dalton:

Dear Paddy, I hope J. Madocks has delivered my message, and that I shall have the pleasure of receiving Sir Lucius O'Trigger on or before the 18th. I must trouble you to take Sebastian in The Tempest [he actually took Trinculo], and Levy in the Farce. The other farce cannot be fixed until we meet.

He adds that he thinks *The Rivals* will do very well with the assistance of the author whom he daily expected. *The Rivals* was not, however, performed and Sheridan was pressed in vain to take part in *The Tempest*, excusing himself on the grounds that he was making preparations for a similar drama on another stage – an allusion to his forthcoming part in the trial of Warren Hastings.[53] A report that Mrs. Sheridan had performed Ariel was promptly denied, the part, in fact, being taken by Master Bunbury.[54] Much anxiety was caused by the illness of Mrs. Cotes, which led to her death. The festival opened with *The Tempest* and *The Man of Quality* (Lee's alteration of *The Relapse*) on 1 January and they were repeated on 5, 9, 11 January; *Cymbeline* and *The Apprentice* were given on 6, 8, 10 January. According to the *Morning Chronicle*[55] the shining lights were Bunbury, Aldersey and a new recruit, St. Leger. Lord Carysfort, who in April married Elizabeth Grenville the sister of Lady Wynn, was another newcomer, who bore himself with much dignity and decorum, whilst Master Bunbury was beyond expectation and praise as Ariel. The Sparkler had improved astonishingly and took over Mrs. Cotes's rôle of Imogen. The enraptured reporter wrote "in all the natural beauties of scenery and situation, inequality, wood and water, this is one of the most captivating spots in our island"; he pronounced the Theatre "one of the completest things of the kind. The scenery on a smaller scale than in London, but in every other respect not at all inferior"; and as for the acting it could not have been better imagined or finished by professionals. Comparing the Wynnstay theatricals with those of Lord Grandison in Ireland, the *World*[56] commented:

the Scenery is well finished, but not on so large a scale. The Orchestra alone is better, The Band is the best hitherto heard in private. This it is, for the Manager to be a Musician – and to have such a leader as Major Williams.

Sir Watkin intended to have his season as usual in 1788 but there were hitches and finally the King's illness put a stop to such festivities.[57] Sir Watkin had been ailing himself for some time and he died in July 1789. With his death the long series of theatricals came to an end for some time. 25 plays and 24 afterpieces had been presented, including 14 Shakespeare plays and adaptations. The choice too had ranged from tragedy to farce, comic opera to pantomime, comedy to burlesque.

A unique relic has come down to us from these theatricals in the shape of the charred leaves of the wardrobe book[58] rescued from the fire that burnt down the house in 1858. It lists 197 costumes and items of dress, frequently assigning them to their wearers and rôles. Thus in some instances we are able to reconstruct the costuming of a play as well as to trace how the costumes were used for several different rôles. Sometimes the indication of position on the shelves of the ladies' and gentlemen's dressing rooms is still distinguishable in spite of the edges of the manuscript having been burnt. The date 1784 appears against a number of items which suggests that an inventory was taken that year.

Some attempt was made to get away from contemporary dress in the Shakespearean plays, in *The Royal Merchant* and *Every Man in his Humour* by the use of vandyke capes and high beaver hats. These usually served several characters. Thus "A Blew Sattin Vandike Cloak, waistcoat, breeches & hat – in and trimmed with white and shoes the Colour 2 belts" were worn by Aldersey as Gascoin in *The Royal Merchant* and Colman as Pisanio in *Cymbeline*. "A purple sattin Vandike Cloak, waistcoat, breeches lin'd with yellow and trim'd with silver – two belts" served Clough as Wolfort in the former piece and Aldersey in an unspecified rôle. "A Buff colour'd and Red Vandike Cloak – waistcoat breeches and two belts – trim'd with Gold – a high Crown'd beaver Hat" did duty for Smith as Hemskirk in *The Royal Merchant*, Carter as Cloten, and Sir Watkin as Pistol.

We can get a good idea of the costuming of *Cymbeline* as, in addition to the Pisanio and Cloten suits described above, we learn that Bunbury as Posthumous wore a striped satin Vandyke dress and white cloak (used again for Prince Hal and Sir Andrew Aguecheek) and also a black and gold suit with alternative scarlet and white cloaks (used also for Hotspur). As for the ladies; Mrs. Cotes as Imogen appeared in a blue silk dress, a white stuffed jacket trimmed with blue, a white robe and "a garter blue velvet sacque and peticoat trim'd with Leopard velvet and gold, stomacher & sleeve knots ye same" which was altered for her for this part; whilst Mrs. Griffin as the Queen had for contrast "A Black velvet Ladys suit of Cloaths trim'd with Gold Lace".

An exotic effect was introduced into *Twelfth Night* by Antonio's "Green sattin turkish Waistcoat trim'd with yellow and a white quilted waistcoat yellow sattin belt & strip'd trousers" but, as we have seen, this does not accord with Bunbury's picture. On the other hand Benedick was evidently habited in contemporary fashion with a lead coloured silk coat and breeches and a white satin flowered waistcoat. In *Catharine and Petruchio*, Petruchio had "a vandike work'd waistcoat", Grumio "a brown vandike waistcoat", Hortensio "A Flower'd velvet Coat, waistcoat and breeches lined with pink sattin", Baptiste "a Crimson velvet coat, waistcoat and breeches", and the Music Master "a light colour'd stuff frock & breeches lined with blue and blue waistcoat". Shylock's costume was black with small white buttons, Launcelot's coat and breeches brown with alternative brown and yellow worsted, laced waistcoats. Falstaff's little page was resplendent in "a Scarlet Cloak & breeches and white waistcoat trim'd with gold and black bonnet". Patched clothes were made for the beggars in *The Royal Merchant*, whereas Mrs. Griffith as Bertha gloried in "a Scarlet silk peticoat with silver, a Lady's Jacket with silver, some blue and silver trimming – a Buckram Peticoat trim'd with silver". "A Green silk Vandike dress with yellow breeches & cloak trim'd with pink & yellow high Crown'd Hat" was used for Slender and Master Stephen in *Every Man in His Humour*. Further evidence of the kind of costume worn for Shakespeare is provided by Bunbury's painting of a dress in *As You Like It*.

Unlike those of the Elizabethan plays, contemporary costumes seem to have been used only once. Militia coats were employed for soldiers; thus "a Shropshire Militia frock with white waistcoat and breeches" was worn for the *Copper Captain*, others for Col. Briton and Major Oakley, whilst Major Sturgeon had a Merionethshire militia coat. There were several sailor suits: "a Blue Jacket strip'd waistcoat & trowsers" for C. Sidebotham in a nautical rôle and "a Blue sea uniform frock with white waistcoat and breeches" for Capt. O'Cutter. Gibby's uniform in *The Wonder* was appropriately Scottish consisting of "a Plaid, a Philibeg [kilt], Waistcoat, Jacket, Cloak – stockings, Pouch, sword belt". Flora in this comedy wore "a Brown Jacket & peticoat trim'd with yellow" Sir John Brute when he donned woman's attire was got up in "a Yellow Stuff sack trim'd with pink". Elaborate liveries were made for *High Life Below Stairs* including "a Buff Livery faced with Pink and Pink waistcoat & breeches, worsted lace" for my Lord Duke's Servant. Other interesting but unspecified items are a scarlet rateen and a white duffle joseph or woman's riding coat, "a Pink silk Venetian gown and hat trim'd with Ermine", "a white figur'd dimity old English dress", "a scarlet Lady's riding great coat," "a rose colour'd silk sashe 2 regimental sashes & a Pink and White, strip'd silk neck handerchief" and "a Brown bag containing a Friar's gown, beads & beard". 35 pairs of shoes and buskins are catalogued including "the Druids Green slippers" which Sir Watkin probably used when he appeared as a Druid at Mrs. Cornelys's masquerade in 1770, "1 pr. of Old Mans shoes", "1 pr. Red & Gold buskins" and "1 pr. Red Morocco slippers". Among the hats are 15 for old women, silver and gold laced ones, "2 black high crown'd hats with red ribbons" and "a White Beaver hatt". Among other items are stockings, gloves, hoops and night caps. These extracts from what is anyway an incomplete list of the resources of the Wynnstay wardrobe, give an indication of the extent, variety and richness of costume of which a private theatre was capable.

Master Watkin Williams Wynn, who succeeded to the title as the 5th baronet had, as we have seen, taken part in his father's theatricals. From 1803 to 1810 he revived the Christmas house party dramatic festivals. The only relic of them that has come down to us is a book of sketches and watercolours[59] of scenes from the plays, most of which appear to have been done by Harriet, Sir Watkin's sister, though there are some by other performers. From the drawings we can tell that most of these perform-ances were given in the great room, but a few, which show proscenium pillars and a curtain, may possibly have taken place in the old Theatre which was not dismantled until some time before the death of Sir Watkin in 1840.[60] A good many of the pieces were evidently especially written for the performances since they are otherwise unknown. The first presentation in 1803 was *The Rivals* in which Sir Watkin himself played Sir Lucius O'Trigger, his sister Charlotte, Lydia Languish, William Shipley (later to become Charlotte's husband), Capt. Absolute, Mary Cunliffe, later to marry Charles Williams Wynn, Julia, Charles himself Sir Anthony Absolute and the Misses Cotton, Mrs. Malaprop and Davy.

An amusing illustration of *The Babes in the Wood* given in December 1804 shows the redbreasts, in the persons of Harriet Cunliffe and Harriet Williams Wynn, scattering the leaves. The father was Sir Richard Brooke of Norton Priory, Cheshire, whose huge stature and pronounced chin are easily distinguishable in the subsequent sketches, and who was later to marry Harriet Cunliffe. A proverb on a classical theme, entitled *Io*, was also given on this occasion.

An Ali Baba story, *Morgiana*, was got up in January 1805 and the sketch (Plate 6), shows some rich and charming costumes in gold and white, as well as the proscenium and curtains. *High Life Below Stairs*, an unknown piece entitled *The Bath Guide* and Fielding's *The Lottery* are also mentioned in the sketch book for this year, the last being definitely assigned to the great room.

There is nothing for 1806, but in 1807 *The Agreeable Surprise* with Wingfield as Mrs. Cheshire, *Pyramus and Thisbe*, an unknown piece called *The Hunchback* and *The Tempest*, with Brooke as Prospero, Ellis as Caliban, G. Cunliffe as Ariel and Harriet Cunliffe as Miranda, were the plays chosen.

Chrononhotonthologos and *The Winter's Tale* (Plate 12c) were revived in January 1808 together with *Miss in her Teens*. Madocks was Florizel and Miss Shipley, Perdita. Water colours and pen and ink sketches for January 1809 show scenes from Colman the younger's comedy *We Fly By Night*, *Young Lochinvar*, *Beauty and the Beast*, with Brooke and Harriet Cunliffe in the title rôles, *The Forty Thieves* and two unidentifiable pieces. An amusing trick is shown in one of the last in which a woman with twins is produced by dressing up the woman's crossed hands as babies. Indeed there was something of the charade in most of the productions. Last of all, the year 1810 saw the presentation of Thomas Dibdin's melodrama *Valentine and Orson*. Harriet married this year and there are no further drawings though there may have been further theatricals. Her book is a unique record since pictures of amateur performances are few and far between. These convey something of the fun they must have been in the getting up, and, indeed, one has the impression that the 5th baronet did not take them as seriously or present them as elaborately as his father had done. They were not on any big scale for the entertainment of the neighbourhood at large but simply organised by a party of family and friends for their own amusement during the Christmas holidays.

5. Blenheim Palace Theatre. *The Guardian*.

6. Wynnstay Theatricals. *Morgiana.*

Chapter VI

The Theatricals of the Gay Delavals

On 3 March 1751 Walpole[1] wrote to Horace Mann that some people of fashion had hired Drury Lane and acted a play. "They really acted so well", continues the mocker,

that it is astonishing they should not have had sense enough not to act at all. You would know none of their names, should I tell you: but the chief were a family of Delavals, the eldest of which was married by one Foote, a player, to Lady Nassau Poulett, who had kept the latter. The rage was so great to see this performance, that the House of Commons literally adjourned at three o'clock on purpose: the footman's gallery was strung with blue ribands.

Sir Francis Blake Delaval led as wild and dissipated a career as Lord Barrymore; and he shared with him that strange, adolescent delight in pranks which was a characteristic of the rakes of the period. He and his great friend Samuel Foote pursued pleasure with avidity in every form, "from books and the most brilliant conversation, sometimes to the lowest species of buffoonery".[2] They spent their fortunes lavishly and Foote, who lived with Sir Francis most of the time, helped his host with the festivities with which his mansion at Seaton Delaval in Northumberland hummed: "Seaton Delaval Hall was like an Italian palace, and the grounds were a perfect fairy-land of light, beauty, and music."[3] In town the boon companions frequented green rooms, ridottos, masquerades and all the gaieties of high society. Sir Francis led whatever frivolity was in fashion, yet he, like Lord Barrymore, was a man of wit and some learning, "an agreeable, gay companion", brave, generous, and popular. His crony Edgeworth[4] tells us that he had a countenance peculiarly prepossessing, tall, strong, athletic, and singularly active, he exulted in every manly exercise, was endowed with courage, and with extraordinary presence of mind.

Having squandered a fortune, he married, in 1750, a woman of great wealth, much older than himself, plain in person and understanding, the widow of Lord Nassau Powlett and daughter of the Earl of Thanet; whereupon malicious tongues like Walpole's whispered that this was yet another trick of Foote's. The unsuitable couple was divorced five years later.

Private theatricals on a big scale were not then much in vogue, though the Prince of Wales had followed up his great fête at Cliveden with the children's theatricals at Leicester House in 1749 and 1750. It was Foote's idea, since Sir Francis was fond of the stage, and a good performer, to get up a play among his friends in 1751. No less a person than Macklin coached the actors, and Kirkman[5] avers that it was partly to give open proof of his abilities in theatrical instruction, as well as to display their own talents and acquirements, that the band decided to perform on the public stage. It was a new departure, since other theatricals had taken place in private houses and had been hampered by the lack of apparatus. There was bound to be some criticism of people of quality who appeared on the stage of a public theatre, but, says Kirkman,

The just sense that the persons who were at the head of this scheme entertained of things, could not suffer them to think, that, if the action itself were not blameable, the place, on this occasion, could not make it so; nor could their spirit submit to their doing anything imperfectly, either for the want of the necessary expense, or of the courage to do what was no way really exceptionable, though out of the common road.

Othello, the play chosen, was to have been given at the Little Theatre in the Haymarket, but this proved much too small for the demand for seats[6]. Then Garrick agreed to interrupt the run of *Alfred* at Drury Lane for two nights and rent that Theatre to the amateurs for a rehearsal and performance. Even so, out of the 20,000 who desired to see the play only 1,000 were able to get in. Care was taken to select the audience and to keep out undesirables such as women of the town. No places were kept, so that the best ones went to those who came first. Thus the house was filled throughout with equally good company, "the shilling gallery was as much crowded with nobility as the boxes; stars shone among the gods, and ribbons were peeping out of the slips".[7] The tickets, which were beautifully engraved, were all distributed beforehand.[8] Elaborate precautions were taken to deal with crowds. Coachmen were instructed to set

96

down their passengers at the Bridges Street entrance and drive off to the Strand; sedan chairmen were to use the new door in Russell Street; and no-one was admitted into either of the passages without first having shown his ticket at the outer door.[9] All was in vain, for on the night of 8 March

the Streets and Avenues were so filled with Coaches and Chairs, that the greatest Part of the Gentlemen and Ladies were obliged to wade through Dirt and Filth to get to the House, which afforded good Diversion and Benefit for the Pickpockets and other Gentlemen of that Trade.[10]

Stars and garters were to be seen glittering in adjacent public houses until their owners could proceed with safety, and the greater part of the audience had to quit their carriages at a distance and walk fully dressed through the crowd. A claim is made in the Delaval Papers that

Such an exhibition was probably never seen before in Europe . . . The House of Commons adjourned two hours early to enable members to be present . . . In a word it was the most splendid appearance of nobility ever seen in a theatre, and including Royalty itself; and so anxious were the polite to be present that ten guineas was offered and refused for a ticket.

Not until another House of Commons was adjourned early for the sake of the private theatricals at Richmond House, was London to witness a similar spectacle. The stage box was occupied by the Prince of Wales, the Duke of Cumberland, Prince George and the Princesses Amelia and Augusta whilst "every corner of the House besides glittered with diamonds and embroidery". As for "the accomodations", they were

fit for the company; the band of music was a very fine one, and the house was in every part illuminated with wax-lights: the scenes were proper, as well as beautiful; and the dresses not only magnificent, but well fancied and adapted to the characters. Othello's was a robe in the fashion of his country; Roderigo's an elegant modern suit, and Cassio's and Iago's very rich uniforms.[11]

Foote confirms that the dresses were magnificent and tells us that the scenery took months to prepare. The expenses were between £1,000 and £1,500, of which £150 was for the hire of the Theatre and wardrobes; a charge worked out on the basis of profits from a benefit for Garrick in his most attractive rôle.[12] Othello was played by Sir Francis himself, Iago by his brother John, and Cassio by another brother Thomas. The part of Desdemona was intended for Sir Francis's mistress the "gay and beautiful" Elizabeth Roach but, as she declined to play it, it was handed over to her sister Mrs. Quarme[13]. The performers were all nervous and it is not surprising that their voices quite failed to fill the large Theatre. The amateurs had not realised the difference between playing to an empty house at the rehearsal, and a full one at the performance. On the credit side, Kirkman says,

There was a face of nature that no Theatrical Piece, acted upon any private Stage, ever came to. It was evident that the Performers felt every sentiment that they were to express; and were not reduced to labour at an imitation of what would be done in real life on the occasion, but were inspired, by the sentiment, to be the thing the Author represented.

He goes on to lavish praise on the individual performers:

The figure of Othello was undoubtedly one of the finest ever produced on a stage; his deportment in the whole, was majestic without pomp; and his sense of the passions, the Author has thrown into his part, quick and exquisite . . . What he was peculiarly superior to every person in, was the natural expression of the lover and the gentleman

when, in the last act, he asks pardon of Cassio. The way he then took the hand of the man he had injured

had something in it so like the man of honour, and so unlike all imitation, that the audience could not easily be reconciled afterwards to the hearing it from anybody else. His embracing Desdemona, on their meeting at Cyprus, set many a fair breast among the audience palpitating.

John Delaval, who had never been on the stage before, showed amazing ease:

his whole deportment so much the gentleman; so perfectly adapted to every circumstance of the character and so elegant in propriety, that his audience were not only delighted, but astonished at his acting. He everywhere conveyed the full sense of the Author's expression, and exaggerated it nowhere. His eye worked as much as his tongue, and he was equally intent on his plots, when engaged in the dialogue, and when out of it.

Thomas was excellent in the drunken scene, and made convincing Cassio's sudden recovery to sobriety. Roderigo was the character Shakespeare intended and not that usually palmed off for it on the stage. Desdemona's native honesty and candour showed in her face, and Emilia was natural. The elocution was easy and free from whining and mouthing even though it could not be heard! On the whole Macklin got honour from his pupils.

The prologue and epilogue were written by the mad poet Christopher Smart[14] who had been private tutor to John Delaval at Cambridge and wrote the addresses at his pupil's request. Once more the professional suffers in comparison with the amateur.

> While mercenary actors tread the stage
> And hireling scribblers lash or lull the age,
> Ours be the task t'instruct and entertain,
> Without one thought of glory or of gain.

Hardly soothing, this, to the ear of Macklin or Garrick. The prologue proceeds to render homage to the amateurs of the previous century:

> Our noblest youth would then embrace the task
> Of comick humour, or the mystick masque.
> 'Twas theirs t'encourage worth, and give to bards
> What now is spent on boxing and on cards.

The epilogue, spoken by Desdemona, in the customary light vein pictured the cavillings of the audience after they had dispersed.

Foote, who was to be one of the party, did not arrive until the play was over and the company were partaking of refreshments in the green-room. They told him what he had missed but Foote, slyly approaching Garrick asked, in a loud whisper, what the great actor had thought of it. Garrick, who liked to flatter the nobility, replied in a whisper that could be heard by the whole company, "I never *suffered* so much in my whole life", which Foote turned to mockery by a quick riposte "What! for the author? I thought so. Alas poor Shakespeare!"[15]

The same kind of line was taken in a lampoon entitled "A Satirical Dialogue between A Sea Captain and his Friend in Town. Humbly Address'd to the Gentlemen who deform'd the Play of Othello . . . To Which Is Added, A Prologue and Epilogue Much more suitable to the Occasion than their Own." In the prologue the speaker sees the ghost of injured Shakespeare with poesy and her train

> Furnisht with *whips* and *Stings* to *Scourge us hence,*
> And murder Us, e're we can murder Sense.

The sea captain is told:

> Our Gentry of late, *to their Honour be't spoke*
> (Who think themselves wiser than all other Folk)
> Have acted, like People *bereft of their Senses,*
> For *Gentility's lost* when the *Player commences* . . .
> You must know that in *London* some *People* there are,
> *So fond of the Greatness, that waits on a Play'r*
> That at once *they turn'd* Actors *themselves to expose,*
> To the *Pity of Friends* and the *Censure of Foes.*

His friend continues by saying that the idea was copied from the French nobility:

> But our *Gentry* so *Confident bold*, and *Conceited*,
> Never used this Precaution, But Fairly admitted
> An *Audience of Critics*, To See Their Fine *Play* . . .
> *Good Manners* Obliged them *Sometimes* to applaud;
> Tho they Little Deserv'd it.

They agree that the £1,500 spent on the entertainment would have been better given to charity and that the amateurs were much to blame. The intention had indeed been to give other performances for charities, including the Foundling Hospital, but nothing seems to have come of it.[16]

In the following years entertainments took place at Seaton Delaval, Vanburgh's vast pile, the wreck of which still idly stands near Tynemouth. On one occasion Robert Delaval, another brother, was the leading spirit, and Mrs. Astley wrote to Mrs. Delaval about 1752:

> Bob has undertaken to entertain us with a Pantomime of his own composing these Christmas Holidays. He has taken in almost all the people in the house as performers. I fancy it will be a very curious sight.

After the event she reported: "Bob has performed his Pantomime entertainment before a great number of the country folk, who showed their appreciation by great fits of laughter". Rope dancers came to Seaton Delaval in February 1753 and are said to have entertained an assembly of 4,000.[17]

13 years later on 12 December 1766 Walpole wrote to George Montagu: "The Duke of York is erecting a theatre at his own palace and is to play Lothario in the Fair Penitent himself".[18] The theatre was situated in James Street, Petty France, Westminster,[19] and belonged to Sir Francis Delaval in whose will it is left as follows:

> I Give to my Sister Lady Mexborough all the Scenes, Decorations, &c in and belonging to my little Theatre in James Street, Westminster; and the Lease thereof I Give to Sir John Hussey Delaval my Brother and Lady Hussey Delaval.[20]

Richard Edgeworth and Benjamin Wilson the painter both claim to have had the fitting up of the Theatre.[21] According to the former

> Macklin was our frequent visitor, as he was consulted as to anything that was necessary for the getting up of a play, in which the late Duke of York was to be the principal actor. On this occasion I was requested by Sir Francis to fit up a theatre in Petty France, near the gate of the Park, and no trouble and expense were spared, to render it suitable to the reception of a royal performer.

Wilson appears to have come in later for the Duke asked him to attend a rehearsal and give his opinion of the performance and particularly of the Duke's part in it. Wilson, though somewhat alarmed at the honour thrust on him, determined to speak his mind frankly, and when, after a speech, the Duke asked for his comment he replied, "it is a new idea entirely [the exhibition of the character]; and I think if there was a little more spirit introduced into the character it would heighten it extremely". So pleased was the Duke with this that shortly afterwards he appointed Wilson manager of the theatre and asked for his criticism at all rehearsals, not being satisfied until he had pleased him. Efforts to dislodge Wilson from favour were vain.

The whole fitting up and preparation of the theatre in James Street, West-minster, the painting of the Scenes &c was intrusted to Wilson; and the entire expenses under his management did not exceed £800 from first to last ... The Duke was satisfied with the effect and the frugality. This theatre was by order constructed only for fifty persons. Much opposition was made to his arrange-ments, but the Duke supported him in everything and the theatre was, for its size, the most complete that had yet been seen in England. The duke's habits were very exact and orderly, and everything was conducted with the most perfect regularity, silence and propriety.

The leading lady was Lady Stanhope, sister of Sir Francis. Scandal whispered that the theatricals were a bait to ensnare the Duke of York as her second husband when Sir William Stanhope, who was lying ill, should die.[22] Macklin was called over to England to superintend the rehearsals and instruct the Duke in acting. Kirkman says[23]

the performances were acknowledged to be equal to any ever seen on a regular Theatre, and conferred the highest honor on the skill of Mr. Macklin ... His Royal Highness the Duke of York displayed a correctness, and a chasteness in acting not at all inferior to the most eminent actor.

The company was exclusive. The Duke himself distributed 30 tickets and generally gave 20 to Lord Mexborough (Sir Francis's brother-in-law) and Lady Stanhope for "their disposal to such persons *as were agreeable to him*".[24] As a great favour the Garricks were admitted to one rehearsal and two plays. The company assembled in an elegant drawing room until Wilson appeared, which was a signal for their entry into the Theatre.

Jane Shore was chosen as the first play because the Duke, who at that time was opposed to the government, found some lines, apposite to the political situation, which he wished to speak. We have an eye-witness's account of the proceedings in Thomas Percy who wrote to his wife on

20 January 1767:[25] "Nothing could be conducted in a more genteel and elegant manner than the whole Performance". The Theatre was

small but fitted up in a most elegant taste: only three seats for the Spectators, which will just hold 50 Persons & no more. The seats covered with fine cloth, and the floor all over with carpeting. The Stage raised about 2 feet & decorated in a very pretty neat manner, with all sorts of Scenery as in the great Theatres, but quite new and much more genteel. The stage covered all over with fresh Cloth, and exceedingly well lighted – The Music quite concealed behind the Scenes & consisting of a very well chosen Band.

This unusual position for the music was probably dictated by the smallness of the house. Percy gives a glowing account of the acting. Lady Mexborough, Sir Francis's sister, was Jane Shore. She had a good figure, was of middle stature and, though not handsome, was agreeable and looked the part tolerably well. Her performance was exceedingly good, particularly in the dying scene: "Her action was graceful, yet modest. Her elocution very tolerable, and upon the whole a just & affecting actress". But it was Lady Stanhope as Alicia who sent him into raptures, and he pronounced her superior to anything he had ever seen. She was taller than her sister and, though not beautiful, was fine and graceful "with the most charming mellow voice that ever was". She filled her difficult rôle admirably especially in her leave taking of Hastings, and in her distraction of the last act when "there was not an eye in the house that could withold its tears. All agree that she is equal to any actress that ever happened on any stage"; indeed the delicacy of the modest, well-bred lady was "very different from the hirelings of the Stage". Sir Francis played Richard III but Percy found him too tall and lusty for the character of Crookback. However, in spite of his unsuitable physique he made "a fine grim tyrant" though not so clear or audible as his sisters. As for the Duke of York he was becomingly dressed as Hastings and contrived to look rather handsome though his legs and knees bent in:

His action was exceedingly proper and becoming; & he seemed to enter into his Part with great taste & spirit. His attitudes & Postures were exceedingly fine; but his voice was not quite equal. He speaks very thick and often sunk his words so that he could not be distinctly heard.

Shore was taken by Capt. Wrottesly, a nephew of the Duchess of Bedford and a member of the Duke's household: "No part could be possibly acted better than his upon any stage. His voice is melodious; His action extremely proper & judicious". Minor parts were taken by members of the Delaval or Duke's families: one did his part very ill and seldom spoke a word without loud aid from the prompter. On the whole the tragedy went well and the company was highly entertained. "Between the Acts were fine solemn Pieces of Music, well adapted to the pathetic scenes of the Tragedy". Percy compares the good breeding of the audience, who kept attentive silence and behaved with decorum throughout, with the brawling, noise and disturbance that went on in the public theatres. When the play was over the company was shown back to the drawing room where they mingled with the actors and actresses whilst partaking of sweetmeats and liqueurs. Garrick himself spoke praisingly of the performance.[26] One incident must have been slightly disconcerting. The Duke compelled poor Wilson to play the Chancellor against his will, and even held him down while he was being robed. Wilson, with the speaker's wig on his head, was so conscious of himself as a ludicrous figure, that he burst into uncontrollable laughter which was aggravated by Wrottesly's grimaces from the side scenes. The Duke whispered to him to blow his nose but in vain and the whole audience was soon infected with his mirth. At the end of the play the Duke told him, no doubt much to his relief, that he should never be his Chancellor again.[27]

On 24 May 1767, Walpole reported to Horace Mann that the Duke of York was

acting plays with Lady Stanhope and her family the Delavals. They have several times played The Fair Penitent: his Royal Highness is Lothario; the lady, I am told, an admirable Calista. They have a pretty little Theatre in Westminster; but none of the royal family have been audience.

The first performance of *The Fair Penitent* took place on 7 April, and 150 of the nobility are said to have been present.[28] If so the little Theatre must have trebled its capacity. Edgeworth[29] gives the following account of the performance and its Bohemian aftermath:

The play was, as to some parts, extremely well performed. Calista was admirably acted by Lady Stanhope, and Horatio by Sir Francis. Sciolto [Sir John Delaval] was very well, and Lothario was as warm, as hasty, and as much in love, as the fair Calista could possibly wish. After the piece, Sir Francis and his friends from the professional theatres, retired to sup, and to criticise at the King's Arms, Covent Garden. It was singular that Sir Francis, who was the projector of the scheme, preferred supping with his critical friends to partaking of an entertainment with the Duke of York, and a splendid company. I accompanied Sir Francis Delaval, and we passed a most agreeable evening. The company was in fact, all performing amusing parts, though they were off the stage. After we had supped, Macklin called for a night-cap, and threw off his wig. This, it was whispered to me, was a signal of his intention to be entertaining. Plays, playwrights, enunciation, action, everything belonging to eloquence of every species, was discussed.

Benjamin Wilson painted Lady Stanhope as Calista and an engraving was made by James Basire in 1771 (Plate 3)[30]. It depicts Calista seated in black with her lover Lothario's body in the background. The table with a skull, bones, book and lamp on it follows the stage directions for Act V, scene 1 but the background appears to be a fanciful one without reference to the actual scenery. Another picture at Doddington represents the moment later in the scene when Sir John Delaval as Sciolto is restraining Calista from stabbing herself.[31] A prompt book of the performance with stage directions, notes and passages marked for omission in Tonson's 1766 edition is extant at Ford Castle Northumberland.[32] There is too a letter from Garrick to Sir John Delaval dated 26 March. He had been consulted as to the tones and actions necessary in certain passages, and replied that it was difficult to prescribe these with precision and that it would be necessary to rehearse the speaker, adding that "a fix'd attention to the business of the scene, which Lady Stanhope has to the greatest perfection, is the sine qua non of acting". He professed himself

proud to throw in my mite to an entertainment which will give so much pleasure to the spectators and do honour to the undertakers . . . There was one passage in Lothario which I thought at the time his Royal Highness might have spoken with more levity, and kind of profligate insensibility to the distress of Calista.
It was this speech: "With uneasy fondness
                       She hung upon me."
I must beg you once again to employ me how and as often [as] you please, if you think I can be of the least service to you.

Garrick wrote a prologue for the Duke of York's Theatre which was spoken by Sir Francis Delaval and "An attempt at an epilogue for L.[ady] S.[tanhope] after playing the character of Calista".[33] On 22 April he wrote to Sir Francis: "We have had Several Accounts here of the excellent doings in James Street: There is not the least difference in the opinions of the Publick. You have all your share of Glory, but Lady Stanhope is mention'd as a Prodigy: I am greatly honour'd that my trifle was thought worthy of being the Gentleman Usher to so creditable a Performance".

Several performances were given, and the fourth one was attended by the Prince of Brunswick.[34] On 6 June Thomas Gray wrote to the Rev. James Brown:[35]

The Westminster Theatre is like to come to a sudden end. The Manager will soon embark for Italy without Callista. The reason is a speech, which his success in Lothario emboldened him to make the other day in a greater theatre.

The Duke went abroad and died on 17 September, at Monaco, of a malignant fever at the age of 28. Sir Francis died on 6 August 1771 at the age of 44 of an apoplectic fit.

His brother, Sir John Delaval, succeeded to the family estates and, in 1783, was created a baron. That same year he lost his wife. He had five daughters, one of whom, named Sarah, married the Earl of Tyrconnel. She and her husband lived mostly with Lord Delaval after he became a widower[36] at Claremont, Surrey or at Hanover Square. The Countess of Tyrconnel's name was associated with that of Frederick, Duke of York, son of George III. She was "feminine and delicate in her figure, very fair with a profusion of light hair". Lord Delaval was not so eccentric as his brother; he employed his wealth in cultivating and improving his estates and, among other things, he built an additional wing to Seaton Delaval.[37] Here he gave a series of theatricals on a sumptuous scale with the Countess of Tyrconnel as the heroine and her husband and himself as the male leads.

The first performance took place on 23 December 1790 and was noticed in the *Newcastle Chronicle*[38] as follows:

On Thursday evening Lord Delaval's elegant theatre at Seaton Delaval was opened for the admission of a certain number of Ladies and Gentlemen, to whom tickets had been sent, and the tragedy of *The Fair Penitent* performed in a stile that would have done credit to a regular theatre.

The rôle of the libertine Lothario is said to have lost its disgusting qualities in Lord Tyrconnel's perfect representation of a finished gentleman. Lord Delaval in his old rôle of Sciolto, drew from one critic the opinion that he had never seen the feelings or appearance of the character assumed with more propriety. Over Lady Tyrconnel's Calista the newspapers waxed ecstatic:[39] "her betwiching charms" were indescribable; she evinced "perfect judgment, taste and elegance"; her style of acting was chaste and correct, her conception admirably just and "in most of the scenes she exhibited powers which at once astonished and charmed the audience". An independent eyewitness, Henry Swinburne,[40] is more critically discriminating:

Spearman was the most ridiculous, fat, lame, monotonous Altamont that ever was seen; Mr. Foster insipid; the misses not capital, but the rest of the parts were extremely well performed. Lord Delaval was correct and pathetic: he even gazed at his wife's picture when he swore. Lady Tyrconnel now and then mumbled her phrases, but looked the thing. Lord T. was too bulky, his coat too scanty, and he sawed the air over-much. Williams was manly and clear, but brogued to excess, and straddled a great deal. After the play, Lord Delaval spoke an epilogue written by himself, pointed and smart, alluding to the actors. A natural son of Lord Tyrconnel's danced and sang, and so did some children of Mrs. Abbs.

After this came a strange farce, written by Williams and Spearman . . . really it was beyond anything I ever saw or heard of: such a farrago of officers, nuns, lovers, conjurers; ancient and modern times and manners all jumbled together hodge-podge, with a prologue by Charles Williams, and many bacchanalian songs, for which indeed the farce was intended as a vehicle.

This afterpiece, *You may like it or let it alone*, was an attempt to stage an episode in the family history or legend. A manuscript copy is in possession of the Society of Antiquaries of Newcastle-upon-Tyne.[41] The prologue, spoken by Williams in the character of a conjurer, explains that the play takes place in the days when William the Conqueror granted the site of the house to the Delavals. The scenes include the revels of friars at Tynemouth Priory, a room in Derville (Delaval) Castle and a Monastery in the dark. An interesting stage direction in this last has the phrase "on the light restored" presumably by raising floats and lowering a chandelier. 17 songs were introduced from other sources including the finale from *Inkle and Yarico*, "Greenwich Pensioner" and "Here's to the Maid". Lord Tyrconnel's singing as well as his comic powers were commended in the leading rôle of Lord Derville.

Swinburne tells us that "the theatre was erected in the hall with elegance, warmth and comfort. The scenery was well painted, and the dresses were good". Lord Delaval's epilogue[42] refers to the audience:

> But what, I think, is the best sight of all,
> In this our sometimes playhouse, sometimes hall:
> Sons, daughters, father, tenants, and landlord –
> Agents, men, maids – all, all, with one accord –
> Actors and audience – all of us we see,
> In love and friendship – but one family.

After the plays were over "the most elegant and superb collation ever displayed in this part of the kingdom" was served to over 170 guests in the Grand Salon, and was followed by a ball.

When the plays were repeated on 4 January 1791 there was an audience of 120. The guests had encountered a severe storm to which their host alluded in some additional lines to the epilogue. Swinburne relates that

Williams, being ill, was doubled by Collins of the Shields company, and Captain Scott of the artillery in the farce. The play was even better acted by Lord Delaval and his daughter this time than the last, and the farce was still more detestable. We had supper, and songs by a Mr. Smith, with horrid convulsions. The company, on account of the darkness of the night, staied until eight in the morning.

On 20 February *Othello* was presented and, according to Swinburne, "was very indifferently acted by all except Lord Delaval". The newspapers were as usual adultory: The *Newcastle Chronicle*[43] praised Lord Delaval's rendering of the Moor,[44] and spoke of Lord and Lady Tyrconnel as "animated, correct and impressive" whilst another eulogistic reporter had "never witnessed more chaste, spirited or elegant acting". The farce was *No Song No Supper* in which Swinburne had a good laugh at "fat Spearman's coming out of the sack covered with flour".

The theatricals were renewed the following winter. On 20 January 1792, *The Fair Penitent* was revived with small changes in the cast and was followed by *No Song No Supper*.[45] *Othello* was revived with the same afterpiece on 1 February. At the last moment Williams, who was to take Roderigo, was again ill and Archer from Stephen Kemble's Newcastle company was hastily sent for to join the amateurs.[46] A prologue was spoken by Lord Delaval[47] which referred to the burning question of the hour – the rights of man. At one o'clock in the morning the company of 130 sat down to supper which was enlivened by catches and glees and succeeded by country dances and cards. The cost of the performance was only £66 7s. 2½d. but, as the plays had been given before, there were no expenses for dresses and scenery. Items of interest are:

12 lb. of Mold candles for stage Candlestick		8.	4
20 lb. Tallow do for Lamp		10.	0
Musicians supper and wages	4.	14.	0
Painters and Horse hire	about 1.	11.	6
Chaise hire for Musicians		15.	0

Other entries relate to food for guests and servants, hay for the horses, wages for extra help, and candles. Refreshment expenses totalled only a modest £33 14s. 10d.[48]

The final performance was held on 14 February when *The Fair Penitent* was repeated with *The Poor Soldier*. Among the Delaval Papers is the original holograph ms. of the epilogue which was written by Lord Delaval and spoken by Lord Strathmore; one couplet ran:

To Vapours, hypochondriacs, and grief
Private Theatricals may give relief.[49]

Mrs. Delaval was highly praised as Norah and she happily introduced the famous song, "The Soldier tir'd of War's alarms" into her rôle. The part of Bagatelle was taken by the actor Lee Lewes who concluded the evening's amusements by reciting a whimsical dissertation on law. Though the performance was judged[50] to be as good as amateur acting could achieve yet the greatest native talent could not compensate for the lack of professional experience.

The day after this last performance an inventory of costumes was taken.[51] Among items of interest for *Othello* are "1 Small bedstead Desdemona's", "ornaments for Desdemona's bed", a strawberry handkerchief, Othello's wig, gloves, coat, waistcoat and breeches from which we may gather that he was dressed in 18th century fashion, "1 Pages Dress in Othello", "1 Stand for Dukes Chair", "4 Senators Gowns" and senators' caps and a coat, waistcoat and breeches which served both for Brabantio and Altamont. For *The Fair Penitent* there was "1 Deal Bier & Canvas Corps of Lothario", a black cloth pall and a lamp for Calista. Father Luke in *The Poor Soldier* wore a cloak, black stockings and a wig. Among the properties for *No Song No Supper* were Robin's cake, guineas and ham, Margaretta and Farmer Crop's baskets and songs and the sack used to conceal Endless. There are mss. of this piece, a book of *The Poor Soldier*, Patrick's part in ms. and two books of *The Fair Penitent*. No mention is made of scenery.

CHAPTER VII

The Theatricals at Blenheim Palace

The first theatricals that took place at Blenheim Palace were organised by Sarah, Duchess of Marlborough to entertain the great Duke, two years before his death. The ailing Duke's chief interests in 1718 were his house and his family, and the Duchess must have known how much it would please him to see his grandchildren and their friends perform the heroic plays of *All for Love* and *Tamerlane* in the Bow Window Room of the Palace. The Ladies Anne and Diana Spencer were the grand-daughters of the Duke through his second daughter Anne, Countess of Sunderland. In *All for Love* Lady Anne played Octavia and spoke a special prologue written by Dr. Hoadley, then Bishop of Bangor.[1] Lady Diana and Lady Anne Egerton came on as the daughters of Mark Anthony. Miss Cairnes, who was the Serapion, supplied the following details to William Coxe for his *Memoirs of John, Duke of Marlborough.*[2]

Miss Cairnes, as high priest, wore a very fine surplice, that came from Holland for the chapel (no sacrilege), for the chapel was not finished many years after: What makes me call it a fine surplice is that all the breast was worked in what, many years after, was called Dresden work. The old duke was so pleased that we played it three times, first because we were to play it, some time after, for Lord Winchelsea, then Lord Finch, and a great favourite there, and the third time at the duke's request. The duchess scratched out some of the most amorous speeches, and there was no embrace allowed &c. In short, no offence to the company. I suppose we made a very grand appearance; there was profusion of brocade rolls &c., of what was to be the window curtains at Blenheim. Jewels you may believe in plenty; and I think Mark Anthony [played by Capt. Fisher, the Duchess's page] wore the sword that the emperor gave the Duke of Marlborough.

Miss Cairnes's governess, Mrs. la Vie, was Alexas, and Cleopatra was taken by Lady Charlotte Macarthy. Great screens were utilised for changes of scene. We know nothing of *Tamerlane* except that a special prologue was also written for it which does not appear to be extant but which, like Dr. Hoadley's, eulogised the Duke's achievements and his wife's virtues.

Blenheim again became the scene of theatricals in the time of the 4th Duke of Marlborough. Though he had taken some part in politics in his youth, he lost interest in public affairs after the age of 30 and spent most of his time in retirement at Blenheim. His wife had been Lady Caroline Russell, the only daughter of the 4th Duke of Bedford, and they were a devoted and inseparable couple. The Duke was a reserved man, sometimes accused of being sullen and overbearing, but he is also highly spoken of for his benevolent and generous hospitality, for his probity and his love of peace.[3] No hint of scandal was breathed against his theatricals in the newspapers and never was it said, as so frequently of others, that they encouraged loose living and unseemly behaviour. Indeed, as might be expected of a host of such a character, they were very much of a family affair.

Though plays did not start in real earnest until 1786 there were at least two occasions before this when they were performed. We have already seen that Lady Craven spoke an epilogue to *High Life Below Stairs* at the conclusion of a party, and another on 7 January 1773 with Harriet Wrottesley and the Duchess's boy fiddler.[4] We do not know where these theatricals took place, perhaps in the same Bow Window Room that had witnessed the children's performances. It was, anyway, a converted room, for sometime in the 1770's Lady Craven wrote to Cradock: "There is no stage at Blenheim, nor are there any plays to be acted there, that I know of, and if there were I believe I should certainly be informed of them".[5]

Neither can we be certain where the performances at Christmas, 1786, were given. They were the first of a succession for at this time private theatricals were very much the vogue. The Earl of Sandwich was starting his at Hinchingbrook, Fector's in Dover and Sir Watkin William Wynn's at Wynnstay were in full cry, and the young Earl of Barrymore had recently tried his talents in a barn. At Blenheim *She Stoops To Conquer* was got up on 27 December.[6] Four of the Duke's children took part: his eldest son the Marquis of Blandford, aged 20, as Young Marlow, Lord Henry Spencer, aged 16, as Hardcastle, and the Ladies Caroline and Elizabeth as Miss Neville and Miss Hardcastle. Sir Charles Marlow was entrusted to the Duke's brother Lord Charles Spencer and Hastings to the Duchess's brother Lord William Russell. Indeed the only actors outside the family circle were the Hon. Richard Edgcumbe as Lumpkin and Miss Pigot as Mrs. Hardcastle. Edgcumbe was later to become a leading light in the

Richmond House theatricals. The following evening the first act of *The Critic* and *The Guardian* were acted.

So successful were the theatricals that the Duke and Duchess decided to convert a greenhouse into a proper theatre. This greenhouse stood on the left side of the quadrangle as you enter through the eastern gate. The transformation seems to have been a happy one and the resultant theatre is said to have been[7]

fitted up in a style of peculiar elegance, and with appendages correspondent to the munificence and fortune of the owner. The stage is large and is furnished with proper changes of scenery and fixtures: the seats for the audience are easy and commodious, and capable of accommodating two hundred persons, without including the side-boxes. The whole has a grand and pleasing effect.

Elsewhere[8] the capacity is given as 160 with ease. The colour was a full dove grey, the niches and friezes being in pale blue and the pilasters and other ornaments in white. The scenery was the work of Michael Angelo Rooker, chief scene painter of the Haymarket Theatre. A new experiment in lighting was made in the shape of reverberators or lens and reflectors, which were placed at the extremity of the boxes on each side of the stage, and served to illuminate the proscenium instead of footlights. This was the invention of Pierre Patte who publicised it in his *Essai sur L'Architecture Théâtrale in* 1782. George Saunders[9] considered that the arrangement should be tried in the public theatres. The motto of the playhouse was, unlike most, in English not in Latin: "Laugh where you may, be candid where you can".[10]

Rehearsals for the new season were under way at the beginning of October, 1787. A project to give two dress rehearsals for the Corporations of Woodstock and Oxford was abandoned, and instead they were invited to full performances.[11] The opening night of the theatre was on 19 October when the pieces given were Kelly's *False Delicacy* (Plate 4) and Mrs. Cowley's *Who's the Dupe?* The prologue to the comedy, which was designed to deflect criticism from the unpractised amateurs, was written by William Cole, who had been the Duke's chaplain and tutor to his sons. It was spoken by Edgcumbe.[12] The epilogue was by John Randolph, formerly professor of poetry at Oxford and later Bishop of London, and was spoken by Miss Peshall. The prologue to the farce by Monck Berkeley, was addressed to the Duke and Duchess on opening the new theatre. There were three newcomers among the *dramatis personae:* Lady Charlotte Spencer, John Spencer the son of Lord Charles, and Mary Peshall the daughter of Sir John Peshall. It was claimed that never before had such an assemblage of rank, beauty and elegance graced the stage.

111

Lady Elizabeth acted with vivacity tempered with sensibility and gave proof of her refined taste in her conception of the character of Lady Betty Lampton and in her dress. Lady Charlotte was natural and unembarrassed, Lady Caroline remarkable for her mental powers and Miss Peshall for her flow of spirits. Either Lady Elizabeth or Lady Charlotte[13] sang an Italian air entitled "Non Dubitari". There was "no intermission, no embarrassment, no outré action or look"; the play seemed but the conversation and manners of real life. So far the flattering newspapers, but Frederick Reynolds, who attended with his fellow author Miles Peter Andrews[14] and the actor Holman, gives a very different impression. Andrews had some difficulty in procuring tickets, but having finally succeeded, he and his companions arrived at Woodstock at 7 p.m. and presented them at the lodge. They found the trees decorated with variegated lamps hung in tasteful devices to illuminate the statue of the great Duke of Marlborough. The theatre was crowded to excess but Monck Berkeley had secured places for them. Reynolds was struck by the beauty of the Ladies Spencer and the elegant and expensive costumes but complained that he was "unable to hear one line out of twenty which these *really private* actors uttered". In contrast the Duke's porter in a minor rôle spoke his one line so naturally and audibly that Andrews applauded. Refreshments of every description were served after the second act "on the most liberal and munificent scale". During the love scene between Sir Harry and Miss Rivers the aldermen and electors of Oxford began to whisper and clatter their cups, whereupon an officious member of the suite asked the performers to stop as the company wanted more tea! A dance by the characters was so elegantly executed that the whole audience broke into applause:

Indeed the ease and grace of all their manners, now they assumed their natural characters, and proceeded to practise the art they really understood, made us doubt, whether they were the same persons, who, a few minutes previously, had displayed so much awkwardness and stiffness.

Reynolds tells us that the Duke, who superintended the proceedings, was a most attentive host. He summoned the professionals from their box to converse with him and the Duchess behind the scenes. Andrews, outspoken in his criticism, told them that the theatre was too cold and the play dull and obsolete which did not earn him an invitation to supper! It is probable that this account approaches nearer the truth than the adulatory notices of the newspapers. Inaudibility and awkwardness are the obvious failings of amateurs, and there are many other complaints of them from eye-witnesses at private theatricals. That they excelled in the dance reminds one that in the days of the masque the amateur contribution was limited to dancing. The fresh beauty of the actresses and the elegance of the dresses were what frequently struck professionals who attended performances given by the nobility. In *False Delicacy* Lady Caroline wore a pink bodice, gauze petticoat and cap with a panache of feathers, and Lady Elizabeth a superb black and silver mourning suit and a headdress adorned with brilliants and a plume. Lady Charlotte's costume was *à la bergère* with a white petticoat, a Devonshire brown gown and, to crown all, an elegant hat in a new style; whilst Miss Peshall appeared in a gauze dress trimmed with wreaths of roses and bound in pink, a cinnamon coloured bodice, a striped gauze train and a large pink hat with black feathers. All the ladies carried small bouquets.

The scenery was by Rooker and included a garden scene for *False Delicacy* and a scene with a view of Marlborough House and St. James's Park "not less appropriate in its application than beautiful in its executive" for *Who's the Dupe?*[15] A scene from *False Delicacy* and another from *The Guardian* are shown in mezzotints of the Blenheim theatricals by J. Jones after paintings by James Roberts of Oxford[16] (Plates 4, 5). The machinery was by Austin of Woodstock and the orchestra was led by Talbot. Dr. Philip Hayes, professor of music at Oxford, is said often to have composed the music for the theatricals.[17]

The following night, 20 October, *The Guardian* and *The Lyar* were given. The *World*[18] reported that the former had never been presented with more taste and delicacy, and that the scenes between Young Clackit, taken by Edgcumbe, and Harriet, taken by Lady Caroline, would scarcely ever again be so well finished. Edgcumbe made a hit too as Young Wilding in *The Lyar*, rousing incessant laughter in the last scene. Monck Berkeley's prologue for *Who's the Dupe?* served again for *The Lyar* with alternative lines.[19] The mezzotint of *The Guardian* (Plate 5) shows that the scene used was the same as the last scene of *False Delicacy*, with the addition of a draped curtain and with another view through the door. Lady Caroline wore a blue corset laced with seams of silver in a new style, a spangled crepe petticoat, with a deep silver fringe and a cap with diamond wheatears and bulrushes twined round with a profusion of other diamonds.[20] Her dress was matched in splendour by Edgcumbe's superb suit of violet velvet with Lyons embroidery in silver.

On the third night, 23 October, the programme was varied by playing *False Delicacy* and *The Lyar* together; a performance witnessed by the Vice-Chancellor of Oxford, two bishops and three deans; whereupon the *Morning Chronicle*[21] commented "May the example of encouraging this most noble and rational amusement be followed by patrons equally capable of doing honour to it". At the fourth performance on 25 October

The Guardian and *The Lyar* were repeated and among the audience were several other amateurs: Lady Saye and Sele, the Bowles's from North Aston, and Capt. Ashe.[22] The fifth night was on 26 October and the concluding one, at which *False Delicacy* and *Who's the Dupe?* were repeated, on 27 October.[23] After a dance by all the performers, Miss Peshall spoke a farewell address and the Duchess announced a further season at Christmas.

The newspaper chorus of commendation lauds the Duke and Duchess for adopting "this elegant, and instructive mode of entertaining their family and friends" instead of indulging in horse racing and gaming. So popular were theatricals at this time in high society that winter bookings at Bath were seriously affected by those at Blenheim, Hinchingbrook and Richmond House.

The Guardian and *The Lyar* were revived on 10 January 1788 and were followed by two new presentations, Colman's *The Musical Lady* and Burgoyne's *The Maid of the Oaks*. The theatre had

received many valuable improvements and decorations, several beautiful scenes by Rooker have been added to the former suite; and new arrangements made for the accommodation of the spectators, are such as judgment and experience united, have evidently dictated.[24]

A future Prime Minister had joined the cast in the person of the Hon. R. B. Jenkinson, afterwards Earl of Liverpool, who was at Christ Church with Lord Henry. Lady Elizabeth sang and acted well as Lady Bab Lardoon and Edgcumbe sang an Italian air in *The Musical Lady* in excellent taste. The evening concluded with a charming ballet in which the Ladies Elizabeth and Caroline, and Edgcumbe and John Spencer danced. The Duke's own band was augmented by several capital performers and was well conducted. It is uncertain whether there were five or six performances.[25] Three nights were appropriated for the inhabitants of Woodstock, Witney and Oxford respectively and on the last two nights the gentry and clergy of the county and university were supplied with tickets on application. Holders of tickets, who were unable to make use of them, were asked to return them the day before the performance. Unlike those of Wynnstay they were quite plain.

Before the next season in October improvements were made in the accommodation of the theatre which was enlarged to hold between 200 and 300 people.[26] Two stage boxes lined with scarlet cloth were arranged for the family. Additions were made to the scenery by James Roberts, who had painted the groups of theatrical portraits, and by Thomas Greenwood the elder, chief scene painter at Drury Lane. Roberts was just coming into public notice and this commission must have helped him considerably. "The pure repose" of his scene was said to harmonise "with the native charms of the performers".[27] Greenwood's bill for painting the scenery is extant and reads:[28]

By order of her Grace the Duchess, Painted the Frontispiece with Pillasters, Curtains and Cornice (5 gns); Painted two busts in circular frames (2 gns); Painted an Architect drop with a View of a Garden thro' an Arch (10 gns).

This time the same programme was given on all five nights[29] and consisted of *The Provok'd Husband* followed by *The Musical Lady*. Some alterations in the casting of the latter were necessitated by the absence of Edgcumbe and Lord Henry Spencer, in the latter case probably owing to the fact that the performances were given during the University term. Robinson was a newcomer. The players had achieved more self-possession, knowledge of effect and intimate acquaintance with costume. Each performance showed an improvement, so that what started as being delightful ended by being impressive. Lady Elizabeth's Lady Townly was animated, discriminating and varied. A more magnificent season promised for Christmas did not materialise, probably owing to the King's illness, and the theatre did not re-open until 21 August 1789 when Conway's *False Appearances* was given with *Who's the Dupe?* Lord William Russell did not act this time and his rôle of Gradus in *Who's the Dupe?* was taken by Edward Nares, son of the judge Sir George Nares. He had met Lord Henry at Oxford[30] and was asked by him to take part in the theatricals. At first he declined but finally succumbed to repeated invitations from the Duke and Duchess. He found the rehearsals irksome because it was difficult for him to act without properties, and he felt awkward among strangers who had all had more experience. However his embarrassment soon vanished on the stage and he even had to guard against over-acting. He did not trouble to study particular gestures but left them to the inspiration of the moment, a method which at times proved disconcerting to his fellow performers. Thus once as Gradus he suddenly assumed so grotesque an attitude that Lord Charles Spencer not only missed his cue but had to run laughing from the scene; but Nares kept the audience amused until he was sufficiently recovered to return and the incident only served to increase the merriment. His verdict on the theatricals is balanced and confirms that of Reynolds:

The newspapers of the day gave us credit for being capital actors; but I am persuaded none of us pretended to be so; it would have been absurd and preposterous. As comic actors we were satisfied to make people laugh, and whatever our want of histrionic talent, it was fully compensated by the elegance of the

115

theatre and the scenery, the splendour of the dresses, and the good management of the whole.

Only two performances were given in August and, owing to the heat, fewer tickets were distributed, but the audience made up in fashion what it lacked in numbers. General Conway's *False Appearances*, which had originally been brought out at Richmond House and since had been publicly performed at Drury Lane, was again the main piece for the autumn theatricals which opened on 26 November 1789. It was given four or five[31] successive performances followed by *The Maid of the Oaks*. Lord Henry Spencer did not act, again probably because it was during the University term, but the Marquis of Blandford, who had not played since 1786, took over his rôle of the Marquis in the comedy. The Hon. Capt. Parker was a newcomer and replaced the Hon. R. B. Jenkinson as Old Groveby in the afterpiece. The decorations were again by Roberts. General Conway himself attended on 30 November. Mrs. Lybbe Powys records in her diary:[32] "Young Phil and Tom went with General Conway to the Blenheim play. We were all offer'd tickets, but the weather was so bad we declined going". Nares describes how Conway and Burgoyne, the authors of the two pieces, sat side by side immediately in front of the stage: "It was reported to us that they express'd themselves well pleas'd. It might be so, but they could hardly be expected to say otherwise". He felt his own responsibility in the rôle of the Abbé, which Conway had added to Boissy's original comedy, and continues:

As to my own performance, it was so extoll'd in the newspaper that had I been capable of being deluded by such exaggerations, I might have fancied myself a Roscius . . . Some who acted with me deserved the compliment. Fine acting we none of us pretended to.

He stresses the uncritical attitude of the friendly audience:

It may easily be suppos'd that we had only good-natur'd audiences to witness our performances, that we play'd light pieces, and made no attempt at tragedy. The theatricals offer'd opportunities of entertaining their neighbours, of which the Duke and Duchess gladly availed themselves.

The guests on the first night were the corporations of Oxford, Woodstock and Witney with their wives and families; the second night was devoted to the University, the third was reserved for the Duchess's invitations to the county and neighbourhood. The last night was most select of all, the audience consisting of people invited by the performers. In the number and rank of the spectators as well as in the execution of the pieces this was the most splendid of the theatricals.

116

The last of all took place on 28 and 29 December 1789 when two farces, Pilon's *Deaf Lover* and O'Brien's *Cross Purposes* were given. Nares wrote an additional scene for the latter as well as these verses which were sung as a glee at the conclusion of the performance.

> From the busy stage retiring
> Now our mask'd disguise is o'er
> Mimic scenes no more admiring
> Smiles of truth may we implore.
>
> No cold critics here intrude
> No proud judges prone to blame,
> Here no censors harsh and rude
> Check our blameless hopes of fame.
>
> Whilst the stage of life we range
> Sure from trouble to be free,
> Harmless is th' attempt to change
> Gloomy hours for mirth and glee.[33]

Some members of the household were called in to fill the minor rôles, as they had been when Reynolds visited Blenheim and commended the Duke's porter. Unlike Wynnstay their names do not appear in the play-bills. The theatre was now furnished with as many as 10 changes of scenery not counting the fixtures.[34] The royal family had hoped to attend but were prevented.

Nares wrote more truly than he knew that the "masked disguise" was over. In March 1790 two of the leading performers. Lady Elizabeth Spencer and her cousin John Spencer, were married. Seven years later Nares, who had been made Librarian in 1791, married Lady Charlotte. There were rumours in December that the theatricals would open with the addition of Lord Henry Fitzgerald who, it was said, had given offence to his uncle the Duke of Richmond by this projected change of allegiance.[35] Nothing came of it however. The theatre long stood unused and open to inspection until, sometime between 1835 and 1852.[36] it was converted into offices for the Lord Steward's department. The conservatory still stands, though without trace of its use as a theatre. The west end of it, which may have been the stage, is cut off and converted into a strong room.

The theatre's epitaph may best be spoken in the words of William Mavor.[37]

For an amusement at once liberal, elegant and instructive, which admits so many to participation, and which leaves no sting behind, the expence conspicuous here cannot be deemed too profuse, nor can that generosity and taste be sufficiently praised that have appropriated and applied it so well.

Chapter VIII

The Theatricals of the Earl of Sandwich
and
Three Lord Hollands

(a) *The Earl of Sandwich's Theatricals at Hinchingbrook*.

We have seen that, along with those of Blenheim and Richmond House, the theatricals at Hinchingbrook were said to have adversely affected winter bookings at Bath. They were given by John Montagu, 4th Earl of Sandwich, who had succeeded to the peerage when still a child in 1729. Familiarly known to his time as Jemmy Twitcher on account of his betrayal of his friend Wilkes, he was one of the most unpopular statesmen in an age that hated with vigour. His mismanagement at the Admiralty during the American War of Independence was one of the chief factors in the disastrous lowering of English prestige under the North administration, but on the fall of the North government in 1782, he practically retired from politics and spent his time at his mansion of Hinchingbrook near Huntingdon. Like Lord Barrymore and Sir Francis Delaval he was a rake, and he had taken part in the wild, strange orgies of the Hell Fire Club. Further notoriety came to him in 1779, when his mistress Martha Ray was murdered by a mad clergyman named Hackmann. Martha Ray was a singer and Sandwich an ardent lover of music, so that it is not surprising that many musical entertainments and oratorios were given at Hinching-brook. The Earl was also one of the chief promoters of the Catch Club and of the Concerts of Antient Music. Once more we meet a rake who was also a patron of the arts. The first theatricals at Hinchingbrook took place on 16 December 1760, and on other days that week. *The Tempest* and *Miss in Her Teens* were acted for two nights and *The Mistake* and *The Way to Keep Him*, which had appeared less than a year previously at

Drury Lane,[1] on another two. Doubtless the comedies were all performed in heavily cut versions. The Prospero was the 2nd Viscount Palmerston, a young man of 21 years of age, the Ariel a Miss Courtney who was a niece of the Earl. A new prologue and epilogue were spoken by the former and latter respectively. In the prologue the practice of private theatricals is defended by tradition.[2]

> Should some harsh censor blame theatric joys,
> And cry "this acting spoils our forward boys" . . .
> Let them be taught that pastimes such as these
> Did oft amuse our grave forefathers days.

400 tickets were issued for the four nights, and among the guests was Henry Fox who was about to hold theatricals of his own at Holland House. We do not know where the performances took place.

The next record is not until 26 years later, in the winter of 1786, when the plays were given in a theatre that had been previously used, either in 1760 or at some subsequent unrecorded date. This is attested by Joseph Cradock[3] who wrote, "I received a most kind letter from Lord Sandwich, inviting me to Hinchingbrook, where an effort was made to entertain the Prince of Wales for an evening in the old theatre". In an undated letter[4] to John Houghton of St. Ives, the Earl of Sandwich wrote that he had informed the Prince that they intended to perform the day after Christmas day and every day that week "and he has promised to honour us with his company, having heard so much of our fame". There were difficulties with the cast and the Earl continued:

I find that Captain Squire is fearful of undertaking a long part, therefore we must depend on you for the part of Sr Jasper in the Mock doctor, and must desire Mr. Knighton to undertake Goodwill in the Virgin unmasked. I hope also that you and Mr. Knighton will come over on Friday morning by twelve o'clock that we may have as good a rehearsal as we can of both . . . in which I hope we shall be perfect before the end of next week; but in order to be so we must stick to our business.

A performance had taken place before the Prince attended on 27 December, for we learn then that the prologue had already been delivered by the Earl of Sandwich a month previously, and, in the usual way, it received additional lines in celebration of the royal visit. The motto of the theatre was also changed in the Prince's honour from *Renascentur quae jam cecidere* (Horace, *Ars Poetica*, 71) to *Carmina tam melius cum venerit ipse canemus* (Virgil, *9th Eclogue* last line), and the Prince is said to have been "highly sensible of the elegant and classick attention paid him by the frontispiece and motto. In the middle of which was his Royal Highness's crest". The royal guest stayed three days and on the first evening saw Fielding's ballad opera *The Mock Doctor* and Lloyd's musical farce *The Romp*, both of them afterpieces. The prologue was written by the Earl and spoken by Launcelot Brown, M.P. for Huntingdon and son of "Capability" Brown the landscape gardener. It suggests that the theatre was a building specially adapted and cites the precedent of Voltaire:

> Of all the various systems he profess'd,
> He found that mirth and laughter was the best
> Friends to his cause, his doctrine we embrace
> And dedicate to mirth this antient place;
> With his example plac'd before our eyes.
> This rural theatre is bid to rise.[5]

The second evening began with a concert in which the Prince played the violincello and Madame Mara, who had recently made her debut on the London stage, sang. This was followed by two other afterpieces, *High Life Below Stairs* and *The Virgin Unmask'd*. Catches and glees enlivened both dinner and supper. On the eve of the Prince's departure, 29 December, *The Mock Doctor* was repeated with *The Romp* "with new Scenes, Dresses and Decorations".[6] His Royal Highness, before he left, gave his permission for the theatre, where he had passed three pleasant evenings, to be renamed the Prince's Theatre and the actors His Royal Highness's Company of Comedians, the only instance of a private company being taken under royal protection. The season ended the next night when *The Mock Doctor* was combined with *The Virgin Unmask'd*. For every night 100 tickets were delivered to the gentry of the neighbourhood; two of these may be seen in the Banks Collection in the British Museum. The next season opened on 29 October 1787 with two other afterpieces, Foote's *The Lyar* and Coffey's ballad opera *The Devil To Pay*. A famous amateur had joined the company in the person of Major Arabin, who spoke a prologue written by General Burgoyne.[7] The next day Arabin wrote to the author of it:[8]

The prologue last night was received with the greatest and justest applause, and many solicitations for a copy of "the Major's own prologue"; so you see I shone in borrowed plumes. If I am permitted by you, I shall favour Mr. Topham with a copy for insertion in the World, which I know will oblige him, and that it is what he will expect from me upon hearing the encomiums that it met with. And if you still persist in not acknowledging yourself as the author, your name need not be mentioned. Thus Peter Pindar or any other celebrated writer, may attain the praise your productions so justly merit. I hope you are convinced that *I speak truth*, though from my great success last night in The Liar, I have met with encouragement enough to alter my system and profit by the credulity of mankind which can only be expected from a good liar.

Arabin played Young Wilding in *The Lyar*, and, on 31 October, drew incessant laughter and applause as Mrs. Cheshire in *The Agreeable Surprise* "dressed in a rich crimson silk, a pair of double ruffles, and diamond earrings".[9] A song entitled "A Blooming Flow'r my Chloe Chose" was introduced into this comic opera. It was composed by Charles Hague to words attributed mainly to Matthew Prior which made a great hit.[10] *The Romp* followed. The Prince of Wales was expected at the performance of *The Lyar* on 2 November but failed to come. A new prologue written by Sandwich was spoken by Arabin[11] and supper in the greenroom was accompanied by catches and glees. Two further performances took place the following week. Though good at straight comedy, the forte of the company was in the musical pieces. Comparing Hinchingbrook with Blenheim *The Times*[12] said that, whereas the latter excelled in magnificence of decoration and in acting, the former was without rival for good humour, vivacity and acquaintance with the interior business of theatrical arrangement. Elsewhere Sandwich is distinguished as a particularly good manager. He set an example in changing pieces, a system which was favourably compared to that of Richmond House where repetition tended to become monotonous.[13]

The theatricals were soon resumed and, on 26 December, *The Lyar* was revived with O'Keeffe's comic opera *The Poor Soldier*. The half brothers, J. and W. Stephenson, and Capt. Houghton were said to be unequalled as amateur singers;[14] Arabin sustained Bagatelle. Great disappointment was caused by the absence of the Prince of Wales and the Duke of York, who sent a messenger to say they could not come. Yet the house was full of company and the theatre packed every night. Madame Mara was there with Lord Exeter and sang in the concerts. *The Agreeable Surprise* and *The Virgin Unmask'd* were revived on 27 December, Arabin taking over the rôle of Thomas in the latter. He was declared to be unequalled in comedy, and the epilogue, which he delivered as Mrs. Cheshire, was encored. It emphasised that "Tis known, the Comic Muse we here explore, Nor dares Melpomene approach this door". Some lines were hurriedly changed to express disappointment at the Prince's absence.[15] Another new piece, Colman's *Tit for Tat*, was seen on 28 December followed by *The Devil To Pay*; a third new piece, Macklin's *Love à la Mode*, with Arabin as Sir Callaghan O'Brallaghan, on 29 December with *The Romp*. The festivities closed on 31 December with the two musical pieces *The Agreeable Surprise* and *The Poor Soldier*. According to the *Gazetteer*[16] the actors and actresses were uniformly excellent both in dialogue and songs "and the gay scenes of ancient and hospitable Christmas" were "completely preserved".

Nevertheless all was not well. Arabin, if we are to believe a paragraphist, had been rude to the ladies, one of whom he had even threatened to kick in character.[17] There were dissensions over the choice of the next pieces, a choice which gave umbrage to some old performers who wanted things to go on as they had always been.[18] The Kings' illness in November 1788 precluded festivities that winter, and the Earl's health was beginning to fail, though he lived on until 1792. All these causes conspired to put an end to the theatricals. The company, after 1760, had never attempted anything but afterpieces, but of the nine given five were musical. The theatricals were approached from a musical rather than a dramatic point of view and many actors were chosen for their voices. In this lies their distinction from others of their time.

(b) *Theatricals at Holland House and Winterslow.*

The first theatricals at Holland House were mainly for children and young people. They were given by the Rt. Hon. Henry Fox, afterwards 1st Lord Holland. His wife (Georgiana Lennox daughter of the 2nd Duke of Richmond), had, at the age of eight, taken part in children's theatricals at the house of John Conduitt, and appears in the well-known Hogarth print of the performance of *The Indian Emperor* there. Two years after his marriage Henry Fox rented Holland House, and in 1767 he purchased it. Unpopular as a politician, he was an attractive personality in private life.[19] In 1759 he took under his roof Lady Sarah Lennox, his wife's sister, who soon became fast friends with Lady Susan Fox-Strangways, his niece, whom he invited for long periods to Holland House. The two girls were about 18 and 16 years old when they appeared in the first theatricals on 20 January 1761. Horace Walpole was enthusiastic about their fresh loveliness and wrote to George Montague:[20]

I was excessively amused on Tuesday night; there was a play at Holland House, acted by children – not all children, for Lady Sarah Lenox and Lady Susan Strangways played the women. It was Jane Shore; one Price, Lord Barrington's nephew, was Gloster, and acted better than three parts of the comedians. Charles Fox, Hastings; a little Nichols, who spoke well, Belmour; Lord Ofaly, Lord Ashbroke, and other boys, did the rest – but the two girls were delightful; and acted with so much nature and simplicity, that they appeared the very things they represented. Lady Sarah was more beautiful than you can conceive, and her very awkwardness gave an air of truth to the shame of the part, and the antiquity of the time, which was kept up by her dress, taken out of Montfaucon. Lady Susan was dressed from Jane Seymour, and all the parts were clothed in antient habits and with the most intimate propriety. I was infinitely more struck with the last scene between the two women than ever I was when I have seen it on the stage. When Lady Sarah was in white, with her hair about her ears, and on the ground, no Magdalen by Correggio was half so lovely and expressive. You would have been charmed too with seeing Mr. Fox's little boy of six years old, who is beautiful, and acted the Bishop of Ely, dressed in lawn sleeves and with a square cap; they had inserted two lines for him, which he can hardly speak plainly. Francis had given them a pretty prologue.

It was a strange assortment of ages. Charles James Fox, the second son of the host, was 12 and his little brother Henry must have looked rather diminutive as the Bishop. Uvedale Price, son of Robert Price of Foxley and later a great friend of Charles James Fox's was 13 and William Flower, Viscount Ashbrooke was 16. George Fitzgerald, Lord Offaly, was first cousin to the Fox children. The Rev. Philip Francis who wrote the prologue was Charles Fox's tutor and father of the reputed author of the *Letters of Junius*. Walpole's references to the costumes are of especial interest for they show that some attempt was made at historical accuracy. Jane Shore and Jane Seymour were roughly contemporary, and the antiquarian Bernard de Montfaucon had published designs showing costumes of the period in his *Les Monuments de la Monarchie Française*. The movement to replace 18th century dress by something approaching historical realism had been initiated on the stage some little time before, but was to gain little headway until the era of Kemble and Capon; to find it influencing the private stage at so early a date is unusual. In this respect the noble amateurs led the way.

Another theatrical followed in the summer, for we find Lady Sarah Lennox writing to her friend Lady Susan in July, 1761:[21] "We are to act a play, and have a little ball. I wish you were here to enjoy them, but they are forwarded for Ste, &, to show that we are not so melancholy quite". "Ste" was Stephen Fox the eldest son of the house. Lady Susan returned to act on 26, 27 September in *The Distressed Mother*. Lady Ilchester[22] informed her husband that "It was performed surprisingly well, and a very pretty sight. Susan was Hermione, Ly. Sarah Andromaky! Lucy, Kitty, Ophaly, Fitzgerald etc. acted". Fox himself extolled Lady Susan's Hermione, writing to her father Lord Ilchester "I never saw a part so well acted in my life".[23] The present Lord Ilchester thinks that these performances took place in the Oak Room (later known as the White Parlour), the scene of later theatricals at Holland House.

In the Christmas holidays *The Revenge* was got up with Charles James Fox as Zanga but Lady Sarah's absence cast a damping effect on the future stateman. Lady Susan wrote to her on 15 December:[24]

Charles is as disagreable about acting this play as he can be, he won't learn his part perfect, won't rehearse &c, in short, shews plainly that your not being here is the reason he won't enter into it and be eager, which as you know is the only way of going on with comfort.

Lady Sarah was still deep in matters theatrical at the end of January, 1762, when she wrote to her friend "I have sent you a paper with proposals about acting plays: I hope you'll approve of it". *Creusa* and *Tom Thumb* were the plays chosen for the opening on 20 April 1762 with Lady Sarah and Charles Fox as the star performers. George Offaly did better than was expected and his brother William Fitzgerald made "a fine, jolly, bold-looking girl". The next night *The Revenge* was given.[25] Three months later Lady Sarah married Thomas Bunbury.

Lord Ilchester[26] says that a play was arranged every winter but we have no further records of any. Among those who assisted in the presentations was the actor William O'Brien, who was employed by Lady Susan's father to teach her elocution.[27] In 1764, to the mortification of her family and the chagrin of Charles James Fox who was himself in love with her, she eloped with O'Brien and married him. No wonder that theatricals then lapsed at Holland House for over half a century.

Stephen Fox grew up to cause anxiety to his parents on account of his weak character and spendthrift habits, and they were relieved when, in 1766, he married Lady Mary Fitzpatrick, daughter of the Earl of Upper Ossory. His father, then Lord Holland, renovated and enlarged for the young couple a hunting and shooting box he had recently purchased in Wiltshire, called Winterslow House. Marriage, however, failed to check Stephen's extravagance and at Winterslow he built a little theatre as an addition to the house. We know that it was a barn which was still in existence in the early 19th century.[28] Dr Arnold Hare has examined a barn which stands less than a hundred yards from the house and which local tradition maintains was the theatre. He made a tentative reconstruction of it as a theatre.[29] It was at one time panelled to about 4 ft and, from there upwards, covered with lath and plaster, traces of which remain. Though there are no indications of a stage, there is a door at the east end which seems to have been broken into the timber wall, not at floor level but at the height of about 4 ft; this may have been a back stage entry, The *Salisbury and Winchester Journal* for 31 October 1768 tells us that "an adjacent building was converted into a commodious theatre, decorated with handsome scenes etc. properly adapted". The seats, which were all in front, were "made very commodious for a number of spectators". Evidently no attempt was made to have side or stage boxes. The opening play was Hill's *Zara* which was given on 24, 26, and 29 October 1768. Fox himself took the old man's rôle of Lusignan, Lady Mary that of Zara, and Charles James Fox continued the amateur career that he had started at Holland House, in the rôle of Nerestan. The principal characters were "properly dressed after the manner of the Eastern Princes, very rich and splendid". The piece was said to be admirably performed, every part being sustained with that spirit and propriety, both in speaking and acting, as rendered the whole representation uniform, agreeable, and affecting.

The theatre was filled each night with guests from the city and close of Salisbury and from the neighbourhood to whom Fox had sent tickets the previous week. When they had taken their seats, tea was handed round whilst the band played for about an hour, and after the play had ended about nine, the company returned to the house for a cold collation.

The theatricals were resumed that winter with two pieces: Hughes's tragedy *The Siege of Damascus* on 10 and 12 January 1769, and Mrs Centlivre's comedy *The Wonder* on 14 January. We learn that

The theatre was adorned with a variety of excellent scenes, suited to the events of each performance, and which were shifted with the greatest readiness and facility. The dresses of the tragedy were superb and rich, and a fine contrast appeared between the robes of the Eastern Christians, and those of their enemies the Saracens. The dresses in the comedy were after the Spanish mode, where the effect was both pleasing and striking from the mixture of dignity and grace.[30]

Mrs Harris wrote to her son from Salisbury on 31 October 1770:[31]

Mr. and Mrs. Garrick are to be at Wilton on Friday, and go next week to Winterslow. The plays begin there next Wednesday; Garrick does not act there this year, but says he will another year act Lord Ogilby, if they will act "The Clandestine Marriage" which I much hope they will. Mr. Charles Fox cannot come down by Wednesday, so Mr. Payne takes his part; the latter is a good actor, but the former is excellent.

There is no evidence that Garrick ever fulfilled this promise. Mrs. Harris joined a distinguished company at the performance and reported on 11 November:

We were at Winterslow Play Friday, they acted "The distressed Mother": Hermione, Mrs. Hodges; Andromache, Lady Mary Fox; Pyrrhus, Mr. Fox; Phoenix, Mr. Harry Fox; Mr. Fitzpatrick, who was to have acted Orestes was confin'd to his bed with the rheumatism, so Mr. Storer read his part, and did it well. Charles Fox is so taken up with the Admiralty business, that he says he cannot come down. The two ladies acted most incomparably.

For the next theatricals on 13, 15 January 1773, the Fox's were joined by the Herbert family from nearby Wilton. The pieces were *Jane Shore* and *High Life Below Stairs*. Lady Mary Fox played the heroine; Mrs. Hodges, Alicia; Stephen Fox, Gloster; Storer, Hastings and Richard Fitzpatrick, brother of Lady Mary and part author of *The Rolliad*, Dumont. In the farce Charles James Fox was Freeman; the Earl of

Pembroke, Kingston; Herbert, Philip, and John Floyd, whose father had left him to the Earl's care, Robert. [32] According to the local newspaper,

The whole performance was conducted with the utmost regularity, and was received with the most distinguished applause, by a very numerous and polite audience. The characters of Jane Shore and Alicia as well as the most laughable ones of Kitty and Lady Bab were supported with equal propriety, by Lady Mary Fox and Mrs. Hodges; and the humorous appearance of Sir Thomas Tancred in Lady Charlotte, afforded great diversion. And, in short, the characters of both play and farce, were executed in so just a manner, as to convince the audience that theatrical merit is not confined to those who make the stage their profession; and that it does not so much depend on practice as on the true taste and judgment of the performers.

The next winter the theatricals were resumed on 8 and 9 January 1774 with *The Fair Penitent* and *High Life Below Stairs*. Mrs. Harris again wrote the news, and the rumours, to her son:

I hear Garrick has engaged Mrs. Hodges for this season, and is to give her 1,500 l. Her first appearance is to be in the Fair Penitent. Next week they act that play at Winterslow House, and Mrs. Hodges is to be Calista. I can hardly believe she will go on a public stage, though her finances are not very strong.

There is no evidence that she ever committed such a solecism. Mrs. Harris duly attended the performance which she described on 9 January: [33]

Yesterday we dined at Canon Bowles's. At 5 I set off in his coach in the dark and rain, for the play at Winterslow, we got safe there, and were most highly entertained. Mrs. Hodges does the Fair Penitent most finely, and Mr. Fitzpatrick is the very thing for Lothario, dressed so elegantly, all white satin, trimmed with silver, I never saw so fine a figure. Lady Mary Fox was Lavinia, she looked and dressed most prettily, but had the toothache, so was not in spirits. Charles Fox was Horatio, Mr. Kent Altamont. All did well. After the play we had "High Life Below Stairs", and in the character of the Duke's Servant, Mr. Fitzpatrick exceeded all comic acting I have yet seen. When that was finished, we all repaired to the house to supper. The performance and company were very agreeable together. We got home in whole bones soon after one and in high spirits, but our joy is now turned to sorrow, for this morning, at 5, a fire broke out in the new building at Winterslow House and entirely consumed that and also the old house ... The play was to have been again tomorrow and a ball afterwards.

This fire broke out soon after the second performance, indeed Lord Pembroke went off in the Fool's coat in which he acted. [34] In spite of the house being full of company, no lives were lost and Stephen Fox and his family took shelter at Wilton. That summer Stephen succeeded his father

7. Lord Barrymore's Theatre at Wargrave.

8. Richmond House Theatre. *The Way to Keep Him.*

9. A private rehearsal of *Jane Shore*.

10a. Exterior of Brandenburgh House.

10b. Interior of Brandenburgh House Theatre.

as Lord Holland, but died on 26 December and was in turn succeeded by his infant son.

Under this 3rd Lord Holland, Holland House became one of the great social centres of the Whig Party. As a boy he had acted at his uncle's theatricals at Ampthill Park, but when, on December 19 1816, he himself gave theatricals at Holland House he did not act in them but reverted to his grandfather's idea of a children's performance. The White Parlour (then known as Marsh's room) was again "fitted up with scenery and green curtains". Scenes from various plays were acted. Among the performers were the son of George Tierney the leader of the Whigs; the two sons of Bolus Smith brother of Sydney Smith; Lord Morpeth's son; John Romilly, the second son of Sir Samuel Romilly who was staying at Holland House during his mother's illness; and Henry Fox, Lord Holland's second son who was to be the 4th Lord. Lady Holland wrote:

In the Lyar, the *females* were Henry Webster, and Miss Godfrey was enacted by old Serafino Bonaiuti. When he raised his veil and displayed his black museau, it was a coup de theatre to the amazement and diversion of the audience.[35]

Henry Webster, who was 23, was the son of Lady Holland by her first husband and Bonaiuti was an Italian general factotum and Librarian. Giuseppe Binda, another Italian staying in the house, also took part.

Further children's theatricals were given on 4 April 1818 when scenes from *Venice Preserv'd, The Rivals* and *The Lyar* were selected,[36] but we do not know who took part in them. No further performances in the great mansion are recorded.

E

CHAPTER IX

Two Celebrated Amateurs

(a) *Thomas Twisleton and Theatricals at Adlestrop and the Freemason's Hall.*

One of the grounds on which private theatricals sustained attack was that they led to immorality among the actors and actresses. Jane Austen made capital of such prejudices in her description of the theatricals in *Mansfield Park*. There seems to have been singularly little foundation for the charges except in the characters of hosts like Lord Barrymore and Sir Francis Delaval, but there were at least two elopements. One, we have seen in the last chapter, was that of Lady Susan Fox-Strangways with the actor William O'Brien; the other was the notorious case of Thomas James Twisleton, the second son of Lord Saye and Sele. He was born on 28 September 1770, and his maternal grandmother was Cassandra, daughter of William Leigh of Adlestrop in Gloucestershire. Twisleton was sent to Westminster and there distinguished himself, not only in classics and athletics, but in the annual Latin plays whence he doubtless acquired his taste for acting[1]. At the age of 17 he made his appearance in private theatricals as Pierre in *Venice Preserv'd* and his performance was much spoken of. Twisleton's sister Julia had married her cousin James Henry Leigh of Adlestrop House near Stow-in-the-Wold in December 1786. It was at his house that the theatricals took place[2] in the autumn of 1787 with Lady Saye and Sele as Belvidera in *Venice Preserv'd*, Andromache in *The Distress'd Mother* and Lady Townley in *The Provok'd Husband*. The only relic is some verses signed Theatricus,[3] comparing her, in the customary fulsome fashion, to Mrs. Siddons and Mrs. Pope. Probably a room was fitted out for the purpose, for Miss Agnes Leigh, the recent owner of Adlestrop, said that she had never heard of a theatre there.

128

That December Twisleton earned the following commendation of his performance of Phaedria in Terence's *Eunuch*, the Westminster play:[4]

> Mr. Twisleton acquitted himself of the difficult part of Phaedria with his usual success; his carriage is graceful and commanding, his action easy, and his make remarkably genteel. This gentleman has before acted very principal parts in other plays at private Theatres; and if we may believe common report, in a capital style.

Twisleton was to have taken part with his mother in a comedy at Adlestrop but nothing came of it.[5] He next appeared on 9 May 1788 at the Freemason's Hall, Great Queen Street, London. The Hall had been built 10 years previously from designs by Thomas Sandby, but the acoustics were poor and the echo destroyed the value of many of the speeches. An orchestra of 15 or 16 musicians was engaged. Behind them, at the upper end of the room, a stage was raised and on it a frontispiece was hung between two pillars. Admission was by subscription and an audience of 300 people of fashion filled the benches. The play chosen was Jephson's tragedy *Julia*, which had come out at Drury Lane the previous year, and the rehearsals and direction were in the capable hands of Colonel Arabin.[6] There were five or six scenes in the best manner and the dresses were beautiful, especially a painted gauze of Julia's, in addition to which "a splendour of diamonds was exhibited, unknown to any former private stage". Twisleton himself played Mentevole, a part originally intended for someone else who had resigned it on finding he had no histrionic talent. The heroine was taken by Charlotte Wattell, daughter of John Wattell, "a very beautiful young lady . . . of very respectable connections, being nearly related to the Stonehouse family, of Radley in Berkshire".[7] Twisleton had already met and admired her and they shared a passion for acting. It was suggested that he formed an attachment to her at the theatricals,[8] but some lines in the prologue written and spoken by Mrs. Barnard in which Julia is thus addressed, rather point to an engagement:

> Put off the Tragic dress, and play thy part,
> In happier scenes, congenial with thy heart,
> And if the fates decree thee soon a Bride,
> Thy husband may assume a conscious pride.

And in the epilogue by Barnard, which she herself spoke with "a complete knowledge of the histrionick art", occur lines addressed to the audience:

129

Tis Yours – the business of the World to guide,
And o'er the sterner Scenes of Life preside:
'Tis Ours – in gentler Scenes to act our part,
To soothe your cares, with sympathetic art,
And with Love's milder sway – to rule the Heart.[9]

Twisleton's voice was hampered by the room's acoustics, but Miss Wattell's

native beauty shone with great lustre, though clouded with the garb of woe; her features are very expressive, her attitudes noble, and her voice, when modulated by a proper instructor, will force the sympathetick tear to flow. At present, she has not a sufficient change, which is the only fault that the severest shaft of criticism can point out.

Plaistow as Marcellus had an easy utterance and unembarrassed deportment. Corey as Manoa and Oliphant as Durazzo were commended for the propriety and energy of their delivery and Miss Madden was particularly good as Olympia. The acting in the last scene was said to resemble that of the real stage more nearly than in other private performances.[10]

Among the audience were the Duke and Duchess of Richmond and some of their amateurs, including Mrs. Hobart, Mrs. Damer and Lord Edward Fitzgerald. The rest of the night was taken up by a masquerade supper and dancing in the Hall for which the company swelled to over a thousand.[11]

Four months later Twisleton, whilst still at school, eloped with Charlotte Wattell and married her in Scotland on 28 September.[12] It was a precipitate adventure and it had unhappy results. As the *Gentleman's Magazine* had it:

Like most other early unions, this turned out to be an unfortunate one. The lady was extravagant, and otherwise misconducted herself, and the marriage, after the birth of a daughter and a son, was in consequence dissolved by Act of Parliament. But this rash and unfortunate step not only impeded Mr. Twisleton's rise in life, by interfering with his education, and throwing a cloud over the brightness of his manhood, but was the occasion of much pecuniary embarrassment brought on to a certain extent by his own careless and liberal disposition, but more by the folly and prodigality of his wife.

It was an excellent handle for the enemies of private theatricals though, curiously enough, they do not seem to have made use of it.

About three months after marriage the young couple appeared at further theatricals at Adlestrop. They played Edwin and Matilda in Francklin's tragedy *Matilda*, Raymond and Hortensia in another tragedy,

130

Jephson's *The Count of Narbonne*, and Pierre and Belvidera in *Venice Preserv'd*. The afterpieces were *Bon Ton* with the Twisletons as Lord Minikin and Miss Tittup, and *Who's the Dupe?* in which they sustained Gradus and Charlotte.[13]

The dramatic ambitions of the Twisletons now vaulted higher than the applause of a private circle, and they arranged with Holman to appear for his benefit first at Cheltenham and afterwards at Liverpool. It was, of course, not unusual for an amateur to act for a particular actor's benefit in a company that was playing locally, and we have seen that Lord Barrymore did this; but it was not so usual for a lady of quality to appear on the professional stage. The fact that the Twisletons accompanied Holman from one town to another suggests, too, that they were paid for their services, and they were probably pleased to be so in view of the lady's extravagance. The handbills announced that they had left town expressly to play Pierre and Belvidera in Liverpool in July 1793.[14] On Holman's recommendation they were then engaged by Harris to play for six nights at Covent Garden; but at the last moment Twisleton's outraged family succeeded in persuading him to abandon the project, and when his wife made her professional debut in London as Belvidera on 1 February 1794, he was not her Pierre.[15] The criticisms of her performance were, on the whole, favourable and show that an actress trained in private theatricals could hold her own in a famous rôle. She appeared to have studied Mrs. Siddons and other celebrated exponents of the part, was correct in all means of producing stage effect and played several scenes powerfully. Her great defect was still lack of variety in her voice which "came upon the ear with a loud monotony, destructive of all possibility of pathetic effect." Her free and unembarrassed deportment proclaimed her no novice and it was felt that industry and experience would make her a distinguished ornament to the stage.[16] She possessed a petite, good figure but her features, though agreeable, lacked expression. In her portrait,[17] however, she appears animated. During the season she was seen as Calista, Euphrasia in *The Grecian Daughter*, Juliet for her benefit, and Cordelia, and she drew good audiences. Daly engaged her for Crow Street Theatre, Dublin for the summer. Her persistence in continuing her stage career led Twisleton to obtain a deed of separation in June 1794 and a divorce in April 1798. He stated as his reasons that she had almost reduced him to poverty, "then, that she would go on the Stage. She said she should make a great Fortune by it; and that if I would not suffer it, she would go herself". When questioned as to whether she had acted before the separation he replied: "I think she acted Three or Four times which caused in my Breast a very great Aversion to it",[18] thus concealing the fact that they had acted together in a public theatre. He added that he had threatened to break with her unless she gave up the stage but his sudden objection to her continuing her career was, no doubt, the result of family pressure.

Twisleton used his declamatory powers in the service of the church and returned to Adlestrop as the parson. He rose to be Bishop of Colombo where he died in 1824. Mrs. Twisleton continued her stage career and turns up at several provincial theatres though she does not appear to have been re-engaged at Covent Garden.[19] In 1803 she remarried, and, as Mrs. Stanley, is lost in obscurity.

(b) *William Fector's Theatricals at Dover.*

With William Fector we leave the aristocracy for the middle class, but, though his theatricals had not the glitter of the *haut ton*, they were accorded just as much publicity in the contemporary press.

William Fector was born on 9 December 1764, and was the third and youngest son of Peter Fector, a merchant and banker at Dover and owner of a small estate at Eythorne. He had French blood in him for his maternal grandfather, the Rev. John Minet, rector of Eythorne, had immigrated from France at the time of the Revocation of the Edict of Nantes.[20]

Fector's first performances were held at his father's house, whether at Eythorne or Dover is not recorded, in January 1783. He created a great impression as Orestes in *The Distress'd Mother* and as Barbarossa in Brown's tragedy of that name. His success encouraged him to purchase, and fit up "with great taste and at considerable expence" the Assembly Room in Snargate, Dover which stood opposite the theatre of today. We are told[21] that this theatre "was entirely new and most elegant. Never could any place be better adapted or contrived for a private theatre". The motto was "Labor ipse voluptas" and the livery was blue and orange; many ladies appeared with yellow ribbons out of compliment to the founder. The capacity was 190 but generally only 170 tickets were distributed. On the opening night, 30 October 1783, *The Revenge* was acted with a prologue and epilogue written by Miss Mantell, the former being spoken by Fector and referring to his "veteran corps". [22] Fector was acclaimed as Zanga. An expert pronounced that, though only 19, he excelled Mossop in the first four acts and equalled him in the burst of comedy in the last. A critic adds that he

acts in so easy, familiar, yet powerful a manner that I imagined I saw a second Garrick rising up to banish bombast and affectation. His figure is pleasing and graceful, with eye the most expressive, and he feels his part so capitally, insomuch, that I was nearly certain of what he meant to inform one of, before he uttered a word.[23]

At the opening of the play, where Zanga compares fortune to a storm, "his look and action was very fine, and his leaning against a rock, when the scene drew up, had by far a better effect than the common way Zanga begins the play"; in Act IV in his account of seeing Carlos and Leonora in the garden, both action and narration were said to beggar description; when receiving Alonzo's signet to murder Carlos with the words "I dare not disobey" he "turned round and gave a look aside, which so expressed the joy he felt . . . as cannot be conceived"; lastly in Act V his avowal of villainy "by keeping Alonzo first in suspence, and then like a peal of thunder declaring, he had been the cause of all the mischief, was so well performed as to strike every spectator with a degree of astonishment". "Indeed," the critic summed up, "if his comedy were as fine as his tragedy he would be a young theatrical prodigy".

Whitmore, who was the Alonzo, had had acting experience and displayed much ability for a private performer but his voice was too low in parts. Mantell as Carlos was tolerably good in the first act but did not sustain it. Mrs Mantell as Leonora had ability and judgment, and the minor parts were pretty well supported. Whitmore's voice had improved at the second performance on 16 December and he excelled in the middle acts, whilst Fector in his burst of perfidy in Act V sent the critic into the hyperbole that this was "the most astonishing display of theatric powers ever exhibited".[24] His declamation of the prologue is also commended. Perhaps this reporter was a friend but his estimate of Fector's powers is borne out by a notice in the *European Magazine* where we read that:

In person he is rather above middle size; his countenance pensive; has great expression; the fire of his eye can be best described by those who have seen his performances: his voice is very powerful, and perfectly adapted to express the rage of the Hero and the tenderness of the Lover.

He never allowed his attention to be diverted from the scene to the audience, "a compliment due to very few of those gentlemen who at present tried the stage". He had, however, still to learn the nice touches derived from a critical examination of the text. There can be little doubt, however, that Fector, like Lord Henry Fitzgerald, was a born actor, and that he really moved people even though they came to praise.

We know little of the next performance on 11 March 1784. The play was *Tancred and Sigismunda* and Fector spoke both prologue and epilogue.[25] In the former reference is made to a newly married brother or sister of Fector's:

Not such the Pair who grace this honour'd roof,
Bless'd in each virtue as with blooming youth –
Long on you both may happiness attend,
So ardent prays the Brother and the Friend.

In the epilogue Fector forestalled the carping person that would complain

"For four full hours we crowded were and crampt
To see them enter blunder scold and rant".

Venice Preserv'd was given with a prologue and epilogue by Miss Mantell on 5 October 1784, and on 3 March 1785, Murphy's *Orphan of China* with a prologue and epilogue by the miscellaneous writer Samuel Jackson Pratt which were spoken by Fector. Pratt stresses the advantages of private over public theatre audiences:

Lo! friendship summons candour to our stage
Who brings no catcall and no party rage;
The shining rows that grace this little round,
Will fright our heroes with no frightful sound ;
Arm'd with no terrors do our critics sit,
To rowl the thunders of a London pit;
No phalanx awful and intent to blame,
Blasts the fair rosebuds of our *private* fame.

In the epilogue he refers to the recent balloon flights of Jeffries and Blanchard at Dover.

Pratt again wrote the prologue for the autumn performance this year of Hughes's *Siege of Damascus* on 13 October, whilst the epilogue was written by another friend and both were delivered by Fector.[26] Murphy's *Zenobia* followed on 24 November in which Fector as Rhadamistus gained fresh laurels. His "astonishing powers" in so wide a range of characters evoked the tribute:[27]

To see a young gentleman, only by the force of his own genius perform such capital parts, and parts so opposite as Zanga, Jaffeir, Zamti [*Orphan of China*], Rhadamistus and others, and each with equal greatness is a phaenomenon in the theatrick hemisphere like a comet and dazzles all beholders. From the feebleness of age, the ravings of wild phrensy to the tender pathos and ardour of love Mr. W. Fector's sensibility leads him to assume any passion the character requires.

Mrs. Whitmore was the Zenobia and drew tears at her meeting with Rhadamistus in Act III and in her dying scene. She was possessed of an elegant figure and uncommon powers and of her acting in this rôle and that of Mandane in *The Orphan of China* the critic averred that he never

134

saw her equal on a private stage. Of Curling as Pharasmanes he could only hint the worst, since "where gentlemen are so obliging as to act only with a view of amusing their friends, it would be unjust and unpolite should we pretend to criticise". Miss Oakley was timid at first as Zelmira but after acted well, and all but one were word perfect. The dresses were splendid. Fector wore a rich leopard spotted satin train trimmed with ermine and gold, and a costume of spotted and blue satin profusely ornamented with gold and spangles, lace and fringe. The scenery was beautifully painted and there were numerous changes: "The throne of Pharasmanes with the blacks and their drawn sabres, had a good stage effect". The prologue and epilogue[28] were written respectively by Jackson and Pratt and were spoken by Fector, who was said to be unrivalled in such recitations. A splendidly dressed audience was enraptured by the entertainment.

In the next theatricals on 28 March 1786, Fector took the part of an old man, the patriot Horatius in Whitehead's *Roman Father*.[29] He was well able to adapt himself to aged as well as youthful characters, and he delivered the prologue by Pratt and the epilogue by Peter Pindar with fire. The latter alluded to the unusual custom of performing a tragedy without the relief of an afterpiece:

> What! must we dismal part, and seek our beds
> With nought but shrieks and murders in our heads?
> Go home, without of mirth one single grain,
> To exorcise the horrors from our brain.

In this matter Fector was a century ahead of his time. On this occasion, however, there was music. Mrs. Mantell had improved unbelievably as Horatia and a newcomer Garner who acted Hostilius had already had experience in some theatricals at Sandwich.

At the next performance, that of Hill's *Zara* on 14 December 1786, Fector took the dual roles of Lusignan and Osman. His versatility in portraying, in one tragedy, the fire of Osman and the sufferings of poor old Lusignan is emphasised by the *Morning Chronicle*.[30] Another critic[31] was of opinion that the role of Lusignan had not been more ably represented since the days of Garrick, but that his Osman was not up to Kemble's rendering. Fector recited the prologue and epilogue, both written by W. Gillum,[32] with such humour, that it was felt that he would excel as a comic as well as a tragic actor. Fector's sister gave a good performance as Zara, her "action was elegant and just, and the dress very handsome". "The Roscius of the Cliffs" had no reason to complain of the play's reception. Most of the genteel families of the neighbourhood attended and Dover was converted that night into "a little London".

The next play had already been decided upon, and on 5 March 1787, Fector appeared as Zaphna in Miller's version of Voltaire's *Mahomet*, with Gill as Mahomet. His powers of oratory were particularly conspicuous in Act IV.[33] The growing opposition to private theatricals is referred to in Gillum's prologue:

> Keen wits at every foible will take aim
> These "Private Theatres" they think fair game;
> And as the rage increases they discern,
> That topsy turvy everything we turn,
> To crush, not check, this acting rage, they're bent,
> And thus their petty irony they vent.

Both this and the epilogue, which was by Capt. Topham, were spoken, as usual, by Fector.

During 1787 Gillum, who was a clerk in the East India Company, published his *Miscellaneous Poems* and dedicated them to Fector, "A Gentleman, whose veneration for the liberal arts has ever been eminently conspicuous". The Fector family came out in strength as subscribers to a volume which included addresses spoken at the theatre.

The autumn season was expected to be uncommonly brilliant: "new fancy dresses and decorations are in order, and everything is to be in style".[34] 500 invitation cards had been circulated so that at least two performances were contemplated. At the last moment Fector was taken dangerously ill,[35] but by the end of November had recovered sufficiently to continue with the preparations "in a style that shall make the little Theatre of Dover vie with those of prouder name and more elaborate ornament".[36] Francklin's tragedy *Matilda* was finally presented on 18 December. Morcar was said to be one of Fector's best characters and the heroine was played by Mrs. Mantell. The dresses were handsome but not gaudy; the scenes suitable; the music sprightly and entertaining; the company delighted. The prologue, which was written by Pratt, referred to preparations for war; the epilogue was written by the dramatist James Cobb, and both were spoken by Fector.[37]

Then at last Fector yielded to the desire that he should be seen in comedy. For the only time in the history of his theatricals two comic pieces were presented on 24 April 1788. In *The Guardian* Fector appeared as Clackit and in Colman's farce *The Deuce Is In Him* as Prattle.[38] Unfortunately, no criticism has come down to us so that we do not know whether he fulfilled expectations as a comic actor. He obviously preferred tragedy and did not repeat the experiment. The prologue and epilogue were both by Gillum; the latter defends private theatricals:

Permit a word or two on acting Peers.
The Stage will never wound a parent's heart,
'Tis Dice and Faro point the cruel dart.
By private Theatres no heir's undone –
Estates by different Play are lost and won.

Fector returned to tragedy with Thomson's *Edward and Eleonora* presented on 21 November 1788.[39] Fector's Edward was declared a masterpiece, not surpassed by Garrick at his age. Mrs. Mantell's Eleonora was very affecting in parts, and Miss Fector, inspired by her brother with a love of the drama, was never seen to better advantage. Fector's costume was purple and yellow satin richly ornamented, Mrs. Mantell's, primrose coloured satin and Miss Fector's, white. "The scenery of the theatre has been a little beautified and embellished; but superior attractions caused us not to attend so much to them", reported one critic. "The Town, as on former similar occasions was all life and bustle; the coaches and carriages lined the large street"; indeed such was the eagerness to gain admission that the house was rather overcrowded. The prologue, written by Pratt and spoken by Fector, once again alluded to the vogue for private theatricals:

For now you know, Dramatic Navigation,
Grac'd by the great, is grown into a Passion.
The Richmond and the Blenheim, whose fair Crew
And Passengers, just admiration drew;
No public Tempests there presume to blow,
No critic Syllas threaten wrecks below
Smooth glide the Vessels through th'untroubled seas,
While Friendship rules the wave and Fashion guides the breeze.

In the epilogue, written by Gillum, lines concerning George III's lapse into insanity were spoken by Fector in so pathetic a style that there was scarcely a dry eye in the house.[40]

Young's tragedy of *The Brothers* was presented on 9 February 1789, with Fector as Demetrius, Gill as Perseus and Mrs. Mantell as Erixene. The *World*[41] said that it was on the whole the best performance yet given in Dover and that the dresses were very splendid. The *Morning Post*,[42] more measured in its praise than its contemporaries, merely accords Fector "very respectable talents", and puts in a plea for the avoidance of the practice of circulating twice as many tickets for every night of playing as the theatre could contain. The prologue was written by Gillum and attacks the preference for boxing matches to drama at Covent Garden, an allusion to the appearance of Mendoza and other pugilists in *Aladdin* at that house. The epilogue was written by Mrs. Piozzi and was adjudged to be full of dull commonplaces in indifferent numbers. In her journal[43] she wrote:

I half wonder'd that Mr. Fector of Dover, who was so kind to us when coming home, & suffer'd all our Things to pass the Customhouse *Unexamined;* should send to beg I would write an Epilogue for Young's Play called The Brothers in which his Son was to perform a principal Character ... but they told me afterwards that the Young Man was Mad for the Stage, and Threatened his Father that he would *himself* write the Epilogue if I did *not*. So to save a kind Friend from seeing his Darling Boy heir to 30,000£ hiss'd off a Country Theatre, I sent the following lines ... well enough adapted to the *Time* and the *occasion* ... They saved the Play I heard – and the Performer; but the poor Stage struck Heir died a Lunatick some two or three years later, I was told.

This self-important and condescending farrago, in Mrs. Piozzi's usual manner, shows how little she was acquainted with the theatricals for which she wrote.

Fector and some friends formed a small dramatic society in honour of Shakespeare and held their annual dinner on 18 April 1789. As at Wynnstay, they had a uniform, with steel buttons inscribed with a cypher of the private theatre and the words Shakesperian Institution.[44] The last play of all was Rowe's *Tamerlane* given on 4 and 5 November 1789.[45] Fector as Bajazet was careful not to out-Herod Herod and was restrained in his tyrannical rage: "In the taunting scene with Tamerlane he approached nearer to Kemble than any other public performer: that with Selima was at once sublime and beautiful". His only defect was lack of inches, for tyrants on the stage were expected to be of giant stature. The *Morning Post*[46] even went so far as to say that he had "few, if any, competitors, either on public or private stages, in Bajazet". For the only time, professional actresses were called in owing to domestic misfortunes of the amateur ones. They were the two daughters of Mrs. Sarah Baker, a famous character who conducted a circuit of Kent theatres. Dilnot was kingly as Tamerlane, and both he and Gill, as Moneses, gave powerful performances. In attention to the presentation of the smaller parts Fector's theatricals were an improvement on others:

In general, it is thought quite sufficient, if the Noble Owners of the Mansion are decked out with all the "glorious circumstance" of the Drama – whilst the friendly assistants are left to content themselves with the comfortable reflection of having "that within which passes show".[47]

Tamerlane, too, was often more indebted to magnificent dresses than to scenery but at Fector's both were rich, elegant and appropriate. The prologue by James Cobb was a patriotic eulogy of the brave men of Kent, and the epilogue by Gillum expressed thankfulness for the King's recovery and sorrow for Louis XVI's imprisonment. Fector spoke both. There were above two hundred spectators.

A comedy was projected for the spring 1790 and *The Wonder, The Busy Body* and *The Drummer* were mentioned, but no further performances actually took place. A new public playhouse, opposite to Fector's, was erected that year by subscription and his wardrobe was purchased for use there.[48]

William Fector died on 23 December 1805.[49] Mrs. Piozzi's story that he died two or three years after 1789 is therefore untrue; whether, as she heard, he became insane is equally so, I do not know. That he had talent as an actor as well as enthusiasm is evident. His concentration on tragedy was without parallel in the theatricals of his time, and betokens a passion for acting rather than the usual desire for amusement. Of his efforts the *European Magazine*[50] said: "instead of following the tide of fashionable frivolity, he has endeavoured to stem the torrent, by encouraging an amusement which has ever been deemed the most rational of its species".

CHAPTER X

The Theatricals of Two Country Squires

(a) *Oldfield Bowles at North Aston.*

The little, thatched village of North Aston in Oxfordshire lies in a peaceful, rural setting just off the busy Oxford-Banbury main road. It cannot have changed much from the 18th century village of which Charles Bowles was squire in 1773. The Hall, though now gothicised, still stands amid its spacious lawns next to the church, which contains memorials of the three generations of the Bowles family who owned the manor.

Charles Bowles's son and heir, Oldfield Bowles, was in 1773, 34 years of age. His first wife having died in 1767, he married Mary daughter of Sir Abraham Elton of Clevedon Court, Somerset, who was but 20.[1] Oldfield Bowles was a man of culture, owner of an extensive library, amateur musician, painter and botanist, besides being an adept at rural sports and athletics and an excellent farmer.[2]

We first hear of dramatic performances at North Aston early in 1773. The *Oxford Journal* for 6 February[3] reports that, on an evening in the previous week, Murphy's two act farce *The Upholsterer* had been acted by the Misses Fowler and Messrs. Oldfield Bowles, Graham, Manders, John Manders, Elton, Haynes and Broderip. The prologue was spoken by Manders, the epilogue by Oldfield Bowles and the performance met with "singular applause". It was followed by a collation and ball. Perhaps Bowles had been inspired by the performances that had taken place in January at nearby Blenheim. However that may be, he was sufficiently encouraged by the result to fit up a theatre. He employed Thomas Jones of Pencerrig, who had been a pupil of Richard Wilson's, to paint the scenes, and Jones was assisted by one Ned whenever the hounds were not out.[4]

A general rehearsal was given at the beginning of January 1774 before all the farmers of the district and their families, and on 6 January, when it was full moon, the gentry of the neighbourhood were invited, and above 20 carriages came.[5] The theatre was a room in the house,[6] which was furnished with rich scenery. *The Merchant of Venice* was given with *Lethe* one evening, and Cumberland's *West-Indian* with *The Upholsterer* on another. A third programme was presented to friends and neighbours on 29 January consisting of *The Fair Penitent* and *The Mayor of Garratt*. We are told that

the distinguished applause which the Theatrical part of the entertainment met with, on account of the extraordinary merit of the several performers; the elegance of the scenery, propriety of dresses, &c. does equal honour to the judgment and taste of that family, as the latter part of the entertainment did to their well known hospitality.

This latter part was a cold collation provided after the show. Among the actors was Sir George Beaumont, the famous art patron and friend of Wordsworth. He was also a life-long friend of Bowles with whom he had many interests in common, and was associated with the theatricals throughout their career. He is said by Allan Cunningham[7] to have "excelled so much in the presentation of various characters, serious as well as gay, that friends were not wanting who thought he more than approached Garrick". The music was supplied by the Oxford band of musicians who were employed at North Aston over the Christmas holidays;[8] for, as at Wynnstay, the theatricals were part of the festivities of a country house party at that season.

The next theatricals took place on 23 December 1774, when *Every Man in his Humour* and *The Mayor of Garratt* were performed. Members of Oxford University as well as the neighbouring gentry were sent tickets.

In 1776 Bowles, finding his theatre too small, converted a large barn into "a very spacious and elegant one".[9] That winter he ventured to present for the first, and probably only, time on any stage a local production, *The Siege of Scutari*,[10] a tragedy by Edward Taylor, son of the Archdeacon of Leicester.[11] After having travelled extensively in Europe, Taylor retired in 1770, at the age of 30, to the village of Steeple Aston, where he spent the rest of his life "in the pursuits of elegant literature". He entered the Shakespeare controversy in 1774 with a pamphlet entitled *Cursory Remarks on Tragedy*, and left at his death, besides his manuscript tragedy, some poems and translations. He is said to have been endeared to his friends by his urbanity, brilliant talents and goodness of heart.

141

The Siege of Scutari was performed on 7 November 1776, with Foote's *The Author,* to a crowded audience

in the Theatre at North Aston in this County, lately erected at a great Expence by Oldfield Bowles Esq; our present High Sheriff. The Scenery, Decorations, and Habits, were uncommonly splendid, and entirely new. – The Fable of this Tragedy is simple and interesting; the characters justly drawn, the Incidents which regularly produced the Catastrophe truly affecting, and the Diction nervous and pure. – The Prologue for opening the Theatre was written by William Whitehead Esq, Poet Laureat, and most deservedly admired.

This prologue,[12] which was spoken by Sir George Beaumont, is worth rescuing from limbo:

> Sure some infection hovers in the air!
> For every man and woman is turn'd play'r.
> No age escapes it – antiquated dames
> And reverend Romeos breathe fictitious flames;
> Pale misses antedate love's future force,
> And school-boy Richards lisp – "A horse! – a horse!"
> No rank escapes it – with a Garrick art,
> Right honourable Hamlets stare and start;
> And lady Belvideras every-where
> Pat the starch'd handkerchief, and squeeze the tear,
> What wonder then in this theatric age,
> If we too catch the epidemic rage?
> If with the rest we play the mimic's part
> And drive to our own barn the Thespian cart?
> For we confess this pageant pomp you see
> Was once a barn – the seat of industry:
> And time may come when all this glittering show
> Of canvas, paint, and plaster, shall lie low;
> These gorgeous palaces, yon cloud rapt scene,
> This barn itself, may be a barn again;
> The spirit stirring drum may cease to roar,
> The prompter whistle may be heard no more
> But echoing sounds of rustic toil prevail,
> The winnowing hiss, and clapping of the flail.
> Hither once more may unhous'd vagrants fly
> To shun the inclement blast and pelting sky;
> On Lear's own straw may gypsies rest their head,
> And trulls lie snug in Desdemona's bed.
> Mean while, good neighbours, till that time shall come,
> We bid you welcome to our harvest home;
> Our's are the fairest crops Parnassus yields,
> In lessons gather'd from poetic fields.
> Let Oxford boast her powers of every kind

142

To mend the morals, and improve the mind;
More instant aid our rival stage affords,
We bring to action what they teach in words.
Here virtue's mildest form instruction wears,
Wins you with smiles, or softens you with tears;
Our mental physic, gratis, we dispense,
A country hospital for wit and sense;
The maim'd in faculties, the blind in thought,
All but the deaf are here humanely taught.
Then lend a patient, nay, a willing ear,
For no incurables shall enter here.
To-night we give you as our first essay,
A novelty indeed – a virgin play!
One which no hireling actor e'er defil'd,
One born upon the spot, a neighbour's child
I stand its willing sponsor, and look there,
How many lovely god-mothers appear.
Sure of success, our author's brows to bind
I weave the future wreathe; at least he'll find,
From dread of critic frowns his bosom eased,
Where all are friends, and eager to be pleased.

Beaumont[13] long after recalled that Garrick took an interest in the theatricals:

I shall ever remember the acquaintance of Garrick with pleasure. He was always obliging. When we performed Hamlet at N. Aston, we went a few days before to see him in that character ... He ... secured us a box, and was so kind as to lend us his alteration of the play, which, however justly criticised, suited our small force better than the original.

It is revealing to find Beaumont, who was a man of taste, agreeing to play the Prince in Garrick's dreadful farrago. Mrs. Bowles was Ophelia. *Hamlet* was probably given some time in 1777, since in the *Oxford Journal* of 16 November that year appear Lines by A.B. on two ladies at North Aston who played Ophelia in *Hamlet* and Portia in *The Merchant of Venice*. *The Merchant of Venice* and *Lethe* were revived on 7 November 1777, and, on 21 November,[14] *Jane Shore*, with Mrs. Bowles as the heroine, was played with *Bon Ton*. Beaumont wrote the prologue. *Macbeth* was also acted this season. Beaumont, whilst acting the title rôle observed among the audience "a young lady of great beauty ... who seemed much moved with the performance".[15] She was Margaret Willes of Astrop, Northants, who became his wife the following May.

Jane Shore was revived on 17 December 1779, followed by *The Author*, and the applause which they received was said to testify to the good taste and judgment of the auditors as well as to the merit of the performances.

Charles Bowles died on 4 August 1780, so that theatricals were suspended for a while. The next performance we know of was on 29 January 1782 when *Venice Preserv'd* was given with *The Mayor of Garratt*. Mrs. Bowles played Belvidera supported by Miss Elton, Sir George Beaumont and Messers. Bowles, Mander, J. Mander, Horne and Starkey. In the usual flattering style she was declared to be the equal of Mrs. Siddons in the pathetic scenes.[16] Once again members of the University mingled with the local gentry in the audience.

This appears to have been the last theatrical festivity at North Aston though many efforts were made to resume performances. *The Provok'd Husband*[17] was mentioned in 1783 but, four years later, it was announced[18] that "Private Theatricals, we are sorry to say, have no longer charms for Sir George Beaumont: and therefore the best gentleman actor of the age performs no more".

The success of the Blenheim theatricals stimulated Bowles to fresh endeavour, and a rumour even circulated that the two companies would join forces.[19] By November 1788 tickets had been delivered out for *Catharine and Petruchio* and Foote's *The Nabob*. Sir George and Lady Beaumont were to act Petruchio and Catharine and Lord Charles Spencer, from the Blenheim troupe, was to take Sir J. Oldham in the farce. Mrs. Bowles had, for some unknown reason, declined to act. It was reported from the rehearsals that neither Beaumont's nor Bowles's talents had suffered from their long disuse. But the illness of George III put a stop to the festival.[20] From time to time there were rumours of a revival[21] but all hope of it was abandoned by the autumn of 1791 when a prologue by Sir George Beaumont was printed[22] which

was to have had further additions, had it been Spoken, for it was to have been delivered by himself. But Mr. Bowles did not, as was expected, again open his Theatre – so the Prologue would have been lost – had not good fortune thus presented it to us.

The prologue, in referring to the long interval that had elapsed since theatricals had taken place, recalls Whitehead's former prophetic one.

> Thy sleeping Thunders now forget to roll,
> The Spider spins within the poison'd bowl;
> My useless Helmets garrison the Bats –
> And all my Wigs are eaten by the Rats.
> The grand Cascade which flash'd upon the Drop,
> Is now a Floor-cloth in the Barber's shop;
> The Rain is burnt – and Robert sadly saith,
> My noble storm of Wind is scant of breath . . .
> Dan Whithead's prophecy is out 'tis plain,

And my Barn's now almost a Barn again . . .
Tho' Rocks and Mountains crumble from the Scene –
Tho' Trees turn blue, and all the Skies turn green –
Thy skilful hand shall o'er the Canvass play,
And call the faded landscape back today.

In these last lines Beaumont refers to Bowles's talents as a scene painter. He was a keen amateur artist and painted many of the scenes for the theatre with an ability which rivalled that of his managing and acting. *The Times*,[23] characterising the various private theatricals, claimed that those at North Aston were without rival in stage arrangements and theatrical erudition. For Bowles the theatricals were more than a pastime for they enabled him to employ his talents as a painter and his learning as a man of culture.

Whether the barn which was converted into a theatre still exists it is difficult to say. The Rev. C. C. Brookes, an authority on the neighbourhood, writes that it may have been the one on the right of the Manor House, now a squash racket court, or the one at the top of the drive now a school and master's house. There are no traces of a theatre in either. Oldfield Bowles lived until 1810 but we hear no more of his taking part in theatricals.

(b) *Edward Hartopp-Wigley at Little Dalby Hall.*

Little Dalby Hall still stands high on a hill overlooking the wide-stretching plain in which Melton Mowbray is situated, and until recently it remained in the hands of the Hartopp family who owned it for 400 years. Edward Hartopp, who was born in 1758, assumed the name of Wigley when he came of age in 1779 in pursuance of the will of his uncle, James Wigley. He married in 1782 the Hon. Juliana Evans the daughter of Baron Carbery.[24]

The private theatre at Little Dalby was opened in 1777 and an epilogue to *Bon Ton* for that occasion was found among Joseph Cradock's papers.[25] The epilogue contrasts "the good old times ere we all ran to London" with the boredom of the contemporary gentry when they spent a few days on their estates:

Save cards and dice, ah! what can boast the pow'r
From morn to eve, to cheer each lifeless hour.

What but the solace of private theatricals:

With music's harmony alone we'd charm ye,
And with theatric lore to virtue warm ye;
Laugh with good humour at the foolish town,
Deride their follies, and correct our own.

145

The reference to music suggests that the farce may have been combined with a concert.

In the possession of Mrs. Burns Hartopp there were a retractable dagger and waistcoat which, according to family tradition, were worn by David Garrick when he acted at the theatricals and which are now in the Theatre Museum. It seems, however, unlikely that Garrick consented to act at Little Dalby when he consistently refused other invitations, among them those from Wynnstay, Cassiobury and Kelmarsh; if he did his appearance must have been in 1777 or 1778 since he died in 1779. It is probably a confusion with his nephew David Garrick who took part in theatricals at Kelmarsh in 1773.

We hear nothing further of theatricals at Little Dalby until 1787 when the *World*,[26] speaking of the vogue for these entertainments, mentions that Hartopp's preparations were under way, and later that the performances had been spoken of with praise. After that there is another long gap until 1797. The interest of these later theatricals is greatly enhanced by the fact that, among the Hartopp papers deposited in the Leicester Museum, are detailed bills for work done in the theatre and on the scenery. The first of these starts on 17 October 1797, and is from George Bunney.[27] Bunney's usual work was that of upholstering and mending, or even making clothes and he was employed to sew together the painted scenes and stitch them on to the framework or rollers. He also made covers for the stage and seats. His bill reads:

				s. d.
October 17,	1797	Myself 3 days work 3s Man 2 days 2s Makeing Scenes.		5:0
,,	30,	,,	Myself 1 day at Scenes 1s. Thread 3d.	1:3
Nov.	17,	,,	Myself 3 days do & Makeing Carpets	3:0
Dec.	5,	,,	Part of a days work at Scenes	8
	15,	,,	Myself 1 days work at Scenes	1:0
Jan	17,	1798	Myself 1 days work makeing Bags for Scenery	1:0
Feb	17,	,,	Myself 1 days work Altering the Scenery	1:0
March	6,	,,	Myself 1 days work at Scenes thread 3d	1:3
,,	31,	,,	Myself 1 days work at frontpiece thread 3d	1:3
April	17,	,,	Myself one days work at scenes thread 3d	1:3
May	8,	,,	Myself half days work at the frontpiece	6
	25,	,,	Myself 1 days work at Scenes	1:0
July	9,	,,	Myself half a days work at Scenes	6
	23,	,,	Myself part of day sewing rollers in Scenes	8
	25,	,,	Myself 2 days making Stage Cover. Seat Cover.	2:0
July	26,	,,	Myself 1 day Covering Seats and other jobs thread	1:0 2
August	21	,,	Myself 2 days makeing Covering for Scenery thread	2:0 4

The builder, Richard Johnson, has also a long account for work done in the theatre which, unfortunately, is not specified. I reproduce it in order to give an idea of the amount of work required and the amount spent on it.[28]

				s. d.
June	15,	1798	Myself 4 days works at the playhouse other work	10:8
			A man 4 days Dito	10:8
	22,	,,	myself 7 days Dito	18:8
			A man 7 ,, ,,	18:8
	29,	,,	myself 7 days ,,	18:8
			A man ,, ,, ,,	18:8
July	6,	,,	myself ,, ,, ,,	18:8
			A man ,, ,, ,,	18:8
July	13,	,,	myself 7 days dito	18:8
			A man ,, ,, ,,	18:8
July	20,	,,	myself ,, ,, work at the theater	18:8
			A man ,, ,, dito	18:8
July	27,	,,	myself ,, ,, ,,	18:8
			A man ,, ,, ,,	18:8
Aug.	3	,,	myself ,, ,, ,,	18:8
			A man ,, ,, ,,	18:8
	31	,,	A man 6 days painting the Dressing Room and other work	16:0
Sept	7.	,,	myself 6 days taking Down musick Room and Dressing Rooms Scenes Stage and Clearing Away	16:0
			A man 6 days Dito	16:0
	14	,,	myself 6 days Dito	16:0
			A man ,, ,, ,,	16:0

It took, then, two men seven weeks' continuous work to fit up the theatre and two men 12 days' work to dismantle it when the plays were over. It is clear that preparations were elaborate and the theatricals no simple business. The *Morning Post*[29] merely stated that Hartopp Wigley had "fitted up a small Theatre in his house".

Clementson,[30] the printer, made the following charges for tickets:

				s. d.
July	14,	1798	Printing Theatre Tickets	3. 6
	21	,,	200 Tickets on small Cards	5. 0

The performances took place in the first week in August[31] and consisted of *Othello* with *High Life Below Stairs*, *The Trials of Temper* with Foote's *The Commissary*, and *Romeo and Juliet* with a repetition of *High Life Below Stairs*. The principal parts were taken by Edward Hartopp-Wigley, his son of about 15, and Bilsborrow who acted Othello, supported by

147

professionals from the local companies, Taylor and Robertson from the Stamford Theatre, and Hamilton's family and company from Melton Mowbray. Bilsborrow wrote *The Trials of Temper*,[32] "a Comedy with songs, . . . a most excellent piece, replete with incident and stage effect, and might do honour to a Theatre Royal". The music for this piece was especially composed for the occasion by Sharpe of Grantham, and played by the Melton Mowbray band belonging to the infantry corps. The scenery was painted by Bilsborrow. The entertainments given to the nobility and gentry of the neighbourhood concluded with cold collations and, on the last night, with a ball.

Bunney started to work on the scenes again on 13 November[33] and spent 24 occasional days up to 25 October 1799. The work included a day at the scene front, a day on the green curtain; whilst the theatricals were on, two days covering throne, tables, forms and tent and, after they had finished, a day making bags for the scenes, and another making coverings for them. The printer's items for the 1799 season were:[34]

			s. d.
July	1	Cop⁸ & print⁸ 500 Copies for Theatre	5. 0
	11	Print⁸ 300 hf cards Days of Playing	7. 6
	18	Print⁸ 50 Bills of the Play	3. 6
	25	Print⁸ 70 Bills Wonder	3. 6
	25	,, 70 ,, Rich^d3	3. 6

The first performance was given on 16 July, the last and sixth on 30 July· Two new pieces, probably those by Bilsborrow which were "soon to be brought before a London audience" were presented the first night and *The Wonder* with Foote's *Lame Lover* on the second. The audience pronounced the last out of date but was pleased with *The Wonder* in which Hartopp-Wigley played Felix and Bilsborrow Lissardo, whilst the female rôles and some minor ones were taken by professionals. On the third night *Richard III* was given and one of the new pieces was repeated. "The beautiful scenery" was painted by Bilsborrow, that for the new piece which accompanied *Richard III* being particularly commended. This indefatigable man also engraved the entrance tickets with different devices for each night; was chief machinist; played King Henry VI, and Circuit in *The Lame Lover*, and wrote an address which presented "the growling critic" satirising "Bosworth field just six feet by eleven".[35] Sharpe composed new music, and, between the acts, celebrated pieces were rendered by the Melton band "with that judgment and masterly style, which has so long distinguished them". Some of the costumes were from town by one Johnson, and those worn by Richard and Richmond would not, it was felt, have disgraced the metropolis. Another costumier from London, Martin Gay, was also paid £66. 2. 0. for theatrical dresses.

The theatre was crowded every night, local tradesmen and farmers alternating with the nobility and gentry. Among those who came were Benjamin Thompson, translater of *The Stranger*, and the Rev. Henry Knapp, author of the musical farce *Hunt the Slipper* and the host's brother-in law. The beautiful garden walks were open for the company's recreation as they are at Glyndebourne today. There is no record of any theatricals in 1800, but Bunney was working during the spring and winter on the scenes and put in 25 days between November and May.[36] Meanwhile a new theatre was being erected. Mrs. Burns Hartopp says that she always understood that it was built on to the house beyond the dining room. A letter dated 22 November 1800,[37] refers to "cash to feed the worke then going on at the theatre to the amt of more than £350" but we have no bills for large undertakings. Richard Johnson was employed several days on jobs on the theatre between September and November and charged 3s for erecting the scaffolding.[38] William Kitchen was also employed in building work there. He itemises:[39]

				£. s. d.
June	14, 1800	to Beating of mortar for the theatre 1 day		3. 0
		Do Labourer		1. 4
Dec	18	to packing up the stones in theatre 1 day		3. 0

and in another bill[40] the following:

				£. s. d.
April	5, 1800	Nag stable drain and theatre 2 days		6. 0
	12, ,,	Theatre gallery, foundations and kennel floors 5½ days		16. 6
	26, ,,	The front of the stage 4 days		3. 0
June	28, ,,	Theatre traps and cutting out bricks 7 days		1. 1. 0
		Labourer –do– theatre		9. 4
July	14, ,,	Washing and repairing the theatre walls 7 days		1. 1. 0
				1. 1. 0
		Labourer –do–		9. 4
August	30, ,,	Jobs at the theatre 1 day		3. 0
		Labourer –do–		1. 8
Oct	25, ,,	Garden wall, cow hovel, orchestra in the theatre 5 days		15. 0

In addition Richard Boyfield was at work on scenic contraptions as follows:[41]

			£. s. d.
Jan	4, 1800	Iron Work to Wind up a Trap in the Theatre	16. 6
Feb	6, ,,	A Sett of Iron Work to Wind Up the Lamps in the Theater	16. 6
Feb	28, ,,	Altring Iron Work, Bushing, 2 New hoops & a New handle to wind up Scenes	7. 6

March	6,	,,	2 New Handles Altring & Bushing and 4 New hoops for 2 Setts of Iron Work to Wind up Scenes.	13. 0
,,	8,	,,	A New handle and altring Iron Work & Bushing & 2 hoops for Winding up scenes	6. 6
,,	14,	,,	A New handle and altring a Sett of Iron Work & Bushing & New hoop for Scenes	6. 6
April	2,	,,	A Large Sett of Iron Work all but Gugins [gudgeons] for Scenes	10. 0
,,	5,	,,	A large Sett of Iron Work all new for Scenes	10. 0
,,	12,	,,	Altering 3 handles for Winding up Scenes	3. 0
May	9,	,,	A Larg Sett of Iron Work for Scenes	10. 0
June	28,	,,	A Sett of Iron Work to Wind up a Trap in the Theatre	16. 0
July	21,	,,	–do–	16. 0

It is evident that Hartopp-Wigley was installing new mechanism for scene changing, traps and lighting, for which an unusual amount of iron work was used instead of wood. The scenery must have mostly worked on rollers on the drop system; there is no mention of flats or wings.

The work continued through the winter of 1800–1.[42]

				s. d.
Dec.	20,	1800,	E. Hubbard jobbing in the Theater	10. 6
Jan	31,	1801	A Large Sett of Iron Work to wind Up Scenes 10/– Paid for Wood handle 4d	10. 4
			A large Sett of Do. all But Plates 8/–	8. 4
Feb	7,	,,	A Sett of Large Iron Work for Scenes all But 1 plate	9. 0
	21,	,,	A Large Sett of Iron Work for Scenes 10/– Paid for Wood handles 4d	10. 4
April	4,	,,	Edw. Hubbard, a Day in the Theatre	3. 0

Bunney[43] commenced work again on the scenes on 14 November 1800, and between then and 10 July spent 37 days on work in the theatre. On this last date he itemises four days for covering tables and forms and making hangings for a bed in *The Castle Spectre;* and on 18 July he spent a further two days' work on the stage and stairs, and on 21 July, two days on the seats and orchestra. On 7 July Kitchen worked for two days on opening the theatre drain and on 9 July William Baker charged 1s. 2d. for "Tying up Flowers for the theatre."[44]

The theatricals took place in July 1801 in the "new and most beautiful Theatre ... built by Mr. Hartopp, capable of containing, with ease, between three and four hundred people".[45] This was rather bigger than most private ones, the usual capacity being between 150 and 300.

150

The plays were Monk Lewis's *The Castle Spectre, The Wonder, Macbeth* and two entertainments written by Bilsborrow which "reflected high honour on his genius and taste". An entrance ticket in the Banks Collection for 9 July gives *The Castle Spectre* with *Transformed or No*, this latter doubtless being one of the entertainments. Bilsborrow was again responsible for painting all the scenery "which attracted universal admiration by its beauty and variety". The Hartopps, Bilsborrow and a newcomer, Francis Munday, were the amateurs, and they were supported, more ambitiously than on previous occasions, by the whole of Hamilton's company as well as by detachments from the Cheltenham, Stamford and Drury Lane theatres. The acting was said to have been "most masterly throughout". Nearly 400 fashionables attended and were served with cold collations in all the principal rooms of the mansion. "Gay and sprightly dances" were kept up until the late hours of the morning. A detailed bill for the Macbeth dresses, from Martin Gay of Duke's Court, Drury Lane, has been preserved among the Hartopp documents and is of great interest as showing the kind of costumes that were worn and the materials used.[46]

1801 Hartopp Senr. Esq.

June 29. To a Macbeth's first dress made Trim'd with gold Leather & spangles, fine Callico plaid for do scarlet silk lining to Robe guilt Spangles gold Leather; linings Buttons, & other meter[s] [materials] £10. 9. 6

To a Macbeth's second dress made Richly Trim'd with gold leather & plated spangles fine green Cloth for Dress, fine scarlet Keseegmeer for Robe. Spangles fine Guilt fringe. White silk sarsnet for skirt lining sleeves &c. Body lining Butt[s]. A Black Velvet Belt & lining & all other Meter[s]. (gold leather except[d]) £18. 1. 3

To a Breast plate made Richly Trim'd with Lace Cord guilt spangles & Studd Butt[s] silk linings & all meter[s] Leather Except[d]
£4. 0. 0

32. 10. 9

1801 Hartopp Junr Esq.

To a Bangco's [Banquo's] Dress made Trim'd with gold Leather & spangles, fine Callico plaid for do scarlet silk lining to Robe, yellow silk lining to skirt guilt spangles gold Leather, Cotton lining. Buttons A Black Velvet Belt & all other Meter[s] £10. 17. 6

To a Breast plate made Richly Trim'd with Lace, Cord guilt spangles silk ling[s] etc (Leather Excepted) £4. 0. 0

14. 17. 6

1801 Bilsborrow Esq.

June 29th To a Malcome's dress made Richly Trim'd with silver Leather & spangles fine Callico plaid for do. yellow silk sarsnett, for Robe lining, plated spangles, Cotton Body lining Butt^s. A Black Velvet Belt & lining & all meter^s.   £13. 5. 0

To a Breast plate made Richly Trim'd with Lace Cord. Spangles & studd Buttons silk lining & all other meterials (Leather Except^d).
£4. 0. 0

17. 5. 0

Gay enclosed too "the Hosier's bill for pantaloons & Gloves". He was hard pressed by his creditors and asked for immediate payment but was not actually paid until mid-October. The armour and the plaid show that Kemble's ideas as to historical accuracy had permeated to the private theatres. The costumes were not so expensive when we remember that the Earl of Barrymore's wardrobe was valued at £2,000, but they were rich enough, and the gold leather and spangles, gilt fringing and scarlet silk have a magnificent theatrical ring calling to mind the tinsel prints of later days.

Theatricals must have been renewed in 1802, for we have the following bill from the printer Clementson.[47]

1802. July 3	Printing 500 Letters of invitation	7. 0
„ 17	100 Post 4to Bills Isabella	7. 6
„ 18	„ „ „ „ Douglas	7. 6
„ 23	100 folio Bills Romeo and Juliet	8. 0

Mrs. Burns Hartopp has in her possession an entrance ticket for *Isabella* and *Lovers' Quarrels*, dated 15 July, which probably belongs to this year.

Bunney was again employed on the scenes and covering the forms, seats and stage for nine days in June and July. In addition he altered a theatrical coat on 1 July, and on 23 July spent five days on covering the orchestra stairs and other jobs and one day on uncovering the seats. Johnson made a blind for the theatre for 7s. and Kitchen washed the walls and passage for 15s. and worked for a day in October.[48]

The theatricals of 1803 took place in January. According to the *Gentleman's Magazine*[49] they had been held for several successive summers and Christmas holidays but the *Monthly Mirror*[50] only mentions the successive summers, and adds that they were revived that year at Christmas with their former elegance and splendour. There is no other evidence that before this there had been two festivals a year. Benjamin Thompson's drama *The*

Stranger, adapted from Kotzebue, was followed by Murphy's farce *Three Weeks After Marriage*. Hartopp-Wigley and his son, Bilsborrow and Munday were joined by the two eldest sons of Col. Noel, connections of the Hon. Mrs. Hartopp-Wigley, the three Miss Hamiltons supported the female rôles, it was said, with their usual spirit and excellence, and the band, formerly of the Melton Mowbray corps of volunteers, supplied the music.

Once more Bunney[51] covered the seats, forms and table and on 3 January worked with a man three days on the scenery and horizon [? backcloth]. During February Johnson made and fixed three rollers for the scenes.[52]

The theatricals were revived in July when Bunney spent 14 days on the scenes and other jobs in the theatre with the help of a man. The printer's bill[53] gives us the pieces presented:

1803 July 6	Print 90 tickets		£1. 7. 6
	150 letters of invitation		£0. 5. 0
	150 ,, ,, ,, (trade)		5. 6
	600 tickets (trade night)		15. 6
July 13	300 Bills Tancred & Sigis.		9. 6
16	,, ,, Wild Oats		10. 6
25	100 ,, 3 Weeks After Marriage		5. 0
	300 ,, Macbeth		10. 6

At least two nights were evidently set aside for tradespeople and it is noticeable that their tickets cost considerably less than those for the gentry. Mrs. Burns Hartopp has an engraved ticket marked as not being transferable for 19 July for O'Keeffe's comedy *Wild Oats* and an unnamed farce. The increased number of bills for this and the two tragedies would seem to show that they were given more than one performance.

There is no evidence that any further theatricals were held though Kitchen was working in the theatre in January and March 1804. Edward Hartopp-Wigley died on 30 June 1808 and was succeeded by his son Edward, who, although he had taken a prominent part in his father's theatricals, does not seem to have continued them. Five years later he too died and was in turn succeeded by Edward Bourchier Hartopp then a child of four. He later revived the theatricals and Mrs. Burns Hartopp owns a series of play bills for practically every year from 1833 to 1878. By that time, however, the theatre had been demolished and the plays were given in the hall. Except for the gap of 20 years the family tradition of theatricals was a long lasting one, only rivalled by that at Woburn Abbey.

CHAPTER XI

Theatricals in Two Noble Mansions

(a) *The Marquess of Abercorn's Theatricals at Bentley Priory.*

In 1788 John Hamilton bought Bentley Priory, Stanmore, Middlesex and converted it "into a noble mansion". He was made Marquess of Abercorn in 1790, and the Priory became the centre of Tory society, as Devonshire House had been that of the Whigs.[1]

The Marquess had acted at his house in Baron's Court, Tyrone, in a performance of *Chrononhotonthologos*[2] in 1793 but did not himself appear on the stage in his theatricals at the Priory. These were first held on 21 January 1803, the pieces being Mrs. Inchbald's comedy *The Wedding Day* and Mrs. Cowley's popular *Who's the Dupe?* Among the actors was young Thomas Lawrence, the portrait painter, who had previously made his début as an amateur in Bath and had even entertained serious intentions of becoming a professional. In a letter to his sister, written on 28 January,[3] he tells about the inception of the theatrical fête:

It was projected by a woman of great cleverness and beauty, Lady Caher – very young and full of talent, with Lady Abercorn, and the rest of the female party; and of course it was acceded to by Lord Abercorn, who, whatever character of pride the world may have given him, is just as pleasant and kind and gentlemanly with his family and friends as a man can be.

It was determined to do it in a quiet way, and more as an odd experiment of the talents of the party, than anything else; – but this and that friend would be offended; and at last it swelled up to a perfect theatre (in a room) and a London audience . . . A Play was at first thought of, and I was for Miss Bailey's Comedy, "The Trial", one slightly spoken of by the world, but which, I am sure, Mr. Homer would like for its truly natural dialogue and character; – perhaps, for the great stage more incident may be necessary, but not where the characters are

154

nicely and accurately acted. At last, however, the pieces fixed upon were "The Wedding Day" and "Who's the Dupe?"

So Joanna Baillie's comedy of the passions was passed over in favour of well-worn pieces, but it is interesting to note that Lawrence, like Walpole and many others, thought that the amateurs could contribute a nicety and natural elegance to the stage which was beyond the scope of the professional actor.

The amateurs were coached by Priscilla Kemble the second wife of John Philip Kemble, a mediocre actress who had retired from the stage in 1796. She herself played Mrs. Hamford in the comedy and Charlotte in the after-piece. Lady Caher was the wife of Richard Butler, Baron Caher, a Tory peer, and was then about 36. Her acting as Lady Contest in the comedy was commended for its elegance and style and her charming rendering of the song "In the dead of Night", interpolated from Mrs. Inchbald's *Child of Nature*, drew an encore.[4] Those experienced amateurs William and Joseph Madocks were among the actors and the latter as Sir Adam Contest re-called the veteran actor Thomas King. Two of Lord Melbourne's sons, the Hon. Peniston and George Lamb, also took part. The former acted Sandford in the farce and spoke the epilogue which was laden with compliments to the Prince of Wales, the Abercorns and Mrs. Kemble; and the latter played Contest, and, as Gradus in *Who's the Dupe?*, kept the whole company laughing. Lady Charlotte Lindsay, daughter of Lord North, was Lady Autumn and the Marquess's two sons Lords Hamilton and Claude Hamilton, aged 16 and 15 ,were brought on as attendants. Lawrence, who played Lord Rakeland and Grainger, gave a vivid account of the proceedings to his sister:[5] As soon as the Prince of Wales had entered to the strains of God Save the King,

a terrifying bell rang, the curtain drew up, and The Wedding Day began. At first, I will own to you, Sheridan's face, the grave Duke of Devonshire, and two or three staunch critics, made one feel unpleasantly, for I opened the piece. However, this soon wore off. Our set all played extremely well – like persons of good sense, without extravagance or buffoonery, and yet with sufficient spirit. Lady Cahir, Mr. J. Madox, and G. Lamb were the most conspicuous – the first so beautiful that I felt love-making very easy.

Lawrence later confessed to Joseph Farington[6] that he felt confused on first going on but it wore off as the performance advanced and Sheridan told the engraver James Heath that he "was a very good actor. Heath asked whether He meant considering him as one who attempted. Sheridan replied No, but really a *very good actor* . . . He preferred his acting to his painting". Lawrence says that at first he neglected his part, "but not being coxcomb enough to do it wholly, I made good sail at the last, and was perfect". Something of the prevailing excitement comes through his description of the hours before the event. The performers dined at 3.30:

we all sat down like a Rugby school party, but rather more vociferous, huzzaed our Manager, and hissed our Hostess off for talking of the Prince and hours. At last the dressing, &c ended. The orchestra, behind the scenes, sat down: Lady Harriet Hamilton played the organ – Lady Maria the pianoforte – Lady Catherine the tambourine; Mr. Lamb, Lord Melbourne's eldest son (a performer), Mr. Madox, Violincello, First Violin, and two others hired. A most perfect orchestra, with admirable scenery, and light as day.

The *Morning Post* reports that the scenery "very beautiful, was painted under the direction of an eminent artist, for the occasion. The curtain scene is uncommonly grand; the design architectural". The salon[7] of the Priory which measured 50 by 30 ft. was converted into a theatre. "A beautiful little amphitheatre" of benches covered with cushions, was laid out in a semi-circle in the centre of which an elevated state chair, covered with crimson velvet and embroidered with gold, was set for the Prince of Wales. He dined with a select party of 20 before the performance. Among the guests were the Duke and Duchess of Devonshire, Lord and Lady Melbourne, and the Sheridans and their son Thomas. Mrs. Inchbald was invited but was not well enough to come.[8] She received a gossipy account from Priscilla Kemble:[9]

Our Friday evening was most splendid, and to me in every way triumphant. We had to dine and sleep in the house about forty persons . . . The audience consisted of about seventy persons – a large party from the Earl of Essex's; another from Prince Castelcicala; and everybody supped. Nothing could be more brilliant: the whole theatricals under my direction, and, I do assure you, most excellently acted. Lady Cahir admirable in Lady Contest, and she was a blaze of diamonds! . . . I never saw anything more beautiful than the supper rooms. Mr. Sheridan came with a very elegant chariot, four beautiful black horses and two footmen. The Duchess had only one . . .
I wish you had come, as I do believe there never was a thing of the kind went off better. The billiard-room was the theatre, and we had very pretty scenes, a band of music, and the organ struck up "God Save the King" as soon as the Prince was seated . . . Sheridan is little-minded enough to be vexed at seeing any of his performers admitted into the society he lives with.

Another entertaining description comes from the pen of Lady Harriet Cavendish,[10] though she was more interested in the social setting than the performance. The guests had to put up with discomfort and overcrowding:

There are to be a great many people at it, some return to town at night, and others sleep at Stanmore as the Priory will not hold half of them; our party, consisting of papa (who has changed his mind and means to be present), mama, William Howard, 2 maids and myself, are allowed only one bedroom. How we shall manage Dio sa.

No wonder she trembled when she thought of it; nor was the reality an improvement on the anticipation:[11]

I have been to the Priory and live to tell you of it. It was formidable, disagreeable, uncomfortable and *royal*, for to compleate the misery, the Prince was there...

Lady Harriet Hamilton was in great beauty... Lady Charlotte Hamilton looked ill, pale and very much out of spirits. The acting was excellent. Lady Cahir was as good as Mrs. Jordan, and what surprised me, perfectly original. She looked beautiful, magnificently dressed and covered with diamonds. George Lamb and Lawrence acted uncommonly well, and Pen Lamb spoke an epilogue of his own composition with a *very* little degree of animation more than usual, hoping the audience would find Pope Joan the only dupe tonight.

The Prince seemed pleased and said, "My dear Abercorn, I never enjoyed such perfect happiness in the whole course of my life." Lady Asgill was present and more ridiculous than ever. I sat next to her during the performance and in the Epilogue there was, à l'ordinaire, a compliment to the Ladies of the House. Lady Asgill, of course, took it to herself, and covering her face with her schawl, sunk upon the arm of my chair, quite overcome with modesty ...

Mrs. Kemble she found pleasant and good-humoured and a great favourite; her host more endurable than she had expected.

The play was to have been given a second performance on 26 January, but Lawrence was taken ill on the very morning, and an express was sent to town after William Spencer in vain. So the 40 Harrow boys who had been invited had to be content with a concert.[12] The theatricals were the topic of conversation in fashionable circles for some days, and praises of the scenery, dresses, decorations, acting and liberal expenditure were freely voiced. One critic was said to have declared "that it was impossible for the characters to have been more judiciously cast, even in a professional corps, under a veteran manager".[13]

The theatricals were to be renewed in the spring but the death of Lady Harriet, the Marquess's eldest daughter, on 29 April put a stop to the preparations. An indisposition of the Marchioness prevented them being held at the winter house party in January 1804, and it was not, in fact, until December 1805 that they were renewed.[14] Poor Harriet Cavendish was agitated as early as 21 October when she wrote to her sister: "I am so afraid of not being asked to the Priory that I do not know what to do. Do you think the Oroonoko and Falkland are great undertakings".[15] Her anxiety may have been due to the fact that she was carrying on a flirtation with the Earl of Aberdeen to whom these parts were at first assigned. A few days later she announced a change of casting:

157

William [Lamb] is to act Falkland, which we all think ill judged as Lord Aberdeen would have done it 1000 times better and from his manner to me the other night, gave me the idea of being hurt at its being thought for Mr. Lamb and I think will be much more so at its being accepted by him. Falkland ought also to be the most gentlemanlike of gentlemen, ainsi jugez.

In another letter she gives a different version:

Abellino [Aberdeen] they say, took a sudden alarm 3 or 4 days ago and said he could not act till he had seen William, who is consequently to undertake Falkland.

By November she passes on a rumour:

They talk now of acting Miss Baillie's Count Basil; William Lamb to be Basil; Lord Abercorn Rosenburg and Lady Cahir Victoria, but vide Lady Bessborough, so do not spread the news.

Joanne Baillie's piece was not performed and in the end Lord Aberdeen played Faulkland and William Lamb Capt. Absolute. At that time Aberdeen was young man of 21, of studious and fastidious tastes and, despite a cold demeanour, a delightful companion. In July 1805 he had become the son-in-law of the Marquess of Abercorn by his marriage with Lady Catherine Hamilton and later he was a famous statesman and enthusiast for Greek culture.[16] On 20 November he wrote to Augustus Foster:[17] "I am going to commence acting this Christmas at the Priory, where we have a very good theatre. I am to perform Oroonoko Falkland in the Rivals &c. &c.". This time Kemble himself did the coaching and Lady Elizabeth Foster wrote to Augustus:

He [Lord Aberdeen] and I have been sparring about Roscius, for since Kemble was at the Priory instructing Lord Aberdeen in acting he has won him from the Boy [Betty] and made him insist that all merit depends on right emphasis, and think that all acting different from Kemble's is wrong.

The craze for Master Betty, the Young Roscius, was already on the ebb. The Earl of Aberdeen's younger brother the Hon. Robert Gordon, a lad of 15, also took minor rôles in the theatricals. Other newcomers were Tom Sheridan, son of the dramatist, and the Hon. William Lamb. Peniston Lamb had died since the last festival. Lady Caroline Lamb reported the preparations to her grandmother Lady Spencer in December:[18]

The plays are going on prosperously. I think Wm, George & Mr. Maddox are our chief hopes. Wm's voice and manner are all that can be wished. George has a great deal of humour & not only acts very well but has written a very entertaining farce for them.

11a, b. Characters in *Twelfth Night*

11c. Wynnstay Theatre. *Twelfth Night*.

12a, b. Wynnstay in entrance tickets

12c. Wynnstay Theatricals. *The Winter's Tale.*

This musical entertainment was called *Whistle for It; or the Cave of the Banditti*. The scene is the Black Forest and the plot revolves round a stratagem with a whistle by which a count effects his escape from robbers who have captured him.[19] The dialogue is in high romantic style in which bandits, screeching owls and deep gloom all find place, but are relieved by a contrasting artificial Chloe and Cupid convention. Genest[20] thought that the piece had "considerable merit for the sort of thing – the great fault of it is that some of the songs are introduced with more than usual absurdity". The music was written and selected by G. Lanza junior and the "Songs and Choruses" were printed after the production at Covent Garden in 1807.

The first performance on 20 December consisted of this comic opera with O'Brien's farce *Cross Purposes*. The *Daily Advertiser*[21] speaks of "The New Theatre being now completely finished" and opening on this date. It was

admirably fitted up ... with boxes appropriately designed. The interior was lighted up by very elegant cut glass chandeliers and the stage with patent lamps. A very complete orchestra and a full band added much to the effect.[22]

The dining room served as a green room and the interior of the Priory was illuminated by variegated lamps under the direction of Bennington, the King's lamplighter. Dinner took place first and, as at the Margravine's, a magnificent service of silver gilt plate was set out, after which 150 guests, some of whom had come considerable distances, were ushered into the theatre. Glimpses of the performance and the performers are once again obtainable from the lively letters of Lady Harriet Cavendish[23]

In George's Opera – which is most uncommonly good – Tom Sheridan and Mrs. Heseltine are the Hero and Heroine, for the sake of their singing, as they are undoubtedly the worst performers. William, the Captain of Banditti, (reckoned very fine but I think too violent and ranting); George and Miss Butler, Andrew and Phyllida, she very much in love with him, and Mr. Maddocks, one of the principal ruffians.

In another letter she elaborates:

The play was very fatiguing but very entertaining and the acting excellent. George's play went off perfectly and William is reckoned an excellent actor. He is too much occupied with his beauty and expression of countenance and makes crooked smiles to the audience, when he ought to be attending to his companions. He is also rather tame as a lover and looks much alarmed as Caroline sits and watches him and would probably go into fits if an expression or look of well acted tenderness was to escape him. Tom Sheridan looked very handsome with rouge and sang well, but his tragedy is too comic to be very unlike buffoonery. George, incomparable and must have enjoyed the double satisfaction of the roars of laughter that his good jokes and good acting excited. Mrs Heseltine and Miss Butler both looked and acted well. The "Bravo" [Lord Aberdeen] looked hideous as a ruffian. In the farce . . . he was rouged, which made his face look worse than ever in my opinion, but mama was in raptures. His acting is slow and sure, but otherwise has no merit and Falkland will be a melancholy business. Tom Sheridan as an old man, and Lady Charlotte Lindsay as his spouse were excellent.

According to the *Daily Advertiser* "the dresses were most superb and the Scenery very beautiful. The whole management was under the direction of Mr. Kemble". A sumptuous supper was served after the show in various apartments and 50 guests spent the night at the Priory. Stanmore and Harrow boys were among the spectators.

On 23 December, the second night, *The Rivals* was presented with *Cross Purposes*. Sheridan wrote to his wife[24] that it was played

extremely well indeed, Lady Caher very good, and a Mrs. Heseltine a great Priory Personage and a very pretty woman admirable. She sings too I understand excellently with the finest will in the world. I don't know when I have sat out a Play before.

Here is Lady Harriet's forthright report:[25]

You will be glad to hear that "The Rivals" was acted even to satisfy Mr. Sheridan who was forced to laugh at all his own jokes and applaud all his own sentiments. Lord Aberdeen was what the newspapers term respectable. The opinions were very divided; he looked ugly and awkward, his action is very bad and his countenance even at the moment of receiving Julia's pardon deplorable and embarrassed; but his voice is clear and distinct and he certainly acted with a great deal of feeling and a perfectly just conception of his part. In short, all that one saw bad.

Mrs. Heseltine was an excellent Julia and looked pretty with rouge; Lady Caher was not nearly so good as I expected. She looked old and absent and has not a look of nature about her. William I thought excellent, so perfectly natural but still his two great faults, one that he can't help and the other that he can, are the most ungraceful carriage and action I ever beheld and too much *sympathy* with the audience.

But now for the wonders. Mr. Maddocks Sir Anthony; George Mr. Acres and Lawrence Sir Lucius, were better than any actors I ever saw on the stage and Mr. Sheridan said Lawrence was the first person who had represented Sir Lucius as he had intended him to be. Mrs. Malaprop was very good though she might have been better.

Sheridan also considered Joseph Madocks unique as Sir Anthony Absolute, an opinion endorsed by Michael Kelly.[26] Lady Bessborough gave her criticisms in a letter written to Lord Granville on 29 December:[27]

Lady Cahir look'd very pretty in Lydia Languish, but was rather too violent for the Character; Mrs. Hesseltine perfect in Julia; Ld. Aberdeen rather too reserv'd, but very good, in Falkland; Mr. Dawkins and T. Sheridan perfect imitations of Bannister and Smith, therefore very good in comic parts, but in serious ones T. Sheridan mouths and speaks as if he was bamboozing his own acting; William excellent in the Chef de Bandit [in *Whistle for It*], perhaps too Vehement now and then, as Captain Absolute less good, but very Gentleman like and nothing bad. G. Lamb – by far the best actor I ever saw anywhere – in Emery's style.

As on the previous night a dinner was served to some of the guests at five o'clock and the rest began to arrive at seven, an hour before the theatre opened:

It was a beautiful appearance, being lighted by a fine large Chinese lamp, with several burners suspended from the middle of the ceiling. The Theatre was hung round with patent lamps, and had a very enchanting effect.[28]

Whistle for It and *Cross Purposes* were repeated on 26 December to much the same company that had witnessed them the previous week.[29] It was not until 3 a.m. that the Duchess of Devonshire and the Bessborough and Melbourne families set off in their coaches for town.

At the fourth night on 30 December there was a complete change of programme. *Oroonoko* was acted with the Earl of Aberdeen in the title rôle, Lawrence as Aboan and Mrs. Heseltine as Imoinda.[30] Mr. and Mrs. Woolf reported[31] of Lawrence's acting in this rôle and that of O'Trigger that

They were best pleased with his tragedy, but with all their partiality were free to confess that he wanted much of the usages of the stage. His voice was remarkably fine & possess'd a variety which was quite uncommon. Its gentler tones were perfect music.

This contradicts Sheridan's testimony given earlier that he was a good actor even from the professional standpoint. Kemble too spoke highly of his performance at any rate in rehearsal.[32] The afterpiece was Jackman's farce *All the World's a Stage*. The curtain did not drop until 12.30 a.m. and the plays were followed by supper and dancing. The host was obliged to make up 40 beds every night for the guests who could not get home.

Haryo wrote to her sister about the next performance on 3 January 1806:

We went Thursday to the Priory and I was more amused than I had been before though it was "Whistle for It" again and "Sylvester Daggerwood," pretty well acted by Mr. Dawkins and Tom Sheridan.
The audience was more brilliant than usual and considerably more animated, perhaps from the addition of Mrs. Damer and Miss Berry in transports.

Lady Aberdeen kept a sharp watch on Harriet's flirtation with her husband, and Lady Abercorn was jealous of fat, light-haired little Mrs. Heseltine, a quiet and inoffensive woman who sometimes sang with Lord Abercorn but was devoted to her husband and "much distressed at the ridiculous part she is forced to perform". Lady Harriet had a down on Lady Caher, whom she describes as

"petite insupportable" indeed. William says she is more plague than the whole home put together, and it was owing to her whims that Three Weeks After Marriage was delayed till next week. George Lamb says she is the most odious little d – l that ever breathed and, I tell you all this to sanction my cordial detestation of her.

So the curtain is lifted for a moment on the petty jealousies, intrigues and gossipings of this band of players, and the scene might have come straight out of *Mansfield Park*.

Oroonoko was repeated on 7 January[33] and on the final night, 10 January, *Whistle for It* was given a third performance followed by the delayed *Three Weeks After Marriage*, in which Lawrence and Lady Caher played Sir Charles and Lady Racket. Lord Hampden told Farington[34] that Lawrence acted with "a real theatrical feeling". He added that

Lady Caher performed Lady Racket, but was very imperfect in her part which was a disadvantage to Lawrence, who assisted Her as well He could. Her Ladyship, however, did not seem embarassed by Her difficulties, but went on with perfect self possession.

Lawrence had been a little difficult this season since his prudence directed him to appear only in parts "such as wd. not subject Him to remark on acct. of the immorality of the character"; nor would he take any rôle that required singing. Additions were made to the orchestra, the overture was highly applauded and Mrs. Heseltine sang with taste, expression and softness. Among the 130 guests were the Dukes of Orleans, de Bourbon and Montpensier. Haryo's[35] parting comment on the theatricals was that they were "one continual scene of prompting, rehearsing and managing". A report[36] was shortly after published that the Marquess intended to build a regular theatre at the Priory and he still had this in mind in December 1810 when he thought of employing Robert Smirke.[37] Nothing came of it, nor do the theatricals appear to have been renewed. The Marquess died in 1818 and the first Duke of Abercorn sold Bentley Priory, which is now an R.A.F. station.

(b) *Theatricals at Woburn Abbey.*

Private theatricals took place at Woburn Abbey over a period covering more than a century. The first we hear of them is in a letter from the Earl of Sandwich[38] to the fourth Duke of Bedford from London on 10 January 1744. He was evidently helping the Duke with plays, players and scenery, and writes:

As to our theatrical affairs, they go on in a very flourishing way. Draper, who dined with me yesterday, will undertake the part of Doll [in *The Alchemist*], and Price Dashwood, Shirley and Mackye agree to what is allotted them. We have settled the form for the scenes, and shall employ a painter to begin them out of hand. Your Grace shall likewise receive the plays of the "Alchemist", and "All for Love", by the first opportunity.

David Garrick had been active in attending to scenery and properties and on 11 September 1744 he wrote to the Duke of Bedford:

I had obeyed your Grace's commands sooner in sending the account of the scenes and other things, but the persons whom I had employed to make the fasces, asps, and garlands for the play of "All for Love" was out of town, and I had no opportunity of knowing his demands till last week. I have sent the account enclosed to your Grace's steward and shall think myself greatly honoured if I am favoured with any more commands for the future.

He gives the expenses as:

Paid Mr. Leathes, the painter, as per account	£31. 5. 6
Paid Mr. Devosto, painter, for one flat scene and wings	10. 10. 0
Paid Mr. Arthur for the fasces, asps etc.	1. 1. 0
Paid the carpenter two bills	5. 6. 4

Devosto is presumably John Devoto who was painting the scenery at Goodman's Fields Theatre when Garrick was drawing the town there. The Duke thanked Garrick and sent him a note on his banker's for the £48 2s. 10d.[39] Lady Hardwicke was present at two of the performances. She wrote:[40]

We have been spectators of the "Siege of Damascus" and "Alchemyst" at Woburne. I never saw a more perfect performance than the latter. It far excelled the tragedy. The Duke and Lord Sandwich acted *Subtle & Face*. Sr F. Dashwood, *Abel Drugger*. The scenes and habits were elegant and proper. Every thing was managed with good order.

Aaron Hill[41] wrote an "Epilogue for a Lady, who acted Eudocia, in the

Siege of Damascus, represented at the Duke of Bedford's at Woburn", sometime before his death in 1750.

Lord Sandwich again approached Garrick for help with the loan of scenes and properties in 1756 and wrote to him on 24 May:[42]

> Sir, The Duke of Bedford and myself are greatly obliged to you for the trouble you have given yourself about our scenes; and if you will let my servant, the bearer of this, know how much is due to you on that account, I will order the money to be paid directly. We are under one distress that you may possibly help us out of; the opera not being yet over, we cannot have the scimitars that we borrowed the last year, and we can think of no way of furnishing ourselves unless you would be so good as to speak to Mr. Fleetwood to lend us four scimitars and a Spanish toledo: if you have any such things that are not now in use, I will take care that they shall come to no damage, and be returned in a fortnight's time.
>
> We think to begin our performance on Friday se'nnight, and I believe it will last all the next week; if you in that time should find leisure to struggle to Woburn, you may have an opportunity of seeing both tragedy and comedy very ill-treated by a set of bunglers.

Garrick was frequently troubled by such requests from amateurs. Sir William Young, for instance, asked him to supply Roman dresses, scenery and a prologue for a projected performance of *Julius Caesar* at Standlynch, all of which were refused. (*Letters of David Garrick*, ed. Little and Kahrl (1963) I nos. 208, 209). There must have been further theatricals at Woburn in 1777 as a manuscript of a tragedy entitled *Panthea* turned up in Percy Dobell's catalogue of 1968 (No. 179). The cast was of children including the Duke of Bedford (12 years old), Lords John and William Russell his brothers, Caroline Fox (10 years old) and her brother Lord Holland who was only four and played the silent rôle of a Second Officer.

We hear no more of theatricals at Woburn Abbey until the next century under the sixth Duke of Bedford who succeeded to the title in 1802. The following year he married, as his second wife, Lady Georgiana Gordon who at the age of 11 had taken part in theatricals at Gordon Castle, Scotland in 1792[43]. It was, perhaps, pleasant memories of this occasion that encouraged her to revive theatricals at Woburn. It was certainly she, and not the Duke, who was the prime mover in the matter for it was announced in January 1806 that the Duchess of Bedford's private theatricals had commenced "with new scenes, and decorations, great and splendid additions having been made to her Grace's beautiful Theatre".[44] That there had been previous performances is evident from the phrase about additions to the theatre, and this is confirmed by a paragraph in the *Daily Advertiser* of 2 January stating that the theatricals *recommenced* on 27 December. George Colman's comedy *John Bull* was given with *The Mayor of Garratt*, first to the servants, secondly to the tenants and thirdly to the *beau monde.*[45] The Duke himself played Dennis Brulguddery; his eldest son the Marquis of Tavistock, played Job Thornberry with "much force, firmness and spirit"; his second son Lord William Russell acted with effect and was warmly applauded as Dan; the Duchess was easy and graceful as Lady Caroline, and Lord John Russell, aged 13, spoke the prologue with great effect. Lord Charles Somerset, son of the Duke of Beaufort, proved himself an excellent amateur and displayed all the ease and spirit of Lewis in Shuffleton.[46] The Duchess was at first cast for Mrs. Brulguddery whereupon Lady Holland cattily remarked to Lady Harriet Cavendish:[47] "The Duchess in performing Mrs. Brudgruddery will scarcely depart from her own character". Harriet commented: "If you remember the landlady of the Red Cow in John Bull, you may judge of the severity of this speech". In the afterpiece the Duchess and her stepson Lord William won most applause as Mr. and Mrs. Sneak.

We have seen that *The Rivals* was given that December at Bentley Priory and it was also chosen for the second play at Woburn. Three performances were given on 6, 7 and 11 January. It was rumoured that Sheridan was to attend the rehearsals, and all the neighbouring families were invited to the performances.[48] A special prologue was written by Samuel Whitbread, politician and brewer, later manager of Drury Lane, who had a seat in the county. It was again spoken by Lord John Russell who also played Lucy. Mrs. Malaprop was acted *en travestie* by Wrottesley. The Duke and the Marquis of Tavistock played father and son as the two Absolutes; Lord William Russell well portrayed the self tormenting Faulkland, and the Duchess as Lydia Languish, was all the author could have wished. As O'Trigger Lord Charles Somerset sang "The Awkward Recruit". Lyons's *The Village Lawyer* was the afterpiece with the Duke and Duchess as Mr. and Mrs. Scout.[49]

The Duke of Bedford was Viceroy of Ireland from 1806 to 1807 and this appointment was probably the cause of the break in the theatricals, which do not appear to have been renewed for some years. We find the three actor sons of the Duke performing in private theatricals at the Kilmainham Hospital in Dublin on 22 January 1807.[50]

The Woburn Abbey theatricals were revived in 1817[51] when a playbill for 11 January records a performance of the melodrama *The Watch-word or Quito Gate* which had been brought out at Drury Lane three months previously. The bill states that it was acted by a juvenile company "lately arrived from various parts of the Kingdom" which included four of the Russell children. The prologue was spoken by Lords Wriothesley and Charles James Fox Russell. The latter is also billed as manager. Banks, a scene painter from Drury Lane, was tailor and mechanist and the scenery was by Millard. The playbill parodies the usual managerial puffs:

165

The Manager begs leave humbly to submit to the Nobility, Gentry, and others, that he has spared neither Pains nor Expense to get up this highly interesting Melo Drama with unrivalled Spendour and Magnificence, and he hopes for the Indulgence of a liberal and enlighted Public.

The price of admission was "Plenty of Applause to the Actors".

After this there is no playbill until 1828. The theatricals continued at intervals until 1857. The Theatre was dismantled by the 8th Duke about 1872 but two rooms still bear the names of the Green Room and the Theatre.

CHAPTER XII

Conclusion

How good were these performances and what was their contribution to the history of our stage? We can discount the adulations of a sycophantic press and the comparisons of the amateurs with Garrick and Mrs. Siddons. The views of professionals were for the most part unfavourable. Thus the following anecdote reveals Garrick's attitude:[1]

> The English Roscius having been invited to see a play performed by Lords, Knights, honourables and Ladies, he with all the delicacy of a gentleman, sat not only patiently, but expressed his approbation to the nobility and gentry, who surrounded and attentively observed him. It was "very well", "very well," "Ah, very well indeed", "very fair", &c. At length, in a subordinate character of the piece, all the great parts having been duly distributed to the great folks, a provincial actor, unknown to Garrick, made his appearance, who had been hired as a kind of drill sergeant. As soon as Roscius saw him and heard him speak, his eye fixed and without thinking of the inference, he exclaimed "Ah ha! I see they have got an actor among them."

G. F. Cooke "had a sovereign contempt for private theatricals" and Macklin asserted "that the best private actor who ever trod the stage, was not half so good as Dibble Davies – a third-rate performer of that day".[2] We have seen that Colman found the troupe at Wynnstay awkward, clumsy and ignorant of the simplest technique of the stage, whilst Frederick Reynolds complained also of inaudibility and stiffness at Blenheim. On the other hand the pantomime of *Don Juan* at Wargrave surpassed all that the professional Everard could conceive; Kemble conceded talent to the performers at Richmond House, and Sheridan thought Lawrence the best approach to his conception of Sir Lucius O'Trigger and Madocks a unique Sir Anthony Absolute. Edwin[3] pointed out that the amateur acting had its

167

uses "if it only gives a good emphasis, and improves the *speaking* of those who are to be our Senators, it is something, for it prepares them for more important scenes". On the whole, however, professional opinion of the actual acting was poor or patronising, tinged with the contempt, or at least impatience, of the trained for the untrained. And we may easily believe that inaudibility, rapidity of speech, self-consciousness and awkwardness were frequent faults. Men and women of taste and fashion, however, often felt that the amateurs were able to give them something that they missed on the public stage. In Harriet Cavendish's opinion some of the *dilettanti* at Bentley Priory were better than any actors she had ever seen, and Walpole was more struck by the last scene of *Jane Shore* at Holland House than ever he had been with it on the public stage. We have seen that Walpole explained his preference for amateurs in genteel comedy by the theory that talented people of quality could naturally represent the life they knew and lived better than actors who, having no acquaintance with it, could only mimic them. Fallacy though this is, it is obvious that the amateurs did bring a satisfying refinement and good breeding to parts from high life which for some spectators compensated for their defects in ease and technique. When Lady Sophia Fitzgerald remarked that her brother Lord Henry looked more like a gentleman as Don Felix than Garrick, and when Walpole had it that Garrick was a monkey to him, they meant that he had a finer figure and was more to the manner born. Reynolds was impressed by the beauty of the actresses and the elegance of their dresses at Blenheim, and there can be little doubt that the clothes they wore in the roles of genteel comedy were vastly superior to the stock costumes of the patent theatres. But it was the natural elegance, bred of long habit, with which they wore them that constituted the attraction for their friends. Professional actors noticed the faults of their acting, people of fashion the nicety of their manners. The audience too must have had its effect. The actor in the public theatre had to project himself not only to society in the boxes but to the stolid and the rough in other parts of the house; disturbance, noise and chatter were his frequent portion and he therefore had to coarsen his picture and heighten his emphasis. In the decorous atmosphere of the private theatre, the amateur could indulge in delicacies and subtleties that would be thrown away at Drury Lane or Covent Garden.

The standard of acting was probably not high, yet occasionally some outstanding talent came to light: everyone for instance seems to have agreed that Lord Henry Fitzgerald was a fine performer, and William Fector undoubtedly commanded a wide range of parts. Yet well-known amateurs such as Wathen and Mrs. Twisleton never made any great stir as professionals, though they had been highly praised in private performances. On the whole we may take Nares's verdict that the *dilettanti* were not capital actors but that their lack of histrionic talent was compensated for by the elegance of the theatres and scenery, the splendour of the dresses and the good management of the hosts.

It was in what we have come to know as the décor that the amateur scored over his poorer professional counterpart. The wardrobe book at Wynnstay and the various descriptions of costume tell their tale of rich variety, of fine stuffs, of unstinted expense. Diamonds glittered on the ladies of Richmond House and Blenheim Palace and the Margravine's properties were of gold. In a large theatre pasteboard and paint are perhaps preferable, but in fit-ups in rooms or bijou buildings the real thing made its point. Some of the leading scene painters of the day were employed at one or other of the private theatres: Young at Wargrave, Thomas Greenwood at Richmond House and Blenheim, Thomas Malton at Brandenburgh House, Inigo Richards and Paul Sandby at Wynnstay and Michael Rooker and James Roberts at Blenheim. In other instances a talented member of the *Corps Dramatique*, such as Bilsborrow at Little Dalby or Wilkinson at Wynnstay, would be entrusted with the scene painting.

The theatres varied from converted rooms to specially designed and elaborately ornamental structures such as those of Wargrave and Brandenburgh House. A greenhouse at Blenheim, a kitchen at Wynnstay were transformed. Often the utmost ingenuity was exercised, as when Wyatt contrived to build into the rooms of Richmond House an orchestra well, a sunken pit and boxes. The capacity of the theatres was generally between 150 and 300 though Barrymore's and Hartopp's held 400 and Delaval's first little theatre in St James's had only room for 50. Stages were apt to be confined in the fit-ups, and lack of ventilation was a frequent complaint as it was in the public theatres.

How about the plays? Fector specialised in tragedy because he preferred acting it; the Earl of Sandwich in musical pieces because of his musical tastes; more often comedy was the staple favourite, as with the Margravine of Anspach. Usually there was a judicious mixture. An analysis of plays known to have been given at private theatricals during this period[4] reveals *The Mayor of Garratt* as the most popular piece with a score of 13, followed by *Venice Preserv'd*, *High Life Below Stairs* and *The Guardian* with 10, *The Fair Penitent* and *Who's the Dupe?* with 9, *Henry IV Part I* and *The Wonder* with 8, *Jane Shore*, *The Revenge*, *Bon Ton*, *The Rivals* and *Othello* with 7 and *The Upholsterer* and *The Devil To Pay* with 6. Shakespeare quite held his own. After *Henry IV Part I* with 8 productions and *Othello* with 7, came *The Merchant of Venice* and *Richard III* with 5, *Cymbeline*, *Macbeth*, *The Merry Wives*, *Romeo and Juliet* with 3, *Hamlet*, *The Tempest* and *As You Like It* with 2 and *Twelfth Night*, *The Winter's Tale*, *Measure for Measure* and *King John* with 1, making in all 15 plays. The list is, of course, artificial as there must have been many performances of which we have no record, but at least it shows which plays were popular with amateurs. On the whole they fought shy of new plays, except for the Margravine who liked to act leading rôles in her own compositions. As well as the 19 new pieces for which she was responsible, I have found 36 others that were first given in private theatres or by amateurs. Though a few of these were later presented on the public stage they were, as far as we can tell from those that attained print, of poor quality. This also applies to three volumes of plays written for private theatres but not, as far as we know, actually performed. These were William Mansell's *Fairy Hill or May Day*, a pastoral opera printed in 1784, William Hayley's *Plays of Three Acts written for a Private Theatre* of the same date containing three rhymed comedies and a tragedy, and William Davies's *Plays written for a Private Theatre* printed in 1786 and consisting of one three act and four five act comedies. A full-length play was often more than amateurs could tackle and many were cut or had scenes excerpted from them; others were altered to suit the needs of the performers or the exigencies of casting. We have seen that the Margravine reduced *The Provok'd Wife* to three acts with cuts that ensured that her rôle of Lady Brute should be the principal one, and when Mrs. Crespigny gave *Douglas* at Camberwell she provided that tragedy with a happy ending.

One opportunity that private theatricals afforded, that was not generally available in the public theatres,[5] was the presentation of French plays. I have found 35 of these, mostly dating from the late 1790s and first decade of the 19th century when emigrés from the French Revolution were in the country and able to perform them. Nearly all were *proverbes* or *petites pièces*, but occasionally something a little more ambitious, such as Molière's *L'Avare* at Count de Starhemberg's theatricals at York House, Twickenham, in 1803, or Arnault's tragedy *Marius à Minturnes* at Crauford's in Kensington in 1795, were attempted. It was at the Pic Nic in 1802 that Beaumarchais's *Le Barbier de Seville* was first performed in French in England.

According to the tradition of dramatic entertainments at private houses, these theatricals were social events nearly always accompanied with banquets or at least by refreshments or collations. Contemporary accounts indulge in luscious descriptions of the delicacies that were served in such profusion. Balls or dancing frequently followed, so that those who risked the hazards and discomforts of coach journeys from afar had, for their reward, a varied party which might last the best part of 10 hours.

What was the influence of the craze on the history of the stage? In the first place it undoubtedly helped with the movement, strong since Garrick's day, to improve the status of the actor. Macklin, Kemble, King and Miss

Farren were called in to coach or superintend; Garrick was consulted about scenery, properties or elocution; actors and actresses from the London theatres or provincial companies were invited to take part on many occasions.

Secondly the private stages afforded scope for experiment. We have seen how batten lights were introduced at Wynnstay and a system of reverberators at Blenheim; whilst in the matter of costume one or two private theatres led in historical accuracy. Scenic artists too were given scope for their talents in other than the rather limited field of the public stage.

Thirdly a more critical and informed audience was created, since those who had tried to act themselves necessarily learnt to appreciate the finer points of the art. Lastly the amateur endeavours kept the drama alive, or instilled some knowledge of it, in remote places to which even the strollers did not always penetrate. For the tenant farmers, the yokels, the servants of great houses and small, these performances were often the only ones they ever had the chance of witnessing. Thus, though the private theatricals of the period had very little of the formative influence in the history of the drama that they had had in the earlier days, their very popularity in every branch of society was such that it was another trumpet blast proclaiming the final victory of the stage over puritan fanaticism; another witness to the undying desire among men for dramatic expression.

Appendix I

Calendar of Private Theatricals

This Calendar includes only theatricals to which a year can be assigned. It does not include military theatricals, performances by amateurs in public theatres, unless, as with the Delavals, such performances were connected with other theatricals given by the family, or performances in regular private theatres such as those in Berwick Street, or Catherine Street, Strand, where aspirants paid to try out their histrionic powers. All these have been counted in estimating the numbers of theatricals that took place in each decade in Chapter I, note 21. The organisers or owners have been given only the first time that the theatricals are listed.

Date		Place	Organiser or Owner
1718	—	Blenheim Palace (Oxon.)	Duchess of Marlborough
1731	—	London	John Conduitt
1735	May	Villiers Street, London	Benefit William Bond
	Sept.	Westbury (Bucks.)	Campbell Price
1736	January	,,	,,
1737	July	,,	,,
1740	August	Cliveden (Berks.)	Frederick, Prince of Wales
	September	Goodwood (Sussex)	Duke of Richmond
1741	October	Exton Hall (Rutland)	Earl of Gainsborough
c1743	—	Teddington	Mrs. Peg Woffington
1744	September	Westbury	
1744	,,	Woburn Abbey (Beds.)	Duke of Bedford
1746	August	Westbury	
1748	August	Exton Hall	
1749	January	Leicester House, London	Frederick, Prince of Wales
1750	January	,, ,, ,,	,, ,, ,, ,,

Date		Place	Organiser or Owner
1751	March	Drury Lane Theatre	Sir Francis Delaval
1756	—	Woburn Abbey	
	—	Ashford near Hampton	
1758[1]		Stanlynch, Wilts (now Trafalgar House)	Sir William Young
1760	December	Hinchingbrook (Hunts.)	Earl of Sandwich
1761	January	Holland House, London	Henry Fox (later Lord Holland)
		La Trappe, Hammersmith	Bubb Doddington
	September	Holland House,	
1762	April	,, ,,	
1767	Jan., April and May	Petty France, Westminster, London	Duke of York and Sir Francis Delaval
	—	Privy Gardens, London	Dowage Lady Townsend
1768	October	Winterslow (Wilts.)	Stephen Fox
	—	Harley Street, London	Earl of Mulgrave
1769	January	Winterslow	
1770	January	The Close, Salisbury (Wilts).	James Harris
	September	Queen's Square, London	Dr. Burney
	November	Winterslow	
1771	June	Chessington Hall (Surrey)	Samuel Crisp
1773	January	Blenheim Palace	Duke of Marlborough
	,,	Cassiobury Park (Herts.)	Earl of Essex
	,,	North Aston (Oxon.)	Oldfield Bowles
	,,	Wynnstay (Wales)	Sir W. Williams Wynn
	November	Kelmarsh (Northants).	William Hanbury
	,,	Wynnstay	
	December	Cassiobury Park	
1774	January	North Aston	
	,,	Winterslow	
	June	Lymington Manor (Hants.)	Thomas Marday
		The Oaks (Surrey)	Lord Stanley (later Earl of Derby)
	October	Hewell Grange (Worcs.)	Earl of Plymouth
		Kelmarsh	
	November	Close, Salisbury	
	December	North Aston	
1775	January	Wynnstay	
	September	Gumley Hall (Leicester)	Joseph Cradock
		Weston Hall (Staffs.)	Sir Henry Bridgeman
	December	Nocton Hall (Lincs.)	Mrs. Hobart (later Lady Bucks.)

Date	Place	Organiser or Owner
1776 January	Wynnstay	
September	Gumley Hall	
October	Close, Salisbury	
	Nocton Hall	
November	Hewell Grange	
,,	North Aston	
,,	Weston Hall	
1777 January	Bolney Court, Henley (Oxon.)	Lord Villiers
April	Barborne Lodge (Worcs.)	Richard Burney
September	Weston Hall	
,,	Nocton Hall	
October	Wynnstay	
November	North Aston	
,,	Little Dalby Hall (Leics.)	Edward Hartopp (later Hartopp-Wigley)
1778 January	Wynnstay	
May	Newbury Town Hall (Berks.)	Lady Craven
1779 January	Wynnstay	
December	North Aston	
1780 January	Wynnstay	
April	Newbury Town Hall or Benham House (Berks.)	Lady Craven
1781 January	Wynnstay	
April	Hall Place (Berks.)	Sir Wm. East
November	Weybridge	Tinker
,,	Ham Common (Surrey)	Mrs. Hobart
1782 January	North Aston	
,,	Wynnstay	
April	Hall Place	
,,	Queensberry House, London	Lady Craven
July	Benham House	
November	Ham Common (Surrey)	
December	Hall Place	
1783 January	Dover (Kent)	Wm. Fector
	Wynnstay	
October	Dover	
	Hall Place	
November	Ham Common	
December	Dover	

Date		Place	Organiser or Owner
1784	January	Wynnstay	
	March	Dover	
	Summer	Steventon Rectory (Hants.)	Austen family
	October	Dover	
1785	January	Wynnstay	
	March	Dover	
	November	Dover	
	December	Wynnstay	
1786	April	Dover	
	August	Wynnstay	
	December	Blenheim Palace	
	,,	Dover	
	,,	Hinchingbrook	
	—	Wargrave	Earl of Barrymore
1787	January	Ampthill	Earl of Upper Ossory
		Wynnstay	
	March	Dover	
	April	Richmond House, London	Duke of Richmond
		Faringdon House (Berks.)	Henry James Pye
	October	,, ,,	
1787	October	Blenheim Palace	
		Grimsthorpe House (Lincs.)	Duke of Ancaster
		Hinchingbrook	
	November	Adlestrop (Glos.)	James Henry Leigh
		Hinchingbrook	
		Little Dalby Hall	
	December	Dover	
		Hinchingbrook	
	—	Steventon Rectory	
	—	Weybridge	Tinker
		Bolney Court, Henley	Lord Villiers
1788	January	Ampthill	
		Blenheim Palace	
		Horton (Bucks.)	Mrs. Hickford
		Steventon Rectory	
	February	Richmond House	
	March	,, ,,	
	April	,, ,,	
		Dover	

Date		Place	Organiser or Owner
	May	Freemasons' Hall, London	Thomas Twisleton
		Richmond House	
	September	Eaton Hall (Cheshire)	
	October	Blenheim Palace	
	November	Dover	
1789	January	Adlestrop	
	February	Dover	
	,,	Wargrave	
	April	Champion Lodge, Camberwell	Mrs. Crespigny
	,,	Ham Common	
	May	Tehidy Park (Cornwall)	Sir Francis Basset
	August	Blenheim Palace	
		Wargrave	
		Wavendon (Bucks.)	Shuttleworth
	September	Eaton Hall	Earl of Grosvenor
	November	Dover	
	December	Blenheim Palace	
1790	January	Steventon Rectory	
	,,	Wargrave	
	April	Champion Lodge	
	May	,, ,,	
	July	Savile Row, London	Earl of Barrymore
	September	Wargrave	
	October	Broughton Hall (Oxon.)	Archdale Wilson Taylor
	December	Seaton Delaval (Northumberland)	Lord Delaval
1791	January	Norwich	James Plumtre
	,,	Wargrave	
	February	Seaton Delaval	
	April	Broughton Hall	
		Wargrave	
	June	Aldborough House (now Stratford House), London	Earl of Aldborough
	November	Wargrave	
	December	,,	
1792	January	Bruce Castle, Tottenham	Henry Hare Townsend
	,,	Seaton Delaval	
	,,	Wargrave	
	February	Norwich	
		Seaton Delaval	

Date	Place	Organiser or Owner
July	Arlington St., London	Duchess of Rutland
September	Thorndon Hall (Essex)	Lord Petre
November	Norwich	Deymer
1793 January	Heathfield Park (Sussex)	Francis Newberry
February	Aldborough House	
April	Brandenburgh House, Hammersmith	Margravine of Anspach (formerly Lady Craven)
December	,,	
1794 January	Heathfield Park	
March	Brandenburgh House	
July	,, ,,	
1795 January	Privy Garden, London	Mrs. Gertrude Robinson
June	Brandenburgh House	
December	Kensington Assembly Rooms	Crauford
1796 January	Brandenburgh House	
	Northwick Park (Glos.)	Sir John Rushout
	Wimpole Hall (Camb.)	Earl of Hardwicke
February	Brandenburgh House	
March	,, ,,	
1797 January	Long Ditton	Thomas Streatfeild
	Manresa Lodge, Roehampton	Earl of Bessborough
April	Brandenburgh House	
1798 January	Long Ditton	
March	Brandenburgh House	
June	,, ,,	
August	Little Dalby Hall	
1799 January	Portland Place, London	Lord Shaftesbury
March–		
June	Brandenburgh House	
July	Little Dalby Hall	
1800 July	Brandenburgh House	
November	Strawberry Hill	Mrs. Damer
1801 July	Little Dalby Hall	
November	Strawberry Hill	
December	York House, Twickenham	Count Lewis de Stahremberg
1802 January	York House	
March	Tottenham Street Rooms, London	Pic-Nic
April	,, ,, ,,	,,
	Bentley Priory, Stanmore	Pic-Nic

Date	Place	Organiser or Owner
May	Tottenham Street	
June	Brandenburgh House	
,,	New Burlington St., London	Countess of Cork
July	Little Dalby Hall	
November	Tottenham Street	
December	,, ,,	
1803 January	Bentley Priory	Marquess of Abercorn
,,	Crewe Hall (Cheshire)	John Crewe
	Little Dalby Hall	
	York House	
February	Brandenburgh House	
June	Brandenburgh House	
,,	New Burlington Street	
July	Little Dalby Hall	
October	Powderham Castle (Devon)	Viscount Courtenay
December	Audley End (Essex)	Lord Braybrooke
1804 January	Bentley Priory	
,,	Champion Lodge	
,,	Stowe (Bucks.)	Earl of Buckingham
May	Brandenburgh House	
December	Dowgate Hill, London	William Cleveland
,,	York House	
1805 January	Stable Yard, St. James, London	Earl of Harrington
,,	Stowe	
,,	York House	
1805 July	Brandenburgh House	
September	Stable Yard	
December	Bentley Priory	
,,	Dowgate Hill	
,,	Woburn Abbey (Beds.)	Duke of Bedford
1806 January	Bentley Priory	
February	Cottesmore (Rutland)	Viscount Lowther
,,	Bristol	
August	Wroxton Abbey (Oxon.)	Earl of Guilford
September	Southwell (Notts.)	Leacroft
October	Bristol	—
1807 December	Porkington (Salop.)	Owen Ormsby
,,	Pradoe (Salop.)	Thomas Kenyon

178

Date		_Place_	_Organiser or Owner_
1808	February	Porkington	
	December	Bryn y Prys (Wales)	Price
1809	January	The Cliff, Ipswich (Suffolk)	Mrs. Cobbold.
	March	Grange House, Camberwell	John Rolls
	February	Porkington	
1810	January	Porkington	
	„	Grange House	
1811	January	Grange House	
1812	February	Tavistock Place, London	Benjamin Oakley
	July	London	Lady Hardwicke
1814	March	Tavistock Place	
1816	December	Holland House	
1817	January	Woburn Abbey	
1818	April	Holland House	

[1] There is no evidence that the performance of _Julius Caesar_ actually took place.

Appendix II
English Plays First Performed at Private Theatricals

(Plays marked with an asterisk are not mentioned in *Biographica Dramatica*, Nicoll or *Stage Cyclopaedia*)
T. = Tragedy; C. = Comedy; F. = Farce; D. = Drama

Name	Description	Author	Place and Year of Acting	Printed or Ms.
Adelaide	T.	Amelia Alderson (Mrs. Opie)	Plumtre's, Norwich, 1791	Ms. in possession of Miss Ethel Carr, Canterbury
Alfred	Masque	Mallet and Thomson	Frederick, Prince of Wales's at Cliveden, 1740. Smock Alley, Dublin 1744; D.L. 1745.	Pr. 1740
Arcadian Pastoral	Mus. Ent. in 5 Acts	Lady Craven and Beckford	Lady Craven at Queensberry House, Burlington Gdns., 1782	
Ass-ass-ination	Burlesque	Theodore Hook	John Rolls's, The Grange, Camberwell, 1809	Pr. *Bentley's Miscellany*, 1847
Beauty and the Beast	Ent.	—	Pradoe, Salop., 180–	Ms. Pigott, d.22. Bodl.
*Bedlamites	C. in 2 acts	Trs. Greville from French proverbes *Les Foux, Le Seigneur Auteur*	Pic-Nic at Tottenham St. Rooms, 1802	
*Black and White or Don't be Savage	F. in 2 acts	Theodore Hook	John Rolls's, The Grange, Camberwell, 1811. Hay.	
Blue Beard	Panto.	asc. to Ld. Barrymore, Pasquin, Delpini	Lord Barrymore's at Wargrave 13/7/1791. C.G. 21/12/1791	

Name	Description	Author	Place and Year of Acting	Printed or Ms.
British Orphan	T.	Mariana Starke	Mrs. Crespigny's, Champion Lodge, Camberwell, 1790	
*Cave of Trophonius	Ent.	Wm. Gell	Porkington, Salop., 1808	Ms. Pigott, d.22. Bodl.
Coventry Act	C.	James Plumtre	Plumtre's at Norwich, 1792	Pr. 1793
Earl of Northumberland		—	Berwick St., 1804	
Election	Ent. 2 acts	Cumberland	Hanbury's at Kelmarsh, 1774	Ms. fragment, formerly in possession of Ifan Kyrle Fletcher
False Appearances	C.	Henry Seymour Conway	Duke of Richmond's, Richmond House, 1788. D.L.1789	Pr. 1789
Fashionable Friends	C.	—	Hon. Mrs. Damer's, Strawberry Hill, 1801. D.L. 1802	Pr. 1802
*Fête Champêtre	Ent. and masque	—	Lord Stanley's at the Oaks, 1774	
Gauntlet	D. in 3 acts	Trs. from Spanish by Margravine of Anspach	Margravine of Anspach's at Brandenburgh House, 1804	
*Grey Beards	C.	—	Archdale Taylor's at Broughton Hall, 1790	

Name	Description	Author	Place and Year of Acting	Printed or Ms.
*Guardian Outwitted	Mus. piece, trs. from Bouilly's Une Folie	—	City, 1803	
*Harlequin Arcadian, or The Shepherd's Love	Panto	—	Cleveland's, Dowgate Hill, London, 1805	
*Imagination	Ent. 1 act with Masquerade	Margravine of Anspach	Margravine of Anspach's at Brandenburgh House, 1800	
*Impostor	Play in 3 acts	—	Cleveland's, Dowgate Hill, London, 1805	
*Inquisitive Girl	—	—	Duchess of Rutland's, Arlington St., 1792	
Love in a Convent	C.	Trs. from French by Margravine of Anspach	Margravine of Anspach's Brandenburgh House, 1805	
Lovers of their Country, or Themistocles and Aristides	T.	—	Lalauze's bft., Haymarket Theatre, 1770	
Miniature Picture	C. in 3 acts	Margravine of Anspach	Lady Craven's at Town Hall, Newbury, 6/4/1780, DL. 24/5/1780	Pr. 1781
*Modern Education	C. trs. from Berquin	—	Shuttleworth's at Wavendon, 1789	Pr. in Children's Friend, 1788

Name	Description	Author	Place and Year of Acting	Printed or Ms.
Nourjad	D.	Margravine of Anspach	Margravine of Anspach's at Brandenburgh House, 1803	Pr. 1803
One Bird in the Hand Worth Two in the Bush	Mus. ent. in 1 act	—	John Crewe's at Crewe Hall, 1803	
Panthea	T.	—	Woburn Abbey, c.1777	Ms. in Percy Dobell Catalogue, 1968
Poor Noddle	F. in 2 acts from French	Trs. by Margravine of Anspach	Margravine of Anspach's at Brandenburgh House, 17/6/1803. Hay: as Nicodemus in Despair 31/8/1803	
*Princess and the Slave	Panto-ballet	—	Margravine of Anspach's at Brandenburgh House, 1805	
Princess of Georgia	O.	—	Margravine of Anspach's at Brandenburgh House, 1798. C.G. 1799	Airs and Chorusses pr. 1799
Princess of Parma	T.	Cumberland	Hanbury's at Kelmarsh, 1774	Ms. fragment formerly in possession of Ifan Kyrle Fletcher
Puss in Boots	Panto.	Keppel Craven	Margravine of Anspach's at Brandenburgh House, 1799	
Robbers	T. adapted from Schiller	Trs. and abridged by Margravine of Anspach	Margravine of Anspach's at Brandenburgh House, 1798	

Name	Description	Author	Place and Year of Acting	Printed or Ms.
*Release of Eblis	Panto.	Keppel Craven	Margravine of Anspach's at Brandenburgh House, 1803	Pr. 1803
Road to Ridicule	C. 2 acts	Thos. Streatfeild	Long Ditton Theatre, 1799	Pr. [1799]
*Roman Mutiny	Duologue	Elizabeth Cobbold	Cliff, Ipswich, 1809	Pr. 1825
Secret	—	—	Earl of Hardwicke's at Wimpole Hall, 1796	
*Siege of Scutari	T.	Edward Taylor	Bowles's at North Aston	
*Silver Star, or Harlequin Restor'd	Panto.	—	Cleveland's at Dowgate Hill, London, 1804	
Sleep Walker	C. in 2 acts	Trs. from Pont de Vile's *Sonambule* by Margravine of Anspach	Lady Craven's at Newbury Town Hall, 1778	Pr. 1778
*Smyrna Twins	Mus. P.	—	Margravine of Anspach's at Brandenburgh House, 1796	
Statue Feast	C. alt. from Molière's *Don Juan*	Alt. by Margravine of Anspach	Lady Craven's at Benham House, 1782	

184

Name	Description	Author	Place and Year of Acting	Printed or Ms.
Tamer Tam'd	F. alt. from Beaumont and Fletcher's Woman's Prize	—	Margravine of Anspach's at Brandenburgh House, 1795	
'Tis Well They Are Married	1 act from French	—	Margravine of Anspach's at Brandenburgh House, 1804	
*Ton and Antiquity	C. in 2 acts	Thos. Streatfeild	Long Ditton Theatre, 1798	Pr. [1799]
*Trial of Temper	C. with songs	Bilsbarrow	Hartopp's at Dalby Hall, 1798	
*Two Officers	Trs. from French petite pièce	Trs. Margravine of Anspach	Margravine of Anspach's at Brandenburgh House, 1802	
Whistle for It	Mus. Ent. in 2 acts	George Lamb	Marquis of Abercorn's at Bentley Priory, 1806. C.G. 1807	Pr. 1807
Will or the Widow	F. in 2 acts	Theodore Hook	John Rolls's, The Grange, Camberwell, 1810	
Yorkshire Ghost	C. in 5 acts	Margravine of Anspach	Margravine of Anspach's at Brandenburgh House, 1784	
You May Like It or Let it Alone	F. with songs	—	Delaval's at Seaton Delaval, 1790	
—	2 Ent.	Bilsbarrow	Hartopp's at Dalby Hall, 1801	

Notes

Chapter I

pp. 7 to 15

[1] *Edinburgh Review*, Oct. 1827. Reprinted in *Prose and Verse*, (1878).

[2] Volume of playbills and clippings of private theatricals in the British Library which is the most important single source of the period.

[3] Print Room, British Museum.

[4] Fanny Burney, *Early Diary* II, 165 *et seq.*

[5] W. Austen-Leigh and R. A. Austen-Leigh, *Jane Austen; Her Life and Letters,* (1913)

[6] Mrs. [Anne] Mathews, *Memoirs of Charles Mathews* (1838) I, 270.

[7] *Morning Post*, 26 Sept. 1804.

[8] (1836) Chapter XIII.

[9] *Oracle*, 5 March 1798; *Times*, 9 Jan. 1808; *Morning Post*, 5 Oct. 1805.

[10] John Cunningham, *Poems Chiefly Pastoral* (1771), p. 171. I owe this reference to Miss M. Hope Dodds.

[11] Clifford Leech, *Private Performances and Amateur Theatricals* 1580-1660, an unpublished thesis in the University of London Library to which I owe much in making this survey.

[12] Montague Summers, *The Playhouse of Pepys* (1935) p. 31.

[13] Leslie Hotson, *The Commonwealth and Restoration Stage* (1928) p. 154.

[14] Wm. Blundell, *A Cavalier's Note Book*, (1880), p. 110.

[15] *The Letters from Dorothy Osborne to Sir William Temple* (Everyman Library) p. 255.

[16] E. Boswell, *The Restoration Court Stage* (1932) p. 128.

[17] *Diary*, ed. Braybrooke-Wheatley (1904) VII, 280.

[18] *Diary*, Feb. 5, 1668/9, ed. E. S. de Beer (1955) VII, 320.

[19] For full description see Boswell *op. cit.* pp. 177-8, 186, 227.

[20] *Memoirs of the Verney Family* ed. F. P. Verney and M. M. Verney, (1925) II, 318. See also the performance of *The Soldier's Fortune* acted by yeoman and tenant farmers in 1712, *Blundell's Diary and Letterbook* ed. Margaret Blundell (1952) p. 44.

[21] *London Magazine* Jan. 1749.

[22] Horace Walpole *Letters*, ed. Paget-Toynbee (1905) IV, 299.

[23] *London Post*, 5 Nov. 1776.

[24] I have found 42 seasons of theatricals in the 1770s, 84 in the 1780s, 55 in the 1790s, 68 in 1800-10 and only 7 from 1811 to 1820.

[25] *Post*, pp. 38, 97.

[26] *Oracle*, 9 March 1798.

[27] *Public Advertiser*, 16 Jan. 1788.

[28] *Senilities*, 1801.

²⁹ *Post*, p. 130.

³⁰ *Morning Post*, 16 Jan 1792.

³¹ *Post*, p. 165.

³² *Post*, p. 153.

³³ Thomas Sheppard, *Evolution of the Drama in Hull and District* (1927) pp. 193-5. For some other theatricals see Lord Wm. Lennox, *Celebrities I Have Known* (1876) I, 239 *et seq.*

CHAPTER II, pp. 16 to 33

¹ [Anon.] *Truth Opposed to Fiction* (1793), pp. 34-5.

² Anthony Pasquin, *The Life of the Late Earl of Barrymore* (1793). New edition, p. 87; *Memoirs of J. S. Munden* by his son (1844) p. 54.

³ John Bernard, *Retrospections of the Stage* (1830) I, 209.

⁴ Pasquin, *op. cit.*, p. 14.

⁵ *Passages from the Diaries of Mrs. Philip Lybbe Powys*, 1756-1808 ed. E. J. Climenson, (1899)

⁶ S. Redgrave, *Dictionary of Artists of the English School* (1878)

⁷ *The Reminiscences of Henry Angelo*, ed. H. Laver Smyth (1904) I, 235.

⁸ *Truth Opposed to Fiction*, p. 34.

⁹ *Public Advertiser*, 4, 13. Sept; *World* 21 Sept. 1788.

¹⁰ *Op. cit.* p. 54.

¹¹ *Reading Mercury* 2 Feb. 1789; Burney Collection, Playbills dealing with Private Theatrical Performances, 1750-1808 Brit. Library; Henry Angelo, *Reminiscences*, (1828, 30) II, 109; Pasquin, *op. cit.* p. 101.

¹² *Angelo's Pic Nic* (1905) p. 211.

¹³ *Reading Mercury*, 24 Aug.; *Public Advertiser* 25 Aug.; Burney Collection playbill, 21 Aug.; *London Chronicle*, 25-27 Aug.

¹⁴ *Public Advertiser*, 3 Feb. 1789.

¹⁵ *Reading Mercury*, 12 Oct. 1789.

¹⁶ Angelo, *Reminiscences*, I, 236, 241, II, 310; *Reading Mercury*, 5 Jan. 1790.

¹⁷ *D.N.B.;* W. T. Parke, *Musical Memoirs* (1830) p. 155; *Gentleman's Mag.;* April, 1828.

¹⁸ E. Beresford Chancellor, *Lives of the Rakes*, (1924-5), IV, 178 identified the cottage as the now much enlarged house The Croft.

¹⁹ Unidentified clipping, Burney Collection.

²⁰ E. C. Everard, *Memoirs of an Unfortunate Son of Thespis* (1818) p. 139.

²¹ *Reading Mercury*, 18 Jan; the prologue is printed in *The Annual Register*, 1790.

²² *Morning Chronicle*, 2 Feb. 1790; Burney Collection clipping May 4.

²³ *Letters of Horace Walpole*, XIV, 269.

²⁴ *World*, 23 Jan. 1790.

²⁵ Horace Walpole *Letters*, XIV, 272.

²⁶ Burney clippings; *Gazetteer*, 24 July; Angelo, *Reminiscences*, I, 243.

²⁷ *Letters*, XIV, 282.

²⁸ *Public Advertiser*, 13 Aug.

²⁹ Hist. Mss. Com. Earl of Carlisle, XV, 681.

³⁰ Quoted by H. J. Reid, *History of Wargrave* (1885) p. 125.

³¹ *Public Advertiser; Reading Mercury.*

³² 21-23 Sept.

³³ Seen by kind permission of Messrs. Christie's at their premises.

³⁴ Pasquin, *op. cit.*, pp. 15, 20, 26, 92; *Truth Opposed to Fiction.*

³⁵ Banks Collection, Brit. Mus. Print Room.

³⁶ H. J. Reid, *op. cit.*, p. 126.

³⁷ *World*, 6 Oct.

³⁸ Pasquin, *op. cit.* pp. 18, 19; *London Chronicle*, 21-23 Sept.

[39] *The Times*, 24, 28 Sept.

[40] *Memoirs of John Bannister*, p. 296.

[41] *The Times*, 29 Sept; Burney Collection playbill.

[42] *Reading Mercury*, 4 Oct.; *Public Advertiser*, 1 Oct.

[43] T. Wilkinson, *Wandering Patentee*, (1795) III, 147, 216.

[44] Burney Collection clippings; *Reading Mercury*, 18 April; *Public Advertiser*, 16 April.

[45] *Reading Mercury*, 18 April; *Morning Chronicle*, 15 April; Angelo, *Reminiscences*, II, 57.

[46] *Reading Mercury*, 18 April.

[47] *Ibid; Gazette*, 18 April.

[48] *Reading Mercury*, 13 June 1791.

[49] *Morning Chronicle*, 20, 26 July, 10 Aug., 8 Nov.

[50] Letter dated 1791 in my possession.

[51] *Morning Chronicle*, 3, 15 Dec.; Burney Collection clipping.

[52] *Memoirs of Mrs. Crouch*, ed. M. J. Young (1806) II, 141; Burney Collection clipping; Harvard Theatre Collection clippings in Angelo Vol. VI; *Morning Chronicle*, 15 Dec.

[53] *Public Advertiser*, 22 Dec. 1791.

[54] Playbill advertised in Ifan Kyrle Fletcher's Catalogue, Spring 1936, dated by him c.1790 but belonging to 1791 since Miss Richards was then Mrs. Edwin.

[55] *World*, 2 Feb. 1791.

[56] *Morning Chronicle*, 20 Feb. 1792; *Annual Register*, 1792, p. 4.

[57] Playbill reproduced in Reid, *op. cit.*, p. 127.

[58] *When We're Married*. A favourite song sung at Lord Barrymore's Theatre at Wargrave.

[59] *Op. cit.*, p. 254.

[60] P.R.O. Postea Book, 1792-1801, Berks. Summer Circuit; the sum is wrongly given as £980 in the *Reading Mercury*, 23 July 1792.

[61] *Reading Mercury*, 24 Sept., 8 Oct. 1792.

[62] Seilhammer, *History of the American Theatre* (1891) III, 149.

[63] Pasquin, *op. cit.*, p. 15; Christie's Catalogue.

CHAPTER III pp. 34 to 52

[1] *London Magazine*, Sept. 1779.

[2] *Letters*, VII, 379.

[3] *Historical and Posthumous Memoirs of Sir Nathaniel Wraxall*, ed. H. B. Wheatly (1884), IV, 104.

[4] *Morning Herald*, 13 April 1787.

[5] Burney Collection clipping, 4 June 1788.

[6] Henry Meister, *Letters Written During a Residence in England* (1799) p. 202.

[7] Petronius Arbiter, *Memoirs of the Present Countess of Derby*, 7th ed. [?1797], p. 21.

[8] *The Times*, 23 April 1788.

[9] *World*, 20 April 1787.

[10] *Morning Chronicle*, 18 April 1787.

[11] *World*, 18 April 1788.

[12] *Morning Chronicle*, 18 April 1788.

[13] *Journal and Correspondence of William, Lord Auckland*, (1861) I, 409.

[14] Newspapers later report one hundred and twenty guests.

[15] Burney Collection clipping, April 1787.

[16] *Morning Chronicle*, 18 April 1787.

[17] A drawing of Richmond House by Capon is in Westminster Library, Buckingham Palace Road.

[18] *World, Morning Post, London Packet*, 20 April; Hist. Mss. Com. 15. Pr. VII, p. 281, Diary of Thomas, Earl of Ailesbury.

[19] Burney Collection. The number of actor's tickets was reduced to four in 1788.

[20] Banks Collection, Brit. Mus. Print Room.

[21] *Morning Post*, 20 April 1787.

[22] Prologue and epilogue printed in a broad sheet [1787] Brit. Library.

[23] *London Packet*, 20-23 April 1787.

[24] May 1787.

[25] *Town and Country Magazine*, May 1787; *Gazetteer*, 23 April.

[26] *World*, 8 Feb.; *Town and Country Magazine*; *Gazetteer*, 23 April. The last wrongly states that the portraits were of the principal performers.

[27] Four of these engravings are in the Brit. Mus., Miss Farren and Mrs. Siddons from Lawson's original set, and the Duchess of Devonshire and Lady Duncannon from reprints by R. Cribblin 1797. Only that of the Duchess of Devonshire is coloured.

[28] *World*, 20 April.

[29] Burney Collection clipping, 18 May 1787.

[30] The legends attached to Mrs. Damer and Mrs. Hobart have been transposed in error.

[31] *Prologue and Epilogue to The Way to Keep Him*, 1787.

[32] Diary of Earl of Ailesbury, *op. cit.*, 17 May 1787. I owe this reference to Mr. C. D. Cecil.

[33] *Letters*, XIV, 2, 8.

[34] Burney clipping, May 8.

[35] *Morning Chronicle*, 21 May 1787, 22 April 1788.

[36] *Memoirs of the Life of J. P. Kemble*, ed. J. Boaden (1825), I, 432.

[37] *Memoirs of the Life and Correspondence of Mrs. Hannah More*, ed. Wm. Roberts (1834), II, 57.

[38] *World*, Dec. 7, 18.

[39] *Letters*, XIV, 39.

[40] *Ibid*, 42.

[41] *Public Advertiser*, Dec. 31, Jan 1 1788.

[42] Burney clipping, 4 Jan.; *World*, 16 Jan.

[43] *World*, 23 Jan 1788.

[44] 7, 27 Mar.

[45] *Ibid*, 9 Feb.

[46] *Times*, 7 Feb.; *World*, 9 Feb.; *Morning Post*, 8 Feb.; *Morning Herald*, 2 Feb.

[47] *World*, 16 Jan. *Morning Herald* says two hundred and sixty but this is unlikely as there were under one hundred guests the opening night.

[48] *The Private Theatricals at Kilkenny* (1825), 5.

[49] *World*, 8 Feb.; *Town and Country Magazine*, Mar.

[50] Gerald Campbell, *Edward and Pamela Fitzgerald* (1904), 41.

[51] Sir William East's theatricals at Hall Place, Berks. had taken place in 1781-3. For Bowles see Chapter IX pp. 140-145.

[52] Diary of Thomas, Earl of Ailesbury, *op. cit.*

[53] 9 Feb.; see also *Morning Post*, 8 Feb.

[54] *Hamwood Papers of the Ladies of Llangollen*, ed. Mrs. G. H. Bell (1930).

[55] Burney clipping, 4 Mar.

[56] Walpole, *Letters*, XIV, 45.

[57] 23 Feb., 1, 6 Mar., 18 Apr. and another unknown date.

[58] Burney clipping, 8 Mar.

[59] *World*, 23 Jan.; Burney clipping, 29 Feb.

[60] *World*, 14 Feb.

[61] May 1788, p. 210.

[62] *Times, Morning Post*, Burney clipping, 12 Mar.

[63] *Public Advertiser*, 8 Sept. 1788; W. T. Fitzgerald, *Miscellaneous Poems* (1801), 55.

[64] Burney clippings, 10, 12 Mar.; *Public Advertiser*, 31 Mar.

[65] *Times*, 12 Mar.

[66] *Public Advertiser*, 29 Mar.

[67] Burney clipping 29 Mar. The other performance took place on 28 Mar.

⁶⁸ Burney clipping, 19 Mar.
⁶⁹ From a photograph of the Ms. Mainwaring Piozziana, II, 101 kindly lent me by Mr. Clifford and quoted by permission of Sir Randle Mainwaring.
⁷⁰ J. L. Clifford, *Hester Lynch Piozzi* (1941), 332.
⁷¹ Katherine C. Baldeston, *Thraliana* (1942), II, 712.
⁷² *Town and Country Magazine*, May 1788; *Morning Post*, 28 Apr.
⁷³ *Auckland Correspondence*, 11, 207.
⁷⁴ Burney clipping, 28 Apr.; *Gazetteer*, 12 May.
⁷⁵ Burney clipping, 28 Apr.; *Town and Country Magazine*, May.
⁷⁶ *Gazetteer*, 12 May.
⁷⁷ *Morning Herald, Morning Chronicle*, 2 May.
⁷⁸ P. 232.
⁷⁹ *Letters*, XIV, p. 49.
⁸⁰ *Ibid*, p. 52.
⁸¹ *Morning Chronicle*, 2 June. See also *Morning Herald, World*, 2 June and *Town and Country Magazine*, 1788 June, p. 264.
⁸² Burney clipping, 17 June.
⁸³ Burney clipping, 9 Dec.
⁸⁴ *General Evening Post*, 15-17 Jan. 1789; *World*, 14 Apr. 1789; Burney clipping, 4 Jan. 1790; *World*, 14 Apr. 1790; *Public Advertiser*, 22 Nov. 1790.
⁸⁵ [James Winston] *The Theatric Tourist*, (1805) p. 57.
⁸⁶ *Life and Times of Frederick Reynolds* by himself (1826), II, 1.

CHAPTER IV pp. 53 to 75

¹ J. Cradock, *Literary and Miscellaneous Memoirs*, (1828), IV, 221. The letters are undated but, since Jenner died in 1774, were probably before that year.
² *The Beautiful Lady Craven*, ed. A. M. Broadley and Lewis Melville (1914) 11, 249.
³ Mrs. Montagu, *Queen of the Blues*, ed. R. Blunt and E. J. Climenson, II, 50-1; see also *Reading Mercury*, 18 May 1778; *Monthly Mirror*, Apr. 1801, p. 222.
⁴ A copy is in my possession. They are also extant in a clipping in the Brit. Library *Collections of Prologues and Epilogues 1734-1810*, p. 79, where the performances are incorrectly stated to have taken place at Benham House.
⁵ Originally written as a two act farce, see advertisement to printed play.
⁶ *Beautiful Lady Craven*, II, 146; *Reading Mercury*, 27 Mar., 10 Apr. 1780. Walpole, *Letters*, XI, 178, and the *Biographica Dramatica* state that it was performed at Benham, so that probably an additional private presentation took place there as well.
⁷ *Monthly Mirror*, Apr. 1801.
⁸ *Reading Mercury*, 18 Dec.; *Gents. Magazine*, Dec. 1780; *New Spouter's Companion* revised by Palmer.
⁹ Preface *The Miniature Picture*, 1781.
¹⁰ *Memoirs of the Margravine of Anspach* (1826), II, 181. Sheridan wrote the prologue for the Drury Lane production.
¹¹ *Letters*, XI, 178.
¹² D. E. Baker, J. Reid, S. Jones. *Biographica Dramatica* (1812). Beckford thought it the most stupid and uninteresting piece he had ever seen (J. W. Oliver, *Life of William Beckford* (1932), p. 73) but O'Keeffe found it well written with good songs and fine music by Dr. Arnold, *Recollection of the Life of John O'Keeffe*, II, 3.
¹³ *Reading Mercury*, 22 Apr. The score is extant in the Hamilton Papers in Edinburgh. See E. W. White, "Two 18th Century Composers of Opera" *Listener*, 10 Feb. 1955. The songs were broadcast as "The Descent of Belinda", 13 14, Feb. 1955.
¹⁴ Oliver *op cit.*, p. 108 *et seq.*
¹⁵ François Hippolyte Barthélemon 1741-1808, violinist and composer, director of music at Vauxhall.
¹⁶ Ferdinando Guiseppe Bertoni, 1725-1813, composer, had come to London four

years previously with his friend Gasparo Pacchierotti the famous singer.

[17] *Letters*, XII, 236.

[18] 22, 29 Apr.

[19] *World*, 5 Mar. 1787, reprinted in *Poetry of the World*, ed. Edw. Topham, (1788) II,18.

[20] 5 Aug.

[21] Hans Ley, *Die Litterarische Tätigkeit der Lady Craven*, 1904; *Memoirs*, I, 90. *Abdoul et Nourjad* was published in the *Nouveau Théâtre de Société d'Anspace et de Triesdorf* by Étienne Asimont. The cast of *Le Déguisement*, the translation of *She Would and She Would Not*, is given in the *Monthly Mirror*, July 1801, XII, 9.

[22] *Morning Chronicle*, May 9, 1792; *Public Advertiser*, May 11 says his salary was £200 a year. For his biography see F. A. Hedgcock, *David Garrick and his French Friends* [1912], p. 267 *et seq*.

[23] *World*, July 20, 1792.

[24] *General Evening Post*, Oct. 30-Nov. 1.

[25] *Times*, 7 Nov., 26 Dec.

[26] In the Hammersmith Central Library. The first known engraving by Neale from *Beauties of England and Wales* does not show the colonnade. Other views of the exterior are reproduced in C. J. Fèret, *Fulham Old and New* (1900).

[27] Angelo, *Reminiscences*, II, 22.

[28] Collection of cuttings about Brandenburgh House in the Hammersmith Public Library. Information is from this or Burney collection unless otherwise stated.

[29] *The Prelude* was printed; see also *Morning Herald*, 26 Apr.

[30] Printed in *Receuil des Pièces de Théâtre Lues par M. le Texier en Sa Maison* (1787).

[31] *Times*, 19 Dec.

[32] Prologue written for the re-opening of the Theatre at Brandenburgh House.

[33] *Poems and Plays*, 9th ed. (1806), II, [140].

[34] Probably the father of the tenor Sapio, an Italian singer and teacher 1751-1827.

[35] 7 Mar.; see also *Universal Magazine*, Feb. 1798, p. 81.

[36] Angelo, *Reminiscences*, II, 5.

[37] *Times*, 21 July; *Whitehall Evening Post*, 19-22 July.

[38] *Beautiful Lady Craven*, p. xciii.

[39] 19 June.

[40] *Ibid*, 11 July.

[41] *Beautiful Lady Craven*, II, 138; Angelo, *Reminiscences*, II, 25; Grantley F. Berkeley, *My Life and Recollections* (1866), IV, 155 *et seq*,

[42] *Public Advertiser*, 25 Apr.

[43] *Universal Magazine*, Mar. 1796.

[44] *Morning Chronicle*, 28 Feb.

[45] *True Briton*, 1 Mar.

[46] *True Briton*, 10 Apr.

[47] Genest, *Some Account of the English Stage from 1660 to 1830* (1832), VII, 438.

[48] Undated clipping.

[49] Genest, III, 437. Playbill, Hammersmith Library; the *Airs and Chorusses* were printed in 1798, and the opera was given at Covent Garden, 19 Apr. 1799.

[50] *Reminiscences*, II, 22.

[51] *The Monthly Museum*, June 1798 assigns it to Keppel Craven.

[52] *Morning Chronicle*, 31 May.

[53] Genest, VII, 437.

[54] *Reminiscences*, I, 212.

[55] *Morning Post*, 29 May attributes it to the Margravine.

[56] 7 July 1799.

[57] *Monthly Mirror*, July 1799, p. 51.

[58] Undated clipping but probably belonging to 1799.

[59] *Morning Post*, 3 July 1800.

[60] Angelo, *op. cit.*, I 212; John Nixon, *Dramatic Annals*, II (Garrick Club).

[61] Printed in *Morning Herald*, 28 June.

[62] *Monthly Mirror*, XII, 9.

[63] Angelo, *op. cit.*, II, 234.

[64] 18 Feb.

[65] *Op. cit.*, I, 210.

[66] Copy in my possession.

[67] *Reminiscences*, II, 235.

[68] *British Press*, 26 Feb., Angelo, II, 234.

[69] *Morning Herald*, 26 Feb.

[70] *Morning Herald*, 25 Feb.; *British Press*, 26 Feb.

[71] *Biographica Dramatica*, which misquotes the title as *Poor Nony*, further altered by Nicoll, *History of English Drama 1660-1900* (1955), IV, 285 to *Poor Tony*. *Morning Herald*, 23 June ascribes it to Craven.

[72] Copy in my possession.

[73] *Morning Post*, 18 June; *True Briton*, 22 June.

[74] *Beautiful Lady Craven*, p. cii; G. Raymond, *Life of R. W. Elliston* (1857), p. 123.

[75] *Morning Post*, 18 June. Angelo, *op. cit.*, II, 22, says it was an adaption of Schiller's *Die Raüber* and is followed by Nicoll, (1952) *op. cit.* III, 329 but neither the *dramatis personae* nor scene accords with this, and it must be a confusion with *The Robbers*, 1798.

[76] *Gents. Mag.* (1804), I, 552.

[77] Playbill without cast or date, Enthoven Collection, Theatre Museum.

[78] *Morning Herald*, 9 July.

[79] *Memoirs of the Margravine of Anspach* (1826), II, 96.

[80] 10, 21 May.

[81] *A Catalogue of the valuable building materials . . . of Brandenburgh House, The Theatre and, the Pavilion.*

[82] *Morning Post*, 7 May 1823. I have been unable to trace a copy of this auction catalogue.

CHAPTER V pp. 76 to 94

[1] George Colman the younger saw a record of dramatic performances with playbills and ms. casts of plays from 1770-1808, Colman, *Random Records* (1830), II, 42.

[2] Askew Roberts, *Wynnstay and the Wynns* (1876), p. 19. *Correspondence of Charlotte Grenville*, Lady Williams Wynn, ed. Rachael Leighton (1920), p. 7.

[3] *Lloyd's Evening Post*, 23-5 Apr.

[4] Hist. Mss. Comm. Report 14 Appendix Pt. IV, p. 502.

[5] National Library of Wales, Wynnstay ms. 102, pp. 1, 5, 10.

[6] Presumably an error for 1770 since we know the puppets performed that year, and it is unlikely that 14 Feb., 1771 means 1771/2 since the book could hardly be labelled 1771-2 with this date on the first page.

[7] Peter Howell and T. W. Pritchard "Wynnstay, Denbighshire III" *Country Life* 6 Apr. 1972, p. 851.

[8] Wynnstay ms. pp. 32, 33, 42.

[9] Michael Bryan, *A Biographical and Initial Dictionary of Painters and Engravers* (1903-5), IV.

[10] James Gandon and Thomas Mulvany, *Life of James Gandon*, 1846, p. 3.

[11] Wynnstay ms. 102, pp. 45, 65, 77.

[12] Burney Collection with ms. date c.1770.

[13] Harvard College Library Theatre Collection. For photostats of this and other Wynnstay playbills I am indebted to Mrs. Hall, former curator; playbill for 26 Nov., Nat. Lib. of Wales.

[14] Playbill, Burney Collection.

[15] *Random Records*, II, 48.

NOTES

16 *Ibid*, 52.

17 *Post*, p. 111.

18 *World*, 11 Oct. 1787 says that seasons had been given every year for twelve years i.e. since 1775.

19 *Correspondence of Charlotte Grenville* ed. Rachael Leighton (1920), pp. 8-9; Michael Kelly, *Reminiscences* ed. Theodore Hook, (1826), II, 318.

20 *Adam's Weekly Courant* (Chester), 17 Jan.; see also Colman, *op. cit.*

21 Wynnstay ms. 116.

22 Printed in *Adam's Weekly Courant*, 31 Jan. 1775.

23 Plays and casts, unless otherwise stated, from Burney Collection playbills and clippings.

24 *The Private Correspondence of David Garrick* (1832), II, 177.

25 *Ibid*, p. 234.

26 Walpole, *Letters*, X, 123.

27 *Adam's Weekly Courant*, 7 Oct. 1777.

28 *World*, 18 Jan 1790.

29 Wynnstay ms. 123, p. 131.

30 Performed by Wm. Cotes. Chambre therefore was probably related to Mrs. Cotes.

31 Wynnstay ms. 123, pp. 135, 139, 141.

32 *Adam's Weekly Courant*, 20 Jan 1778.

33 *Random Records*, I, 258 et seq.

34 5 and 6 Jan. respectively.

35 *Morning Chronicle*, 14 Jan. 1779.

36 *D.N.B; World*, 29 Aug. 1789. Percy Fitzgerald, *Life of David Garrick* (1868), II, 221.

37 *The Cheshire Sheaf*, 1880, I, 11. I owe this reference and some others to Prof. Cecil Price who has a chapter on the Wynnstay theatricals in his *The English Theatre in Wales* (1948), p. 61. See also *Notes and Queries*, 4 Nov. 1922.

38 Wynnstay ms. 103. I owe references to this ms. to Prof. Cecil Price.

39 C. Price, *op. cit.*, p. 62.

40 Nov. 1787, XII, 363.

41 *European Magazine*, Feb. 1786, IX, 71.

42 Also played 15 Jan. and doubtless, though there is no bill, on the 17th; *Henry IV Pt. II* was repeated on 16, 18 Jan.

43 Wynnstay ms. 115.

44 *Ibid*, ms. 125 pp. 429, 437.

45 *Public Advertiser*, 16 Jan.

46 *Torrington Diaries* (1934), I, 175; Cecil Price, *op. cit.*, p. 67.

47 *Morning Post*, 2 Feb. but the playbill on 25 Jan. announces *Harlequin's Invasion* as the afterpiece for the next night.

48 John O'Keeffe, *Recollections*, II, 8.

49 *Morning Post*, 26 Jan., 2 Feb.

50 *European Magazine*, Nov. 1787, XII, 363.

51 *Oxford Journal*, 9 Feb. 1785.

52 Hist. mss. Comm. *op. cit.* p. 521.

53 Letter quoted in Thorpe Catalogue, 1838, see Brit. Mus. Print Room, Anderdon Bequest III, 67. *Morning Post*, 22, 28 Dec. 1786; *Daily Universal Register*, 6 Jan. 1787.

54 *World*, 2 Jan.; *Morning Chronicle*, 4 Jan. which incorrectly assigns the part to Miss Jones.

55 11 Jan.; playbill for 10 Jan. in possession of Mrs. Brookes who kindly allowed me to see it.

56 15 Oct. 1787.

57 *Morning Chronicle*, 15 Aug.; *World*, 8 Dec 1787.

58 Wynnstay ms. 116.

59 Victoria and Albert Museum, Dept. of Prints and Drawings.

60 Lord Wm. Lennox, *My Recollections* (1847), I, 199.

193

[1] *Letters*, III, 37.

[2] *Memoirs of Samuel Foote* (1805), II, 65; for his career see Francis Askham, *The Gay Delavals* (1955).

[3] John Robinson, *Delaval Papers*, Newcastle-on-Tyne Society of Antiquaries.

[4] *Memoirs of Richard Lovell Edgeworth*, ed. R. L. and M. Edgeworth (1844), 3rd ed., p. 88.

[5] J. T. Kirkman, *Memoirs of Macklin* (1799), p. 333.

[6] *Whitehall Evening Post*, 5-7 Mar.

[7] *Delaval Papers*.

[8] *General Advertiser*, 6 Mar. 1751.

[9] *General Advertiser*, 6, 7 Mar.

[10] *Penny London Post*, 8-11 Mar.

[11] *Memoirs of Macklin*.

[12] Tate Wilkinson, *Memoirs* (1790), II, 222.

[13] *Universal Magazine*, Sept. 1771, p. 121.

[14] *London Magazine*, Mar. 1751, p. 136; *Works of the British Poets*, ed. Robert Anderson (1794), II, pp. 20-21.

[15] *Memoirs of Samuel Foote*, II, 65.

[16] *London Advertiser*, 11 Mar.; *Whitehall Evening Post*, 5-7 Mar.

[17] *Delaval Papers*.

[18] *Letters*, VII, 78.

[19] *Survey of London and Westminster*, 1935, IV, 644. There is no mention of it in the Westminster Rate Books of the period.

[20] P.R.O. wills 378 Trevor, slightly misquoted in R. E. G. Cole, *History of Doddington* (1897), p. 143.

[21] Edgeworth, *op. cit.*, p. 76; Herbert Randolph, *Life of General Sir Robert Wilson* (1862), I, 18.

[22] Randolph, *op. cit.*, I, pp. 8-21; J. H. Jesse, *Memoirs of the Life and Reign of King George the Third*, I, 418; Cole, *op. cit.*, p. 145.

[23] *Op. cit.*, I, 463.

[24] Randolph, *op. cit.*, p. 20.

[25] Brit. Library, Add. ms. 39, 547, p. 3.

[26] Cradock, *Memoirs*, II, 82.

[27] Randolph, *op. cit.*, p. 20.

[28] *Public Advertiser*, 10 Apr.

[29] *Op. cit.*, p. 77.

[30] The original picture is at Doddington Hall, Lincolnshire. Edward Edwards *Anecdotes of Painters* (1808), pp. 145-6.

[31] Cole, *op. cit.*, p. 145. The owner, Mr. Jervis, informs me that it is in poor condition.

[32] Hist. Mss. Comm. Report 11, Pt. VII, p. 80.

[33] Mary E. Knapp, *A Checklist of Verse by David Garrick*, 1955, nos. 365, 426. *Letters of David Garrick*, ed. Little and Kahrl, II, 566.

[34] *London Evening Post*, 7-9 May.

[35] *Correspondence of Thomas Gray and William Mason*, [ed. J. Metford], (1853), p. 385.

[36] Wraxhall, *Memoirs*, IV, 422.

[37] Cole, *op. cit.*, p. 168.

[38] Friday 31 Dec. The date of performance is usually given as 29 Dec. which was a Wednesday. A Burney clipping describing it is dated 29 Dec. so that, since that performance was on a Thursday, it must have been held on the previous Thursday, 23 Dec.

[39] Burney clipping, 29 Dec.; *Morning Chronicle*, 20 Dec. 1790.

[40] *The Courts of Europe*, 1841, pp. 98, 101, 102.

[41] M. Hope Dodds, "A Performance at Seaton Delaval in 1790", *Theatre Notebook*, Jan. 1952, VI, p. 35.

[42] *Newcastle Chronicle*, 8 Jan.

[43] *Ibid*, 26 Feb., *Morning Chronicle*, 4 Mar.

[44] Swinburne says Tyrconnel acted Othello and Delaval, Iago.

[45] *Morning Chronicle*, 25 Jan.; *World*, 9 Feb.

[46] *Newcastle Chronicle*, 4 Feb.

[47] *Public Advertiser*, 24 Mar.; *Newcastle Courant*, 4 Feb. ascribes its delivery to Capt. Delaval.

[48] *Delaval Papers;* Hist. Mss. Comm. Report 13, App. VI, p. 202.

[49] Printed in *Newcastle Chronicle*, 11 Feb.

[50] *Public Advertiser*, 23 Feb.

[51] *Delaval Papers*, 14 c.

CHAPTER VII pp. 109 to 117

[1] The prologue is printed in *Gents. Magazine*, Feb. 1774, p. 87 where Lady Anne Spencer is said to have played Cleopatra.

[2] 1819, vol. III, 643 *et seq.*

[3] G[eorge] E. C[okayne], *The Complete Peerage* (1910—), VIII, 500.

[4] *Ante*, p. 54.

[5] J. Cradock, *op. cit.*, IV, 223.

[6] Information from Burney clippings unless otherwise stated.

[7] Wm. Mavor, *A New Description of Blenheim*, 6th ed. (1803), p. 19.

[8] *World*, 4 Oct. 1787.

[9] George Saunders, *A Treatise on Theatres* (1790), p. 39.

[10] *Morning Chronicle*, 31 Oct. 1787.

[11] *World*, 71 Oct. 1787.

[12] *Oxford Journal*, 27 Oct. *Public Advertiser*, 23 Oct., says it was suppressed for an unknown reason.

[13] Reynolds, *Life and Time of Frederick Reynolds* (1826), II, 2, ascribes it to Lady Charlotte, *Town and Country Magazine*, Oct. 1787 to Lady Elizabeth. Contradictory statements also in *Public Advertiser*, 23 Oct., *Oxford Journal*, 27 Oct., *Reading Mercury*, 29 Oct.

[14] Reynolds says he was present on 19 October but the newspapers record his attendance on 27 Oct.

[15] Mavor, *New Description of Blenheim*, 11th ed.

[16] Published 8 Dec., 1788.

[17] *Beautiful Lady Craven*, II, 244 note.

[18] 30 Oct.

[19] The prologue was originally printed in 1787, copy in Manchester University Library. Reprinted with slight variations in Monck Berkeley *Poems* (1797).

[20] This head-dress is not shown in the mezzotint but resembles that worn by Lady Elizabeth in *False Delicacy*.

[21] 29 Oct.

[22] *World*, 30 Oct.

[23] Entrance tickets in Banks Collection.

[24] *Public Advertiser*, 22 Jan. 1788.

[25] The fourth performance, on 15 Jan., was *Guardian* and *Lyar;* the fifth, 16 Jan., *Musical Lady, Maid of the Oaks*. According to the *Public Advertiser*, 22 Jan., this was the last, but the ms. cast lists in the Burney Collection give an additional performance of the new pieces on 18 Jan.

[26] G. Cecil White, *A Versatile Professor, Reminiscences of the Rev. Edward Nares* (1903), p. 102.

[27] *Morning Post*, 24 Oct.

[28] Blenheim muniment room, kindly sent me by Mr. David Green.

[29] 16, 17, 18, 20, 21. Oct.

[30] G. C. White, *op. cit.*, pp. 99 *et seq.*

[31] *Reading Mercury*, 30 Nov. says five, Nares four, *A Versatile Professor*, p. 105.

[32] *Op. cit.*, p. 245.

[33] G. C. White, *op. cit.*

[34] *A New Description of Blenheim*, 1789, p. 4.

[35] *World*, 15 Dec.

[36] The 1835 edition of *A New Description of Blenheim*, p. 17, speaks of it as a theatre; the 1852 edition of *A New Guide to Blenheim*, p. 15, records its conversion.

[37] William Mavor, *op. cit.*, 1797, pp. 31-2.

CHAPTER VIII pp. 118 to 127

[1] On 24 Jan. 1760.

[2] *London Chronicle*, 25-27 Dec., 1760, 1 Jan. 1761; *Gents. Magazine*, Dec. 1760, p. 586.

[3] *Op. cit.* I, 148.

[4] Peter Murray Hill Catalogue 64, p. 27, Autumn, 1958.

[5] *Morning Chronicle*, 2 Jan., 1787. See also *Whitehall Evening Post*, 30 Dec.-2 Jan.

[6] Burney playbill.

[7] Printed in *European Magazine*, Nov. 1787, vol. 12, p. 391.

[8] E. B. de Fonblanque, *Political and Military Episodes from the Life and Correspondence of the Rt. Hon. John Burgoyne* (1876), p. 393.

[9] Burney clipping, 13 Nov.

[10] Printed in *Town and Country Magazine*, Nov. 1787, as by Hague; The verses do not appear in Prior's works.

[11] *European Magazine*, Nov. 1787, vol. 12, p. 392.

[12] 15 Nov. 1787.

[13] *World*, 22 Nov. 1787.

[14] *Gazetteer*, 2 Jan. 1788.

[15] *World*, 1 Jan. 1788.

[16] 2 Jan. 1788.

[17] *Morning Post*, 6 Feb. 1788.

[18] Burney clipping, 31 Oct. 1788.

[19] *G. E. C., Complete Peerage.*

[20] *Letters*, V, 18.

[21] *The Life and Letters of Lady Sarah Lennox*, ed. by the Countess of Ilchester and Lord Stavordale (1901), p. 104.

[22] Earl of Ilchester, *The Home of the Hollands* (1937), p. 80.

[23] Lord Ilchester, *Henry Fox, First Lord Holland* (1920), II, 129. The letter is dated 1 Jan. 1761 (O.S.) so the play may have been given in Dec. as well.

[24] *Life and Letters*, pp. 104, 117.

[25] Brian Fitzgerald, *Emily Duchess of Leinster* (1949), p. 96.

[26] *Home of the Hollands*, p. 81.

[27] Alexander Graydon, *Memoirs of His Own Times* (1846), p. 67.

[28] R. C. Hoare, *The Modern History of S. Wiltshire* (1829-44), IV, 45.

[29] Arnold Hare, *The Georgian Theatre in Wessex* (1958), p. 128.

[30] *Salisbury and Winchester Journal*, 16 Jan. 1769. I owe references to this and the 1768 *Journal* to Dr. Hare.

[31] *Letters of the First Earl of Malmesbury*, ed. Earl of Malmesbury, (1870), I, 206.

[32] *Henry, Elizabeth and George*, ed. Lord Herbert, p. 47; *Salisbury and Winchester Journal*, 18 Jan. 1773.

[33] *Letters of Malmesbury*, I, 275, 277.

[34] Herbert, *op. cit.*, p. 48.

[35] *Home of the Hollands*, p. 319, in which there is an engraving of the White Parlour.

[36] *Ibid*, p. 332.

CHAPTER IX pp. 128 to 139

[1] *Gents. Magazine*, Mar. 1825, p. 274; James Welch, *Alumni Westmonasterienses* (1852); *Monthly Mirror*, Mar. 1796, p. 259.

[2] *Daily Universal Register*, 5 Nov. 1787 says they were given by Leigh near Chipping Norton; *The World*, 17 Dec. refers to them as Lady Saye and Sele's theatricals. Twisleton sat to Brown for a portrait in the role of Pierre, *World*, 16 Apr. 1788.

[3] *World*, 29 Oct. 1787.

[4] *Public Advertiser*, 13 Dec. 1787. A picture of him in this role is at Broughton Castle; though attributed to Hoppner it does not appear in W. McKay and W. Roberts's *Catalogue Raisonée* of his works, (1909).

[5] *Diary and Correspondence of William Lord Auckland*, I, 541; *World*, 17, 22 Dec. 1787.

[6] *World*, 10, 13 May; *Public Advertiser*, 13 May.

[7] *Gents. Magazine*, Mar. 1825, p. 274.

[8] *Monthly Mirror*, Mar. 1796; *Gents. Magazine*, Mar. 1825.

[9] *Public Advertiser*, 13 May 1788.

[10] *Morning Post, World*, 12 May; *Public Advertiser*, 13 May.

[11] *Whitehall Evening Post*, 10-13 May.

[12] A second marriage took place on 4 Nov at the Parish Church of St. Marylebone. *Journals of the House of Lords*, XLI, 540.

[13] *Morning Post*, 22 Jan. 1789.

[14] *Monthly Mirror*, Mar. 1796; *World*, 27 July 1793.

[15] *World*, 31 Jan. 1794.

[16] *European Magazine*, Feb. 1794, vol. 25, p. 136; *Morning Post*, 3 Feb. 1794.

[17] By W. Naish; eng. Ridley, *Monthly Mirror*, Mar. 1796.

[18] *Journals of the House of Lords*, XLI, 1796-8, p. 540.

[19] *Monthly Mirror*, Mar. 1796, I, 259; *True Briton*, 28 Dec. 1803.

[20] *European Magazine*, May 1789, XV, 347; W. H. Ireland, *A New and Complete History of the County of Kent* (1829), III, 276.

[21] *Morning Chronicle*, 5 Nov. 1783.

[22] Brit. Library *Collection of Prologues and Epilogues*, 1734-1810, p. 87.

[23] *Morning Chronicle* 5 Nov. 1783.

[24] *Ibid*, 22 Dec.

[25] Printed in *Kentish Gazette*, 20-24 Mar.

[26] *Ibid*, 18-21 Oct.

[27] *Morning Chronicle*, 30 Nov.

[28] *Kentish Gazette*, 29 Nov.-2 Dec.; *Morning Chronicle*, 6 Dec.

[29] *Morning Herald*, 27 Apr.; *Morning Chronicle*, 28 Apr.

[30] 18 Dec. 1786.

[31] *Daily Universal Register*, 23 Dec.

[32] W. Gillum, *Miscellaneous Poems* (1787), pp. 25-27.

[33] *Morning Chronicle*, 9 Mar.

[34] *Morning Chronicle*, 16 Oct. 1787.

[35] *Ibid*, 27 Oct., 6 Nov.

[36] *Ibid*, 26 Nov.

[37] *Ibid*, 24 Dec.; *World*, 21 Dec.

[38] *World*, 19 May 1788.

[39] *World*, 25 Nov.; *Morning Chronicle*, 26 Nov.

[40] *Whitehall Evening Post*, 22-25 Nov.

[41] 13 Feb.

[42] 14 Feb.

[43] Mainwaring Piozziana ms. II, 104. Photographs kindly supplied by Mr. J. L. Clifford.

[44] *Kentish Gazette*, 11-15 Dec. 1789.

[45] *Times*, 6, 7, Nov. 1789.

[46] 19 Nov.

[47] *Times*, 7 Nov.

[48] Rigden, *Historical Sketch of Dover* (1844).

[49] Tablet in Eythorne Church, Kent.

[50] May 1789, XV, 347.

CHAPTER X pp. 140 to 153

[1] Dates from memorials in Aston Church.

[2] Wm. Wing, *Annals of North Aston* (1867), pp. 40-1. Letter from Wing, *Notes and Queries*, 5th series, (12 May 1877), VII, 373.

[3] Information, unless otherwise stated, from files of *Jackson's Oxford Journal* in the Bodleian and Brit. Library.

[4] Extracted for me by Prof. Cecil Price from Jones's unpublished Diary.

[5] *Ibid*.

[6] *New London Packet*, 4-6 Nov. 1776; *Oxford Journal*, 15 Jan. 1774.

[7] *Lives of the Most Eminent British Painters* (1829-33), III, 2. I am indebted for information about Sir George Beaumont to an M.A. Thesis by E. G. Mitchell, *Sir George Beaumont and his contacts with English Romanticism*, University of London Library.

[8] Jones's *Diary*.

[9] *New London Packet*, 4-6 Nov. 1776.

[10] Not listed in *Biographica Dramatica* or Nicoll, *History of English Drama, 1660-1900*, III.

[11] *Gents. Magazine*, 1797, Vol. 67, p. 1076; R. M. Marshall *Oxfordshire Byways*, pp. 38-42. I owe this latter reference to the Rev. C. C. Brookes.

[12] *Universal Magazine*, Nov. 1776, p. 270. It is not included in Whitehead's *Works*.

[13] In a letter to Joseph Cradock on 9 Feb. 1826 in Cradock's *Memoirs*, IV, 257.

[14] *Oxford Journal*, Sat. 29 Nov. used the phrase "last Friday" but it is unlikely that this means 28 Nov.

[15] E. G. Mitchell, *op. cit.*

[16] Newspaper clipping kindly sent me by Miss E. Bowles.

[17] *Morning Herald*, 21 Nov. 1783.

[18] *World*, 17 Sept. 1787.

[19] *World*, 19 Nov. 1788; 22 Oct., 2 Nov. 1787.

[20] *World*, 20 Nov. 1788; 19 Nov. 1789; 14 Oct. 1791.

[21] *World*, 31 Dec. 1788; 4 June, 11 July, 28, 4, 15 Sept., 9 Dec. 1789.

[22] *Ibid*, 9 Dec. 1791.

[23] 19, 24 Nov. 1787.

[24] Henry Hartopp, *The Hartopp Family of Little Dalby* from *Leics. and Rutland Notes and Queries*, reprinted; *G.E.C. Complete Peerage* under Carbery.

[25] *Op. cit.*, IV, pp. 162, 393.

[26] 22 Oct., 1 Dec. 1787.

[27] Box 4, Leadbeater Accounts, June 1798-9, No. 33.

[28] *Ibid*, 8 June 1799-10 Oct. 1800, No. 60.

[29] 13 Aug. 1798.

[30] Leadbeater 8 June 1799-19 Oct. 1800, No. 25.

[31] *Leicester Journal*, 10 Aug.; *Lady's Monthly Museum*, 1798, I, 227.

[32] Not listed in *Biographica Dramatica* or Nicoll, *op. cit.*

[33] Leadbeater, June 1799-Oct. 1800, No. 39.

[34] *Ibid*, No. 25.

[35] *Monthly Mirror*, Aug. 1799, p. 122; July 1799, p. 67; *Leicester Journal*, 30 July, 1799.

[36] Leadbeater, Oct. 1800-1801, No. 5.

[37] *Ibid*, 8 June 1799-10 Oct. 1800.

[38] *Ibid*, Oct. 1800-1801, No. 1.

[39] *Ibid*, 10 Oct. 1801-10 Oct. 1802, No. 4.

[40] *Ibid*, Oct. 1800-1801, No. 10.

[41] *Ibid*, No. 29.

[42] *Ibid*, 10 Oct. 1801-10 Oct. 1802, No. 32.

[43] *Ibid*, No. 7.

[44] *Ibid*, Nos. 4, 40.

[45] *Leicester Journal*, 31 July, 1801.

[46] Bills and Receipts, 1800, 1801, 1802.

[47] Leadbeater, Oct. 1802-3, No. 35.

[48] *Ibid*, No. 40. *Ibid*, Nos. 7, 35.

[49] Jan. 1803, p. 79.

[50] Vol. XV, p. 66.

[51] Leadbeater, Oct. 1803-Oct. 1804, No. 41.

[52] *Ibid*, No. 39.

[53] *Ibid*, No. 34.

CHAPTER XI pp. 154 to 166

[1] Daniel Lysons, *Environs of London*, (1792-6), II, 568; J. N. Brewer, *Beauties of England and Wales*, (1816) X, Pt. IV, 678.

[2] *World*, 16 Dec. 1793.

[3] D. E. Williams, *The Life and Correspondence of Sir Thomas Lawrence* (1831), I, 229.

[4] *True Briton*, 31 Jan.; *Morning Post*, 24 Jan. 1803.

[5] D. E. Williams, *op. cit.*, I, 229 *et seq.*

[6] *The Farington Diary*, ed. Grieg (1923), II, 75, 83.

[7] According to Mrs. Kemble the billiard room, *Memoirs of Mrs. Inchbald*, ed. J. Boaden, (1833), I, 67.

[8] *Morning Herald*, 26 Jan.

[9] *Memoirs of Mrs. Inchbald*, II, 67. The holograph letter is in the Victoria and Albert Mus., Forster ms. 322.

[10] *Hary-O. The Letters of Lady Harriet Cavendish*, ed. Sir George Leveson Gower and Iris Palmer [1940], p. 44.

[11] *Ibid*, p. 47.

[12] *True Briton*, 29 Jan.

[13] *Daily Advertiser*, 25 Jan.

[14] *Morning Post*, 23 Apr. 1803; *Annual Register*, 1803, p. 506; *Morning Post*, 5 Jan. 1804; *Daily Advertiser*, 6 Jan. 1804.

[15] *Hary-O*, pp. 123, 124, 126, 127.

[16] *D.N.B.*

[17] *The Two Duchesses*, ed. Vere Foster (1898), pp. 249, 262.

[18] *Lady Bessborough and Her Family Circle*, ed. the Earl of Bessborough and A. Aspinall (1940), p. 140. Letter docketed 9 Dec.

[19] *Daily Advertiser*, 23 Dec.; Burney clipping.

[20] *Op. cit.*, VIII, pp. 49-50.

[21] 23 Dec. 1805.

[22] Burney clipping.

[23] *Op. cit.*, pp. 134, 136.

[24] *Letters of R. B. Sheridan*, ed. Cecil Price (1966), I, 250.

[25] *Hary-O*, p. 140.

[26] *Reminiscences of Michael Kelly*, ed. Theodore Hook (1826), II, 294.

[27] *Private Correspondence 1781-1821*, ed. Castalia, Countess Granville (1916), II, 151. I owe this reference to the Earl of Bessborough.

[28] *Daily Advertiser*, 26 Dec.

[29] *Morning Herald, Daily Advertiser*, 28 Dec.

[30] *Morning Post*, 2 Jan. 1806; *Morning Herald*, 2, 4 Jan.

[31] *Recollections in Sir Thomas Lawrence's Letterbag*, ed. G. S. Layard, 1906, p.259.

[32] Farington, *op. cit.*, III, 128.

[33] Burney clipping.

[34] Farington, *op. cit.*, III, 131, 215.

[35] *Op. cit.*, p. 149. There may have been more performances as in a letter dated Thursday, 30 Jan. Haryo speaks of the play to be Friday and Monday. However this may be an error of dating and the sentence probably refers to the opening nights of the theatricals on Fri. 20 Dec. and Mon. 23 Dec. 1805.

³⁶ *Morning Herald*, 18 Jan.
³⁷ Farington, *op. cit.*, VI, p. 204.
³⁸ *Correspondence of John, Fourth Duke of Bedford* (1842), I, 18.
³⁹ *Private Correspondence of David Garrick* (1831), I, 31.
⁴⁰ George Harris, *Life of Lord Chancellor Hardwicke* (1847), II, 87.
⁴¹ *Works of Aaron Hill* (1753), III, 129.
⁴² *Garrick Correspondence*, II, 342.
⁴³ Victoria and Albert Mus., Forster Collection of Garrick mss., Vol. 33. f. 49. I owe this reference to T. H. Vail Motter, "Garrick and the Private Theatres", E[nglish] L[iterary] H[istory], Mar. 1944.
⁴⁴ *Morning Herald*, 4 Jan. 1806; see also *Thespian Magazine*, Dec. 1792; Burney playbills.
⁴⁵ Burney clipping.
⁴⁶ *Morning Chronicle*, 8 Jan. 1806.
⁴⁷ *Hary-O*, p. 133.
⁴⁸ *Daily Advertiser*, 6 Jan.; *Morning Herald*, 4 Jan.; *Morning Chronicle*, 14 Jan.
⁴⁹ Miss Flora Russell has kindly allowed me to examine an undated card playbill of the performances.
⁵⁰ R. R. Madden, *Correspondence of the Countess of Blessington* (1855), III, 443.
⁵¹ Woburn Abbey Theatricals, I. His Grace the Duke of Bedford kindly arranged for me to examine these two volumes of playbills, prologues and epilogues, 1817-1857, which are in the Woburn Abbey Library.

CHAPTER XII pp. 167 to 171

¹ Wm. Dunlap, *Memoirs of George Frederick Cooke* (1813), p. 83.
² *Life and Times of Frederick Reynolds*, (1826).
³ *Eccentricities* (1791), II, 134.
⁴ I have not counted more than one performance in a season, ignoring repetitions, but if the piece was given at the same theatre another season I have counted it again.
⁵ In the second half of the 18th Century, Nicoll, *Eighteenth Century Drama 1750-1800*, lists only seventeen foreign plays in London (outside Italian operas) and the majority of these were puppet shows.

Index

The appendices are not included in this index.

Faulkner, Miss 56, 58
Fector, Miss 137
Fector, William, his theatricals 132-9, 168
Fisher, Capt. 109
Fitzgerald, Lord Edward 46
Fitzgerald, Lord Henry 43-9, 51-2, 117, 168
Fitzgerald, William 123-4, 126
Fitzgerald, William Thomas 22, 47
Fitzroy, Henry 58
Fitzpatrick, Richard 125
Florimène 9
Floyd, John 126
Folie du Jour, La 59
Follies of a Day 24, 26
Foote, Samuel 95-7, 99
Forty Thieves 93
Foster 105
Fowler, Misses 140
Fox, Caroline 164
Fox, Charles James 122-5
Fox, Henry (1st Lord Holland) 122-3
Fox, Lady Mary 124, 126
Fox, Stephen, his theatricals 123-7
Fox-Strangways, Lady Susan 122-4
Freemasons' Hall, London, theatricals at 129-30
French plays 170
Fury, Major 48

Gandon, James, architect 78
Garner 135
Garrick, David 44-5, 80-1, 84, 96, 99, 101, 103-4, 125-6, 143, 146, 163-4, 167-8, 170-1
Gaunlet 72-3
Gay, Martin, costumier 149, 151-2
Gill 137-8
Gillum, W., poet 135-8
Goodall 21
Goodall, Charlotte 20-1
Goodenough 46, 49
Goodwood theatricals 35
Gorboduc 9
Gordon, Robert 158
Graham 140
Grecian Daughter 131
Greenwood, Thomas, scene painter 40, 50, 114-5
Grenville, T. 80
Greville 88
Greville, Col. Henry 12
Griffith 79, 81; Mrs. 92
Guardian 29, 43, 46, 111, 113-4, 136

Halliday 49
Hamilton 73
Hamilton Miss 43, 47-9

Hamilton, Misses 153
Hamlet 143, 169
Harley, John Pritt 8
Hardtopp, Edward Bourchier, his theatricals 153
Hartopp-Wigley, Edward, his theatricals 145-53
Haynes 140
Henderson, John 56
Henry IV (1) 85, 91, 169; (2) 85-6
Herbert 126
Heseltine, Mrs., 159-62
High Life Below Stairs, 47, 54, 80, 92-3, 110, 120, 126, 147, 169
Hilligsberg, Janet, dancer 28
Hinchingbrook theatricals 118-22
Hobart, Mrs. Albinia, (later Lady Bucks.) 36-9, 41-4, 46-50, 52, 54-5, 61-2, 64
Hob in the Well, 29-30
Hodges, Mrs. 125-6
Holland House theatricals 11, 122-4, 127
Holman, Joseph G. 112, 131
Honoria and Mammon 9
Horace 10
Horne 144
Horrebrow, Mrs. 30
Hunchback 93

Imagination 69
Incledon, Charles 30
Inconstant 89
Indian Emperor 10-11, 122
Inkle and Yarico 106
Io 93
Isabella 152
Italian Pastorale 63

James, Sir Walter 68-9
Jane Shore 101-3, 122-3, 125-6, 143, 168-9
Jealous Wife, 43, 47, 83-4
Jenkinson, R. B. 114, 116
Jeu de L'Amour et du Hazard, Le 66
John Bull 164-5
Johnson, Richard, builder 147, 149, 152-3
Johnstone John 27, 30, 33
Johnstone, Roger 77
Jones, Anne 84, 86, 90
Jones, Thomas, scene painter 140
Julia 129-30
Julius Caesar 164

Kean, Edmund 8
Kean, Moses 31
Kemble, J. P. 38, 43, 47-8, 52, 158 160-1, 167
Kemble, Priscilla 155-7
Kent 126
King John 169

Kitchen, William, builder 149-53

Lady Jane Grey 11
Lamb, George 155, 157-62
Lamb, Peniston 155, 157-8
Lamb, William 158-62
Lame Lover 148
Lawrence, Sir Thomas 154-62
Leathes, painter 163
Lennox, Georgiana 122
Lennox, Lady Sarah 122-4
Lethe 141, 143
Le Texier 54, 59, 61-3, 65, 69; Mme 63-4
Lewes, Lee 107
Lighting 79, 97, 111, 159, 161, 171
Lindsay, Lady Charlotte 155, 160
Linières, Countess de, 62-3, 66
Little Dalby Hall theatricals 15, 145-53
Lost Lady 10
Lottery 93
Loutherbourg, see De Loutherbourg
Love à la Mode 121
Love in a Convent 73
Lovers' Quarrels 152
Lyar 84, 113-4, 120-1, 127

Macarthy, Lady Charlotte 110
Macbeth 87, 143, 151-3, 169
Machinery 74, 113, 149-50
Macklin, Charles 96-8, 100-1, 103, 167
Madden, Miss 130
Madocks, Joseph 67, 73, 88, 93, 155, 159-60; William 155
Mahomet 136
Maid of the Oaks 114, 116
Malton, Thomas, scene painter 60-1
Manders and John Manders 140, 144
Man of Quality 90
Mantell 133; Mrs. 133, 135, 136-7; Miss 132, 134
Mara, Mme., Gertrude Elizabeth 120-1
Margaret of Anjou 62
Marinari, Gaetano, scene painter 60
Marlborough, John, 1st Duke of, and Sarah, Duchess of 109
Marlborough, George, 4th Duke of 110-7
Mathews, Charles 8
Mathilda 130, 136
Matthew, George 48-9
Mayor of Garratt 30, 83, 141, 144, 164-5, 169
Mazzinghi, Joseph, musician 65
Measure for Measure 169
Melton Mowbray company 148, 151
Merchant of Venice 77, 82-4, 91, 141, 143, 169
Meredith 79, 84

Merry, Robert 43-4, 46-7, 51
Merry Wives of Windsor 31, 78-9, 169
Mexborough, Lady 100, 102
Midnight Hour 19, 33
Millard, scene painter 165
Miniature Picture 55
Minor 23, 78
Miss in her Teens 17, 93, 118
Mistake 118
Mithridates 10
Mock Doctor 119-20
Moody, John 30
Morgiana 93
Morris 73
Much Ado About Nothing 79
Munday, Francis 151, 153
Munden, Joseph 30, 66
Music and musicians 40, 42, 51-2, 90, 102, 107, 113, 118, 120, 129, 141, 148, 153, 156, 159
Musical Lady 114-5

Nabob 144
Narcissus 10
Nares, Edward 115-7
Neck or Nothing 81
Newbury Town Hall, theatricals at 54-5
Newcastle company 107
Nichols 122
Nixon, John 69, 70, 73
North Aston, theatricals at 140-5
No Song No Supper 107-8
Nourjad 70-1

Oakley, Miss 135
O'Brien, William 124
Offaly, George Fitzgerald, Lord 122-4
Ogilvie 46
Oliphant 130
Oroonoko 161-2
Orphan of China 134
Osborne, Dorothy 10
Othello 80, 96-9, 107-8, 147, 169
Oxberry, William 8
Oxford, theatricals at 10

Pacchierotti, Gasparo, singer 56-7
Padlock 30
Palmeston, Henry, 2nd Viscount 119
Panthea 164
Parker, Hon. Capt. 116
Parsay, Baron de 63
Pasquin, Anthony 17-8, 25-6, 28, 31
Payne 125
Pembroke, Henry, 10th Earl of 125-6
Peshall, Mary 111-4
Peyton, Lady, her theatricals 10
Pic Nic Society 12-3, 43, 70, 170

Pigot, Miss 110
Piozzi, Hester 48-9, 137-8
Plaistow 130
Planche, J. R. 8
Plays for private theatres 170
Poissardes Anglois, Les 63-4
Poor Noddle 71-2
Poor Soldier 23, 30, 107-8, 121
Porter, Robert Kerr 72
Porter, Walsh 69
Poulet, Le 61-2
Prelude 61
Price 122
Princess and the Slave 73
Princess of Georgia 67, 69
Private Theatricals 13
Provok'd Husband 128
Provok'd Wife 68, 81, 115, 170
Pugh, Charles, scene painter 68
Puleston 78
Puppets 76-7
Puss in Boots 68-9
Pyramus and Thisbe 93

Quarme, Mrs. 97, 99
Queensberry House, theatricals at 55-8
Quin, James 11

Ralph Roister Doister 9
Ravenscroft, Miss 80
Reading theatre 29, 33
Rehearsals 25, 43, 44, 49, 57, 79-80, 82, 85, 111, 141
Release of Eblis 72
Revenge 123, 132-3, 164
Reynolds, Frederick 112-3, 167
Richard III 84, 148, 169
Richards, Elizabeth (Mrs. Edwin) 22-3, 26, 28-9, 31
Richard, John Inigo 77-8, 80, 84
Richmond, Charles, Duke of, his theatricals 34-52, 121
Richmond Theatre 22, 23, 26, 29
Rivals 28, 30, 47, 89-90, 93, 127, 158, 161, 165, 169
Rivers, Mrs. 22
Robbers 67-8
Roberts, James, scene painter 114-6
Robinson 115
Robinson Crusoe 24, 26, 28, 30, 33
Roche Courbon, Count de la 66
Rock 22
Rolls, John, his theatricals 8
Roman Father 135
Romeo and Juliet 147, 152, 169
Romp 20, 29, 120-1
Rooker, Michael Angelo, scene painter 111, 113-4

Rope dancers 100
Royal Circus 17
Royal Merchant 83-4, 91-2
Rule a Wife and Have a Wife 84
Russell, Lord Charles J. Fox 165
Russell, Lords, John and William 164-5
Ryder 19

St. Leger 90
Salisbury 84
Salomon, Johann, musician 63, 65
Sandby, Paul scene painter 77, 80, 87
Sandwich, John Montagu, 4th Earl of, his theatricals 118-22, 163-4
Sapio, musician 63, 67
Savile Row theatre 22-3
Saye and Sele, Lady 128
Scenery 18, 19, 20, 21, 26, 28, 29, 33, 40-1, 47, 48, 50, 54, 62, 68, 71, 74, 77-8, 84, 87-8, 89, 90, 100-1, 106, 111, 113, 114-5, 120, 125, 137, 141, 142, 145, 146-7, 156, 160, 163-4, 169, 171
Scot, scene painter 18
Scott, Capt. 106
Seaton Delavel, theatricals at 95, 100, 105-8
Shepherd's Paradise 9
Sheridan, R. B. 47, 55, 80, 89-90, 155-6, 160-1, 165, 167
Sheridan, Tom 158-61
She Stoops to Conquer 110-1
She Wou'd and She Wou'd Not 59
Shields company 106
Shipley, William 93
Shuttleworth, Miss 71, 73
Sarah, Siddons 35-6, 43, 45, 52, 66, 131
Sidebotham, C. 77, 85, 92
Siege of Damascus 125, 134, 163-4
Siege of Granada 10
Siege of Scutari 141-2
Silver Tankard 55, 57
Simons 66-7, 73
Sleep Walker 54-5, 64, 69
Smart, Christopher 98-9
Smyrna Twins 65-6
Somerset, Lord Charles 165
Son-in-Law 85
Spagnioletti, Paolo, musician 70
Spanish Barber 84
Spearman 105-7
Spencer, Lady Anne 109
Spencer, Lady Caroline 110, 113-4
Spencer, Lord Charles 110, 115, 144
Spencer, Lady Charlotte 111-3, 117
Spencer, Lady Diana 109
Spencer, Lady Elizabeth 110, 112-6
Spencer, Lord Henry 110, 115
Spencer, John 111, 114, 117